AMERICA AND THE WORLD
IN THE AGE OF TERROR

Significant Issues Series
Timely books presenting current CSIS research and analysis of interest to the academic, business, government, and policy communities.
Managing Editor: Roberta L. Howard

The Center for Strategic and International Studies (CSIS) is a nonprofit, bipartisan public policy organization established in 1962 to provide strategic insights and practical policy solutions to decisionmakers concerned with global security. Over the years, it has grown to be one of the largest organizations of its kind, with a staff of some 200 employees, including more than 120 analysts working to address the changing dynamics of international security across the globe.

CSIS is organized around three broad program areas, which together enable it to offer truly integrated insights and solutions to the challenges of global security. First, CSIS addresses the new drivers of global security, with programs on the international financial and economic system, foreign assistance, energy security, technology, biotechnology, demographic change, the HIV/AIDS pandemic, and governance. Second, CSIS also possesses one of America's most comprehensive programs on U.S. and international security, proposing reforms to U.S. defense organization, policy, force structure, and its industrial and technology base and offering solutions to the challenges of proliferation, transnational terrorism, homeland security, and post-conflict reconstruction. Third, CSIS is the only institution of its kind with resident experts on all the world's major populated geographic regions.

CSIS was founded four decades ago by David M. Abshire and Admiral Arleigh Burke. Former U.S. senator Sam Nunn became chairman of the CSIS Board of Trustees in 1999, and since April 2000, John J. Hamre has led CSIS as president and chief executive officer.

Headquartered in downtown Washington, D.C., CSIS is a private, tax-exempt, 501(c) 3 institution.

The CSIS Press
Center for Strategic and International Studies
1800 K Street, N.W., Washington, D.C. 20006
Tel: (202) 887-0200 Fax: (202) 775-3199
E-mail: books@csis.org Web: www.csis.org

AMERICA AND THE WORLD IN THE AGE OF TERROR

A New Landscape in International Relations

EDITED BY DANIEL BENJAMIN

THE CSIS PRESS

**Center for Strategic
and International Studies**

Washington, D.C.

Significant Issues Series, Volume 27, Number 1
© 2005 by Center for Strategic and International Studies
Washington, D.C.
All rights reserved
Printed on recycled paper in the United States of America
Cover design by Robert L. Wiser, Silver Spring, Md.
Cover photograph: © Reuters/CORBIS

09 08 07 06 05   5 4 3 2 1

ISSN 0736-7136
ISBN 0-89206-452-8

Library of Congress Cataloging-in-Publication Data

America and the world in the age of terror : a new landscape in international relations /
edited by Daniel Benjamin
   p. cm. — (Significant issues series ; v. 27, no. 1)
  Includes bibliographical references and index.
  ISBN 0-89206-452-8 (pb : alk. paper)
1. United States—Foreign relations—2001– 2. War on Terrorism, 2001—Diplomatic
history. 3. Alliances. I. Benjamin, Daniel, 1961– II. Title. III. Series.
  E902.A465 2004
  327.73'009'0511—dc22   2004016449

CONTENTS

PREFACE

Daniel Benjamin

In the history of modern international relations, few, if any, events have had the instantaneous, transformative impact of the terrorist attacks of September 11, 2001. In a matter of hours, the outlook of the United States was changed profoundly. Reorientation of policy began immediately and was most evident in foreign and security affairs. Broad changes were also plainly obvious in domestic policy, with a sudden emphasis on homeland security and far-reaching innovations as well as in law enforcement and domestic intelligence gathering.

As the global hegemon, America's powerful reaction to the attacks was bound to have a major impact on its relations with others. Indeed, Washington quickly gave notice that one consequence of the atrocities would be a reordering of the international agenda. With moral support from allies and friends in all corners of the world, the United States set itself on a course to destroy Al Qaeda, the terrorist movement responsible for killing some 3,000 people on American soil. The administration of President George W. Bush also embarked on a determined effort to force others—especially rogue states—who gave succor to terrorists to change their ways, either through regime change or through withering pressure.

The sweeping nature of the reorientation that occurred can be seen, in part, as a result of the magnitude of the surprise that accompanied the events themselves. A small number of intelligence officials and policymakers in a variety of countries recognized that jihadists sought to carry out catastrophic attacks against the United States and perhaps others. But this understanding had not penetrated the consciousness of much of official Washington, nor was it accepted by many national leaderships around the world. In this sense, the surprise of that day can be said to have exceeded what was experienced by the United States at the time of Pearl Harbor, an event that caused a comparable number of casualties. The U.S. military establishment, after all, had viewed a conflict against

Japan as a significant possibility for decades and was expecting a Japanese strike in late 1941. Only the location of the attack was truly surprising. Similarly, Joseph Stalin may have been shocked when Adolf Hitler's army invaded Soviet territory in the same year, but only because he had ignored a string of intelligence warnings and abundant evidence of Hitler's expansionist aims. Germany and Japan, moreover, were both rising nation-states, a familiar kind of enemy for all observers of world politics in the first half of the twentieth century. Al Qaeda, by contrast, is a nonstate actor of a sort that most analysts discounted as posing a significant strategic threat to the United States or other Western democracies.

Consequently, the new policy initiatives the administration developed to confront the threat addressed issues that had often been of secondary or tertiary concern. For example, officials in numerous countries had worked to combat terrorist fundraising for several years, but their efforts had little urgency until September 11. Suddenly, how terrorists acquired their resources became a critical matter for national leaders. Geographical regions that had attracted limited interest from U.S. leaders in the past—the Caucasus and Central Asia, for example—became central to the formulation of the administration's counterterrorism strategy. Relationships that had historically been defined by a small clutch of issues—such as energy and Persian Gulf security in the case of the United States and Saudi Arabia—were upended by American insistence on addressing radicalism in the Saudi kingdom. Ties between the United States and such great powers as Russia and China were also thrown into flux by the sudden shifting of priorities. The aftermath of September 11 created both challenges for these countries—such as the deployment of forces by Washington into new regions—and opportunities to navigate around long-standing differences for the sake of building better counterterrorism cooperation.

Theorists of international relations might have been able to predict how different governments would behave vis-à-vis Washington had the Bush administration's focus remained solely on jihadist terrorists and those that abet them, the Taliban regime in Afghanistan above all. They would have used a term from the specialist's lexicon—bandwagoning—to describe how different states sought to strengthen their relations with Washington by reconfiguring their own policies to accord with America's efforts to dismantle terrorist cells and increase the difficulty of moving men, materiel, and money to carry out terrorist operations. A small number of nations might also have sought to curb U.S influence. Some of the denizens of the U.S. list of state sponsors of terrorism, such as Syria and Iran, could be expected to try to insulate themselves from additional political and economic pressure. These, and perhaps a few others, appealed for assistance from Russia, China, or even France with the claim that the United States was pursuing hostile, even imperialist policies. These states might also seek to bandwagon a bit themselves, as Syria and Iran have done, by pointing to their own efforts to counter jihadist terror as indications of common interests, thus creating a hedge against precipitous U.S. action.

The attacks of September 11 elicited a global outpouring of sympathy for the United States. Yet only a few months afterward, the picture became much more mixed than the hypothetical international affairs experts would have predicted. This was due to the expansion of the Bush administration's aims in the war on terror to include regime change in Iraq and the argument the Bush administration put forward in favor of preventive war as a necessity in an age of terror. Much support from foreign publics evaporated, and in only a few months, vast demonstrations against the United States took place in cities around the world. Seldom has global public opinion been so quickly reversed. As it pressed for international support for its Iraq policy, Washington found itself increasingly isolated, criticized even by long-time allies in Western Europe.

As the United States pressed forward toward an invasion of Iraq and made clear that it would act whether the United Nations Security Council approved or not, many in the international community felt themselves whipsawed between a recognition of the imperatives of the war on terror and a sense that untrammeled U.S. power was not in their interest. Thus, some nations began to join together, building coalitions to balance against the world's only superpower. Restraining the American Gulliver, it appeared, had become the common aim of many.

The two tendencies of the period after September 11—to exploit America's interest in prosecuting the war on terror to advance national goals and to set hurdles before the exercise of American power—created enormous tension both within the international community as a whole and in individual countries. No simple calculus enabled national leaders to decide how to act in the face of American demands. Many wound up bandwagoning and balancing sequentially and even simultaneously. The different tendencies and tensions have made this period a fascinating laboratory for studying how countries behave in periods of upheaval. Indeed, sorting out how different leaderships reacted to events should be beneficial for both observers of international affairs and policymakers as they seek to understand the dynamics of the age of terror.

With this in mind, the Center for Strategic and International Studies conducted a yearlong study on the evolving patterns of competition and cooperation between a group of selected countries and the United States. A distinguished group of scholars was assembled and seven countries were chosen for analysis: China, Georgia, Germany, Indonesia, Pakistan, the Russian Federation, and Saudi Arabia. No principle of selection would satisfy all desires, but this group afforded the possibility of studying great powers, close allies, key countries in the struggle against radical Islamist violence, and important geographic considerations. To state the obvious, three are Muslim (Indonesia, Pakistan, and Saudi Arabia), three are nuclear powers (Russia, China, and Pakistan), two could fairly be considered America's preeminent rivals over the last half-century (Russia and China). Moreover, one (Germany) has enjoyed one of the closest relationships with Washington over the same period of time; another (Georgia) sits in the heart of one of the most sensitive regions in the war on terror and has had the kind of tumultuous recent history characteristic of some of the former Soviet republics.

The findings demonstrate the complexity of the factors that shaped policymakers decisions and illuminate some of the oddities of the period—the strange compliance of Russia at a number of key junctures, the seeming reluctance of Indonesia to move clearly in one direction or another, the remarkable personal pique that characterized German-American ties. They clarify some of the ephemeral matters that conditioned developments and point to some of the bedrock considerations that must be dealt with as the war on terror continues to unfold. All told, these studies provide a fascinating tableau of international relations at a time of extraordinarily rapid change and great unpredictability.

∿

Many debts have been incurred in the course of producing this study. Within CSIS, Julianne Smith and Jessica Cox dealt with the myriad challenges posed by funding this effort and ensuring that the writers had the wherewithal to travel as necessary and whatever other logistical support they required. Vinca Lafleur brought an exceptional editor's eye and otherworldly patience to each chapter. Jessica Cox also provided vital editorial insights for problems large and small. Donna Spitler of the CSIS Press proved an expert shepherd in moving a flock of essays into this volume. Kurt Campbell, CSIS's senior vice president, oversaw and encouraged the project from conception to completion. Above all, I thank the scholars who collaborated on this effort. They heard the secret harmonies and exposed the seeming discontinuities in the narrative of the period since September 11. I am most grateful for their good humor, sharp insights, and hard work.

CHAPTER ONE

CHINA: TACTICAL BANDWAGONING, STRATEGIC BALANCING

Bonnie Glaser and Carola McGiffert

FROM COMPETITOR TO PARTNER

George W. Bush came to office extremely wary of China. During the 2000 presidential campaign, then governor Bush viewed China both as a prolific human rights abuser and as the rising major threat to the United States, stating that "the conduct of China's government can be alarming abroad and appalling at home."[1] He accused the Clinton administration of selling out the Chinese people for access to the Chinese market and of putting U.S. economic interests over American values.

In a November 19, 1999, speech, entitled "A Distinctly American Internationalism," Bush asserted that "China is a competitor, not a strategic partner. We must deal with China without ill will, but without illusions. . . . We should work toward a day when the fellowship of free Pacific nations is as strong and united as our Atlantic Partnership. If I am president, China will find itself respected as a great power, but in a region of strong democratic alliances. It will be unthreatened, but not unchecked."[2] This statement was interpreted not only as a rejection of the Clinton policy of constructive engagement and strategic partnership,[3] but also as a thinly veiled endorsement of a containment policy toward China.

For the first few months of the Bush administration, the U.S.-China relationship was very much at risk. Yet by the start of 2004, Secretary of State Colin Powell characterized U.S.-China relations as "the best they have been since President Richard Nixon first visited Beijing more than

The authors thank John Garofano and Derek Mitchell for their editorial comments and John Kemmer and Janet Kang for their research assistance.

30 years ago."[4] Indeed, many U.S. scholars now argue that "a real corner has been turned and that the improved relationship can endure for some time to come."[5]

How did we get here? In fact, the change in U.S.-China relations began well before the September 11 terrorist attacks and the subsequent war on terrorism. Whether the change can be attributed to a more mature approach by a new generation of Chinese leaders, the spy plane incident of April 2001 during which both sides looked over the brink and glimpsed what truly hostile U.S.-China relations might look like, the rising threat of WMD proliferation, President George W. Bush's recalculation of American interests once in office, or some combination of these and other factors, clearly U.S.-China relations shifted dramatically about midway through President Bush's first year in office.

September 11 offered a further opportunity for transformation of U.S.-China ties. China has taken full advantage of September 11 to improve relations with the United States in an effort to advance its strategic interests—economic modernization, national unity, and political stability. At the same time, China is looking to the future, working quietly to shift the balance in Asia in its own favor. In other words, China is engaged in *tactical bandwagoning*—supporting the United States in an effort to further its own interests. It is also engaged in *strategic balancing*—working to ensure that China is prepared for a scenario in which the United States and China are once again competitors for influence in the Asia Pacific region.

A CHANGING CHINESE FOREIGN POLICY

Although China opened to the outside world after President Nixon's 1972 trip, its foreign policy remained largely inward looking for at least the next two decades. In the 1970s and 1980s, China's leaders reached out diplomatically and, especially under Deng Xiaoping, economically, but continued to view China's security in domestic terms. Border skirmishes, territorial disputes, and Taiwan dominated China's security perception. Little thought was given to China's role in safeguarding regional or international security. Today, China is redefining its security in global terms. This trend is reflected in three major policy themes—the new security concept, the two decades of "strategic opportunities" principle, and the "peaceful rise" theory.

First, in 1996, China outlined its "new security concept," which sought to redefine Chinese security interests to include economic modernization, political reform, and technological development as well as military security. Although many American scholars viewed this as a mere "repackaging" of previous foreign policy theory,[6] it is nonetheless notable for its focus on multilateralism rather than multipolarity.[7] China appears to have, at least for the moment, accepted the reality of a unipolar world in which the United States will continue to dominate for the foreseeable future. Efforts to develop a multipolar world order are long term at best, and though American power must be kept in check, current Chinese thinking goes, alliances designed to balance the United States, such as among China, India, and Russia, are unlikely to work and could be counterproductive.

According to Wang Jisi, director of the Institute of American Studies at the Chinese Academy of Social Sciences and perhaps China's most respected expert on the United States, "Chinese policy analysts, being realists, have few illusions about the feasibility of formulating a lasting international coalition that could serve as the counterforce to U.S. power. China has neither the capability nor the desire to take the lead in formulating such a coalition, let alone confronting U.S. hegemony."[8]

As such, the new security concept offers a revised perception of the United States and its role in Asia. Although it questions the purpose of U.S. military alliances in the region, Beijing has become more accepting of American presence in Asia, at least for the near term. In a joint press conference with President Bush during the 2001 Asia-Pacific Economic Cooperation (APEC) meeting in Shanghai, Chinese president Jiang Zemin stressed "long-term coexistence" with the United States.[9] Then foreign minister Tang Jiaxuan repeatedly told Secretary Powell that China did not seek to "push the United States out of Asia," and Bush provided similar reassurances to President Jiang.[10]

Second, at the 16th Party Congress in November 2002, Jiang Zemin stated that "the first two decades of the 21st century are a period of important strategic opportunities."[11] Over the next 20 years, China will focus on economic development as its "top priority" and "central task."[12] As such, China must constructively engage with the international community so that foreign policy tensions or military competition do not draw resources away from its economic goals.

Third, to take advantage of these strategic opportunities, leaders in China have put forward a new theory on the "peaceful rise" of China. This theory, the brainchild of former Central Party School vice president Zheng Bijian,[13] is designed to paint a picture of China as a good neighbor, a responsible member of the international community, and a regional leader but one that will not pursue hegemony. This theory centers on global economic integration and the use of China's "soft power," and in this sense, China's leaders have sought to distinguish themselves from Germany and Japan in the interwar period and from Russia during the Cold War.[14] As Zheng has stated, "China's only choice is to strive for rise, more importantly strive for a peaceful rise. That is to say that we have to work for a peaceful international environment for the sake of our development and, at the same time, safeguard world peace through our development."[15] According to this theory, not only will China's rise not hurt any other nation, including the United States, but it will also bring sizeable benefits, primarily economic, to the region and the world.

Taken together, these three policy concepts reflect a new strategic vision for China on which current Chinese foreign policy is based. It is a policy that is designed to create an international environment conducive to allowing China to achieve its two top domestic goals: first, *economic modernization*—to "build a well-off society in an all-round way"[16]—and second, *national unity*, primarily the reunification of Taiwan with the mainland but also holding onto Tibet and Xinjiang, regions where there are active separatist movements. Achieving these two central goals is, in turn, essential for ensuring *political stability* and the sustainability of the current political regime.

Beijing's desire to effectively address its domestic challenges[17] has driven the leadership to adopt a "moderate and pragmatic Chinese international strategy."[18] As part of this strategy, China has sought to peacefully and quietly resolve border and other territorial issues, and, as a result, China's periphery is more secure than at any time in modern history. Similarly, China has proactively pursued a "good neighbor" policy, reaching out to Southeast and Central Asia, initiating free trade agreements, investing in regional markets, taking a greater leadership role in the ASEAN Regional Forum (ARF), and shaping the agenda of the Shanghai Cooperation Organization (SCO), which it initiated.

China is taking a greater leadership role elsewhere in the region as well, although reluctantly in some cases. In North Korea, for example, China played a major role in launching the Six Party Talks,[19] although it would have preferred that the United States negotiate bilaterally with North Korea. This was not an option, however, and though Chinese and American interests on the Korean Peninsula are not completely aligned, both sides have nonetheless managed to emphasize their common objectives while downplaying their differences.

Globally, China has long sought to be recognized as one of the world's great powers. Accession to the World Trade Organization (WTO) and the winning of competition to host the 2008 Olympic Games were important steps in this process, as was the reference in the President Bush's 2002 State of the Union Address and the Bush administration's 2002 National Security Strategy (NSS) to China as a "great power." China's role on the United Nations Security Council during the Iraq debate likewise boosted Beijing's stature. Even if China's leaders tried to "straddle the fence"[20] between the United States and Britain on one side and France and Germany on the other, China's relevance to the discussions was clear.

Most important to China, however, is its relationship with the United States. Globalization is central to China's economic development, and the United States is the dominant player in the global economy and will remain so for the foreseeable future. Bilaterally, not only is the United States China's second largest export market, but also a major source of investment and technology. Although China is increasingly reaching out to its Asian neighbors, Latin America, the Middle East, and Europe as business partners, the United States, according to one Chinese scholar, remains "the most important relationship for China. We need your market, technology and investment."[21]

A cooperative, or at least constructive, relationship with the United States is also important for China's efforts to achieve its second key goal: reunification of Taiwan with the mainland. China is pursuing a policy that not only relies on the threat of military force to deter Taiwan from declaring independence, but also seeks to win the "hearts and minds" of the Taiwanese people, offering both economic and cultural carrots. China's booming economy is its main selling point with Taiwanese businesspeople, students, and job seekers; therefore "antagonistic relations with Washington would . . . weaken the Chinese economy and thereby greatly reduce China's magnetic pull on Taiwan, and lower popular support for the Chinese government."[22]

Beijing also would like to see the United States modify its policy toward Taiwan or, at least, work to moderate the behavior of Taiwan's leaders so they do not cross Chinese redlines and compel China to use force to keep Taiwan in the fold. China believes that time is on its side in the long run and that "many political, economic and perhaps even military trends regarding Taiwan—the most volatile issue between Washington and Beijing—favor Beijing in the long run."[23] Ultimately, the Chinese Communist Party (CCP) has staked its political legitimacy on eventual reunification, and Beijing views the United States as a critical player in resolving the cross-strait issue in its favor, whether it takes 5 years or 50 years.

China, for the time being at least, needs the United States. Not surprisingly, therefore, Beijing was very concerned at the outset of the Bush administration when U.S.-China relations seemed destined for challenging times.

EVOLVING U.S. POLICY AND RHETORIC TOWARD CHINA

The Bush administration's 2001 Quadrennial Defense Review (QDR), while published—and hastily edited to include stronger references on terrorism—after September 11, was drafted well before the terrorist attacks and therefore reflects early Bush administration thinking about China as a serious and growing threat to American security interests. The QDR states that "although the United States will not face a peer competitor in the near future, the potential exists for regional powers to develop sufficient capabilities to threaten stability in regions critical to U.S. interests. In particular, Asia is gradually emerging as a region susceptible to large-scale military competition. . . . The possibility exists that a military competitor with a formidable resource base will emerge in the [Asia-Pacific] region."[24] The unmistakable reference to China alarmed Chinese leaders and scholars.[25]

In addition, Bush seemed to clearly lean toward Taiwan in the early days of his administration. In April 2001, the Bush administration announced that it would no longer conduct an annual review of its weapons sales to Taiwan—a move that was interpreted in Beijing as a commitment to selling more, higher technology arms, in violation, in its view, of the August 1982 communiqué. President Bush's comments later that month that the United States would do "whatever it took"[26] to defend Taiwan similarly rattled Beijing.

The April 2001 EP-3 incident played a major role in redirecting the trajectory of U.S.-China relations. The near collision of a Chinese F-7 fighter jet and a U.S. reconnaissance plane, the holding "hostage" of the American crew and plane, the refusal of the Chinese leadership to accept phone calls from senior U.S. officials, and the painstaking negotiations over the wording of a U.S. apology all contributed to a highly charged environment. The relationship plummeted to such depths that leaders in both Beijing and Washington felt compelled to reassess the state of U.S.-China relations.

Soon after the safe return of the 24 American crew members, Bush administration rhetoric began to shift—and to sound remarkably more like President Clinton than candidate Bush. For example, Assistant Secretary of State James Kelly stated that "we view China as a partner on some issues and a competitor on others. . . . From promoting peace and stability on the Korean Peninsula to nonproliferation to trade, we share common interests with China that are best served by a productive—and positive—relationship. . . . China's behavior, particularly in the next few months, will determine whether we develop the kind of productive relationship the President wants."[27]

In the following months, efforts were undertaken to put the relationship on a more positive track. The first significant step was Secretary of State Colin Powell's July 2001 trip to China. During his visit, Powell expressed the administration's desire for a "friendly"[28] relationship with China and rejected labels, including "strategic competitor," to describe what he called a "relationship . . . so complex with so many different elements."[29] President Bush too adopted a new tone and a new vocabulary when describing U.S.-China relations, calling China "a great power" and stating that "America wants a constructive relationship with China."[30] President Bush backed his words with action. For example, at the president's personal insistence, military-to-military exchanges, which had been suspended after the EP-3 incident, were resumed.[31] Since then, Defense Consultative Talks have been held in December 2002 and February 2004.[32] The next round is expected to be held in the first half of 2005.

In addition, the Bush administration made the new approach to China official policy when it stated in the 2002 NSS that the United States "welcome[s] the emergence of a strong, peaceful and prosperous China. . . . The United States seeks a constructive relationship with a changing China."[33] The contrast between the characterizations of China in the QDR and the NSS is striking. Within a few short months, China went from being seen as part of the problem to being viewed as part of the solution, from being an outsider to being an insider. This shift has reinforced the trend in China toward a more responsible, more pragmatic, and more mature foreign policy.

THE OPPORTUNITY OF SEPTEMBER 11

The new U.S. approach was welcomed by Beijing. The Chinese leadership had been seeking better relations with the Bush team since the presidential election was decided in Florida in December 2000, and it was cautiously optimistic about the less confrontational rhetoric coming out of Washington after the resolution of the EP-3 incident.

Then came September 11. Although changes in Chinese foreign policy and the trend toward more positive U.S.-China relations began prior to the terrorist attacks, the tragedy of that day presented an enormous strategic opportunity for the two countries to solidify their improving ties. Both sides seized this chance.

From the American perspective, the terrorist attacks on the American homeland put into stark relief the so-called China threat. Al Qaeda, terrorism, and weapons of mass destruction suddenly seemed significantly more menacing. Concerns about rogue nations and weak or failing states similarly came to dominate American security concerns. A "rising" China was officially off the front burner of threats.

Moreover, given its seat on the UN Security Council and its close ties to key players like Pakistan and Iran, China was not only no longer a frontline threat, but also a potential, and necessary, partner in the war on terrorism. In the post–September 11 calculus, common interests— fighting terrorism, protecting their respective homelands, and securing sea-lanes of control—now far outweighed their differences.

As a result, the political dynamics in the United States regarding China were transformed on September 11. The so-called Blue Team, which had long viewed China as perhaps the number one security threat and sought to shift the cross-strait balance toward democratic Taiwan, was essentially declawed during this period. Today, this "anti-China" group is largely silent; when it does speak up, such as in the July 2002 report by the mostly hard-line U.S.-China Economic and Security Review Commission, its warnings about the China threat have little, if any, policy impact.[34]

For its part, China saw September 11 as a potential turning point in the relationship and acted quickly to reach out to the United States. According to a Chinese expert with close ties to the People's Liberation Army (PLA), Jiang Zemin witnessed the terrorist attacks on CNN. He quickly convened a meeting of senior advisers at his residence, including Vice Premier and former foreign minister Qian Qichen and then deputy foreign minister Li Zhaoxing, among others, to discuss what had happened and how China should respond. A letter of sympathy to President Bush was drafted.[35] Jiang Zemin was the second foreign leader, after Russian president Vladimir Putin, to get through to Bush on the phone to offer his condolences and to pledge China's support. China's senior leaders clearly understood the significance of September 11 for the United States and sought to make the most of it.

Although sympathetic to the United States and affected by the deaths of PRC nationals at the World Trade Center, Beijing's perception of its own security was not directly affected by the terrorist attacks. It was affected, however, by the Bush administration's response to the terrorist attacks. As one Chinese military scholar commented, "The U.S. priority is to eradicate terrorism and China's priority is reunification with Taiwan. It is difficult for researchers here to say that terrorism is our top security concern. After September 11, the world changed for the U.S., but for China, it is the U.S. response that has changed the world."[36]

As a result of the U.S. response, China saw a fundamental change in its strategic position in the immediate aftermath of September 11. The age-old specter of encirclement resurfaced. With the United States improving ties with Pakistan (aided by China) and Central Asia as a path to Afghanistan, enhanced U.S. relations with both India and Russia, a U.S. foothold in post-Taliban Afghanistan, traditional alliances with Japan, South Korea, and Thailand, strong relations with Singapore, increasing ties to Southeast Asian nations such as the Philippines and Vietnam, and U.S. troops deployed as close as 300 kilometers to China's border, many in China felt increasingly insecure.

Yet, China understood that after the terrorist attacks, the United States was in no mood to be challenged. In a speech to a joint session of Congress on September 20, 2001, President Bush stated that "every nation in every region now has a decision to make: Either you are with us or you are with the terrorists." China's leaders took this admonition seriously and decided that, given its economic, political and security goals, China simply could not afford to be on the wrong side. Moreover, the opportunity to be considered among U.S. friends and allies as partners in the war on terrorism—to be "with" the United States—was an opportunity the Chinese could not pass up. Therefore, when President Jiang called President Bush, terrorism was not his primary concern. Instead, Beijing had a strategic agenda of its own.

First, China sought to improve relations with the United States so that it could focus on its domestic priorities, as discussed above. From this perspective, throwing its hat into the ring with the United States has paid off for China. China's economy continues to expand at a rapid pace, growing 9.1 percent in 2003.[37] In 2004, Chinese GDP grew 9.5 percent in the first three quarters of the year,[38] and full-year growth is estimated to be between 8.6 percent and 9.2 percent.[39] China recently surpassed the United States as the largest recipient of foreign direct investment, and its exports are booming. Politically, the transition of power to the fourth generation leaders has gone smoothly, and the Hu Jintao administration is moving forward with economic reform, albeit not with political reform.

Has China's cooperation with the United States "paid off" with regard to Taiwan? Some American scholars argued in the wake of September 11 that Beijing was explicitly trying to extract concessions on Taiwan in exchange for support for the war on terrorism,[40] a claim that some Chinese scholars echoed.[41] The Chinese government, however, did not explicitly link cooperation on the war on terrorism with other issues, such as Taiwan. Had it done so, the Bush administration would have rejected such a linkage out of hand. Regardless, many in China believe that the Bush administration has in fact moderated its cross-strait policy as a result of improved U.S.-China relations.

To the extent that Washington has modified its Taiwan policy, it has been in response to Taipei's actions, not Chinese pressure. To be sure, greater U.S. appreciation of the value of Chinese cooperation in pursuing its strategic interests in the war on terrorism and other matters provided a backdrop for U.S. deliberations on how to handle issues relating to Taiwan. More important, however, Taiwan's president Chen Shuibian refused to heed the Bush administration's public and private warnings not to stoke tension in the Taiwan Strait, which created strains in the U.S.-Taiwan relationship. President Bush did not seek—nor did he receive—any quid pro quo from China when he publicly rebuked Chen on December 2003 standing alongside Chinese premier Wen Jiabao. Opposition to any unilateral changes in the status quo in the Taiwan Strait and nonsupport for Taiwan independence were added to the U.S. "one-China" policy mantra, along with adherence to the three Sino-American communiqués and the Taiwan Relations Act, and insistence on a peaceful resolution of differences between Taipei and Beijing. Nonetheless, despite U.S. frustration over specific statements and actions by Taiwan's elected leaders and Taiwan's failure to purchase approved weapons systems, the Bush administration remained staunchly supportive of expanding Taiwan's participation in the international community and committed to strengthening U.S.-Taiwan military relations. The U.S.-Taiwan relationship is being challenged, certainly, but these challenges are, in essence, related to Taipei, not to Beijing.

Within the post–September 11 context, China has also sought recognition of its own terrorist problem. China is centrally concerned with territorial integrity, not only because of Taiwan, but also because of its historically based view that a divided China is vulnerable to outside attack. Therefore, Beijing takes very seriously the actions of Muslim separatists in Xinjiang, a province in northwestern China, who have staged violent attacks and bombings both locally and in Beijing and are reportedly supported with arms and money by Islamic sympathizers outside of China—a factor that gives the movement its "international" dimension.[42]

Before September 11, the international community viewed the separatist movement in Xinjiang and the Chinese government's crackdown as a human rights problem. After September 11, China effectively put its Xinjiang problem under the umbrella of global terrorism by proving a connection between Xinjiang separatists and Osama bin Laden, thereby recasting it as part of the global terrorist challenge. Evidence that Chinese Muslims were found training in Al Qaeda camps in Afghanistan led the United States to add one Chinese separatist group, the East Turkistan Independence Movement (ETIM), to its list of terrorist organizations.[43]

For China, the listing of ETIM as a terrorist organization in the United States was a major victory and confirmed in the minds of many Chinese leaders that Beijing could use its cooperation in the war on terrorism to its advantage with the United States. While Beijing denies an explicit connection between support for the war on terrorism and U.S. listing of Xinjiang separatists on the terrorist list,[44] American recognition of the problem has allowed the central government to crack down in Xinjiang under a veil of international legitimacy.[45]

In short, September 11 underscored what both the United States and China had already begun to believe—that a constructive relationship was in both countries' national interest. September 11 gave both China and the United States an opportunity to reassess their strategic position and therefore was a critical catalyst for closer U.S.-China relations. In the wake of September 11, both sides had good reasons to reach out and forge a positive counterterrorism agenda, including WMD nonprolif-eration, intelligence-sharing on terrorist networks, anti–money laun-dering, and maritime security.[46] With a common threat and a shared agenda, the United States and China could, for the first time since the end of the Cold War, focus on mutual security interests. As a result, the U.S.-China relationship was given new impetus from which both sides have benefited.

ON THE BANDWAGON: CHINA'S CONTRIBUTION TO THE WAR ON TERRORISM

By most accounts, China played an important role in the first phase of the war on terrorism, the effort to topple the Taliban in Afghanistan.[47] Perhaps most important, Beijing used its influence with Islamabad to encourage Pakistan's cooperation for the U.S.-led campaign. In addition, China quickly closed its short border with Afghanistan, a move more symbolic than substantive, given that most Taliban members were likely to cross the border into Pakistan, not China. After the fall of the Taliban, China pledged a total of $153.6 million in aid for Kabul—a large amount for a country that does not have a tradition of foreign aid.

In supporting the U.S. war on terror, Beijing has both won American gratitude and strengthened its regional political position. A case in point is Beijing's activity in multilateral institutions. For example, China has worked to refocus the SCO, originally established to address terrorism in Xinjiang and perhaps as a counterbalance to growing U.S. influence in Central Asia, in support of U.S. efforts. Within ASEAN, China spear-headed the establishment of the Kuala Lumpur Anti-Terror Center. China has also held bilateral discussions on counterterrorism with re-gional neighbors as well as with Britain and the United States, among others.[48] The October 2001 APEC meeting in Shanghai provided China with an opportunity to showcase its new partnership with the United States and to shepherd an effort among Asian nations on counterterror-ism, while boosting its own position. In addition, at the APEC meeting, the United States and China established an interagency counterterror-ism mechanism.

China has not sought to disrupt closer U.S.-Russia ties, nor has it publicly voiced much concern about Japan's expanding security role, such as in Afghanistan and Iraq. Amid growing Sino-Japanese friction and the strengthening of the U.S.-Japan alliance, Chinese concerns about Japan's growing military power persist. Yet Beijing has likely ac-cepted that Japan is well on its way to becoming a "normal" country and that there is little it can do to prevent it. Beijing has also learned that belligerent rhetoric often undermines rather than promotes its interests and sees no benefit to condemning Japan's actions. Instead, China has decided to talk less and prepare more, politically and militarily, to deal with a more assertive Japan.

China has supported the United States at the United Nations, includ-ing voting for Resolution 1368, which authorized the use of force in Af-ghanistan—the first time that China had voted for use of force in the UN.[49] China also voted for Resolution 1373, which condemned the ter-rorist attacks and developed antiterrorism guidelines. U.S.-China talks on counterterrorism were established. China has been particularly active in efforts to cut the flow of money to terrorists, and biannual meetings on terrorist financing continue to take place. China is a signatory to a wide range of antiterrorism conventions as well. Information sharing is also a critical element of China's support for antiterrorism efforts. Without providing any detail, U.S. officials have made references to the fact that information provided by China has been valuable and cite this as proof of China's sincerity in antiterrorism cooperation.

China has also assisted on transportation security initiatives, most notably the Container Security Initiative (CSI), a centerpiece of the Bush administration's homeland security efforts.[50] Furthermore, China has taken steps to increase security at its airports, supported financially by the U.S. Trade and Development Agency (TDA).[51] On the enforce-ment front, China began to share intelligence with the FBI, and finally approved the establishment of an FBI office in the U.S. embassy in Beijing. In addition, there are indications that the FBI is conducting courses for officials in the Ministry of State Security on how to prioritize intelligence and analyze threats, although this has not been con-firmed.[52] Finally, after a few years of delay, China published new regula-tions controlling the export of missile technology in August 2002. In China, the problem has been primarily one of enforcement rather than promulgation; however, these new restrictions were welcomed at the time by the Bush administration as a good faith sign of cooperation.[53]

Interestingly, for a time China imposed strict controls on what could be published about the United States after September 11 in an effort to mute criticism of the country's new partnership with the United States in the war on terrorism. This censorship was designed primarily to protect the Chinese leadership from attacks on its partnership with the United States. Yet, setting aside the issue of freedom of the press, this effort to restrain the media contrasts sharply with the government's use of the media to encourage anti-American articles, rhetoric, and even violent protests after the 1999 bombing of the Chinese embassy in Belgrade.[54]

Of course, China could have done more to support the war on terrorism. It did not provide overflight or basing rights, as requested by the United States and as provided by every other neighbor of Afghanistan except for Iran. China provided no soldiers to the multinational force fighting the Taliban. Its aid package of more than $150 million was large by Chinese standards, but many feel that China could have pledged more financial and human resources to the postwar reconstruction effort. In addition, it is unclear whether that money has in fact been disbursed. On export controls, enforcement remains a major problem.

Nonetheless, China's generally proactive and positive actions at the outset of the war on terror convinced the Bush administration that Beijing was genuine in its desire to cooperate with the United States on the war on terrorism and that further strengthening the U.S.-China relationship rather than focusing on the China threat was clearly in the U.S. national security interest.

In addition to the targeted assistance that China lent the United States in the immediate aftermath of the September 11 attacks, Beijing has sought to support U.S. efforts in other areas as well, as long as they coincide with, or at least do not undermine, Chinese interests. Iraq and North Korea are the most obvious examples.

Although in principle China may have agreed with France and Germany's opposition to the war in Iraq, in practice it decided to acquiesce to the invasion. The potential cost of disrupting the positive trend in U.S.-China relations was not worth the moral victory of standing by its long-held principle of not impinging on another country's sovereignty. Despite the fact that many Chinese felt that the United States was pursuing war for economic reasons,[55] China chaired the November 2002 UN Security Council vote on Iraq and voted in favor of issuing an ultimatum to Saddam Hussein in October 2002. China was spared a more difficult vote—on whether to endorse the use of force in Iraq—when the second resolution in early 2003 was withdrawn by the United States.[56]

China has worked even more closely with the United States on North Korea. North Korea's October 2002 admission that it had a uranium enrichment program, its withdrawal from the Non-Proliferation Treaty

(NPT), and its periodic threats to test its nuclear capability have drawn China and the United States closer together on an issue where their interests are not fully aligned. Although much criticized for inaction at the outset of the North Korean nuclear crisis, China has since been given significant credit for jumpstarting multilateral talks that continue to provide an important forum for information sharing and dialogue with Pyongyang. Through private bilateral diplomacy and payoffs, including the promise of oil shipments and the financing of a glass factory, the Chinese helped bring North Korea to the table and continue to apply pressure on Pyongyang—although Beijing believes it is ultimately up to Washington to make a deal.

China's cooperation on North Korea goes beyond the Six Party Talks. For example, in the summer of 2003, on a tip from Washington, the Chinese government stopped shipment by a Chinese company to North Korea of tributyl phosphate, or TBP, which is used as a solvent to extract weapons-grade plutonium from spent nuclear fuel rods. That China cooperated with the United States to stop a North Korean purchase of TBP sent a strong message to Pyongyang. This incident contrasts sharply with the 1993 inspection by U.S. Navy personnel of the Chinese ship Yinhe, suspected of carrying chemical-weapons material to Iran, which was viewed in China as a breach of Chinese sovereignty and remains a sensitive issue today.

BALANCING ACT

Of course, U.S.-China relations have gone through enough ups and downs that Beijing is not willing to put all its eggs in the American basket. China is no longer seen as America's number one threat, but it is still far from an ally. Relations are much improved, but any progress could be reversed overnight, especially over Taiwan. Although the Blue Team has been largely sidelined, there are still those in the Bush administration and in Congress who remain firmly in the "China threat" camp and whose views could grow in influence again in the future. China understands, in other words, that its strategic position is not yet on solid ground.

Evidence of residual skepticism about China was seen in the March 2002 U.S. Nuclear Posture Review, which listed China as one of seven countries that "could be involved in an immediate or potential contingency" in which the United States might use nuclear weapons—a document that rattled Beijing. Similarly, though the NSS was generally welcomed by Beijing because of the reference to China as a "great power" rather than a threat, there were elements of the NSS that concerned China, most notably the explicit doctrine of preemption, which China feared could be employed in the Korean context. The NSS description of a "distinctly American internationalism" that seeks to export American economic, political, and cultural values was also problematic for Communist Party leaders, who are deeply worried about their own political future as well as about U.S. support for a democratic Taiwan. Bush's now infamous "axis of evil" comment in his 2002 State of the Union address also gave China pause—would China someday be added to that list?

Will China continue to pursue its "peaceful rise" and continue to, on balance, cooperate with the United States? For the foreseeable future, the answer is yes. Over the long term, however, Chinese intentions are less clear. China's military build-up and economic development, particularly in strategic sectors like information technology, could simply be the natural outgrowth of China's "peaceful rise." That said, it also means that China could soon be in a position to pursue a different path, should it choose to do so.

In fact, China's vision for its future might be more ambitious. Although China needs the United States now, arguably it is playing a longer-term game, working toward a future in which the balance of power in Asia, or even globally, might be quite different. It would be a mistake, therefore, to assume that China has jumped on the U.S. bandwagon strategically, although it seems to have done so tactically to achieve specific objectives in Xinjiang and to create an environment in which it can concentrate on its long-term goals of economic development and Taiwan reunification.

Looking to the future, China is quietly building relationships with its neighbors and key international players that could serve to strengthen China's regional and global influence. China's increasing interaction on economic and security matters with ASEAN and especially its expanding cooperation with Japan and South Korea—the "plus three" grouping associated with ASEAN—combined with its active support for convening an East Asian summit, suggest an intent to reorganize the security landscape of the region in a way that is more favorable to Chinese interests.

Using its massive market as the hook, China is attracting other countries eager to ride the wave of its economic boom. It has announced plans for a China-ASEAN free trade agreement and has become increasingly active in APEC since the 2001 meeting in Shanghai. China has made a major effort to reach out to South Korea and today is South Korea's leading investment destination and its largest trading partner, surpassing the United States in both categories. Sino-ROK political relations have gotten warmer as economic ties have increased, although tensions still arise periodically, such as the recent controversy over Koguryo.[57]

In addition, in the aftermath of the Philippines' decision to pull its troops out of Iraq in July 2004, Beijing seized on the opportunity to forge close ties with Manila. Within a few months, China hosted Filipino president Gloria Macapagal Arroyo and Filipino defense secretary Avelio Cruz. A bilateral defense cooperation agreement was negotiated that includes intelligence sharing and joint maritime exercises, several business contracts were signed, and an accord to jointly conduct a seismic study of potential petroleum reserves in parts of the South China Sea, including the disputed Spratly Islands, was concluded.

China has also strengthened its leadership role in regional security organizations like the ARF and the SCO. To address territorial issues, China signed a nonaggression pact with ASEAN, and China and India have set aside their border issues.

China has increasingly engaged with Europe as well, and Sino-European trade is on the rise. From the European perspective, access to the China market trumps other issues in the region, which it views as U.S. domain, and Europeans are generally uninterested in the political and security dimensions of the cross-strait issue. As a result of increasing political and economic ties, the European Union is considering lifting the arms embargo that was put in place in the wake of Tiananmen Square in 1989. Beijing has actively lobbied to have the ban lifted, despite American protests. China has also toned down its negative rhetoric about the North Atlantic Treaty Organization (NATO), of which it has long been skeptical, and has expressed interest in joining the G-8, which it previously denounced as a rich countries' club.

In addition to courting friends as a potential balance to the United States, China has in some cases simply resisted U.S. pressure to cooperate on key issues where it is concerned about setting dangerous precedents, such as on counterproliferation. Although China is a signatory to nonproliferation treaties and has stated its willingness to cooperate with the United States, Chinese government officials continue to express reservations about the U.S.-led Proliferation Security Initiative (PSI).[58] In particular, Beijing questions its legal basis and expresses concern about the tools that the United States proposes to employ—namely, sanctions, embargoes, and even the use of force. China would prefer to use "political and diplomatic means within the framework of international laws" and insists that "all nonproliferation measures shall contribute to peace, security, and stability in the region and the world at large."[59]

As China's interests expand beyond its periphery to countries farther afield, U.S.-Chinese friction has emerged in new realms. For example, Beijing opposed the adoption of tougher language that could result in the imposition of sanctions against Sudan, which was proposed by the United States in the UN Security Council in response to the ongoing genocide in the Darfur region of that country. China's reluctance to put greater pressure on Sudan was in part based on its long-standing opposition to interfering in the international affairs of sovereign nations. Another important factor shaping Beijing's diplomatic choices, however, was the burgeoning Sino-Sudanese commercial relationship in which China is Sudan's largest trading partner and the main foreign investor in that country's oil industry.[60] After threatening to veto any resolution that would trigger automatic sanctions, China ultimately abstained from voting on UN resolutions in July and September 2004 after the language was modified to accommodate its concerns.

Similarly, China resisted U.S. efforts to bring Iran before the Security Council toward the end of 2004 over charges that it has a secret nuclear weapons program. China joined France, Germany, and the United Kingdom in proposing that the issue be addressed within the context of the International Atomic Energy Agency. China has long-standing ties with Iran, and the two countries have become even closer in recent years as China seeks to meet its energy needs. For example, in October 2004 China signed a $100 billion deal to purchase liquefied natural gas from Tehran, China's largest energy agreement with a major OPEC producer to date. China was also granted rights for Sinopec, the Chinese oil giant, to exploit an Iranian oil field. Long-term projects include an oil pipeline connecting Iran to China through the Caspian Sea and Kazakhstan.

CONCLUSION: A NEWLY FOUND PARTNERSHIP, ALBEIT STILL FRAGILE

China is among the countries that have reaped significant diplomatic benefits from September 11. The opportunity presented by the terrorist attacks on that day was deftly seized and exploited by Beijing to transform a mistrustful and troubled bilateral relationship with the United States into a constructive, cooperative partnership. For China, consolidating and advancing its ties with the United States is critical to the attainment of economic development, its top national objective. The Bush administration has subsequently altered its view of China as a potential strategic competitor, now regarding it as a country with which it shares important interests and with which it seeks to cooperate when interests overlap. The war on terrorism provided a rationale for strategic cooperation between the United States and China that had not existed since the halcyon days when the two nations faced a common threat from the Soviet Union.

Of course, Beijing's support for the war on terrorism has not derived solely from its desire to improve relations with the United States. The war on terrorism has enabled Beijing to deal more harshly with separatists in Xinjiang and other challenges to the regime under the guise of fighting terrorism, despite warnings from U.S. officials to refrain from doing so. The Chinese are more relaxed today about threats to domestic stability in their northwest region than they were prior to September 11.

Although September 11 has had some negative consequences, there have also been positive by-products. For example, China's appreciation of the dangers to its security posed by the proliferation of weapons of mass destruction has grown. In addition to bolstering its export control regulations for missile and dual-use technology, China has increased its involvement with multilateral export regimes and groupings that it previously criticized or simply paid little heed to. It has formally joined the Nuclear Suppliers Group, applied for accession to the Missile Technology Control Regime, and established a dialogue mechanism with the Wassenaar Arrangement.

Washington and Beijing have settled into a comfortable pattern of cooperation on important security issues, such as fighting the war on terrorism, eliminating North Korea's nuclear weapons, and curbing the proliferation of weapons of mass destruction, while at the same time continuing to address persisting—and sometimes new—areas of disagreement. Indeed, problems in the bilateral relationship have multiplied in 2004, but they have been managed without acrimony, in part owing to the overall positive milieu.

For example, in March 2004, the United States filed the first case against China at the World Trade Organization, charging that China's

value-added tax discriminates against foreign semiconductor produc-
ers and therefore violates WTO rules. That same month, the United
States introduced a resolution condemning China's human rights prac-
tices at the United Nations Commission on Human Rights (UNHRC) in
Geneva for the first time in three years. The draft resolution was rejected
even before it could be put to a vote and was vehemently criticized by
Beijing; China also suspended its bilateral human rights dialogue with
the United States in retaliation. Nevertheless, fallout from this episode
was contained, and there was no setback in the overall relationship.

Certainly, Sino-U.S. relations won't be derailed as a result of a trade
dispute or even over human rights—yet it could be over Taiwan. China
will never abandon its goal of reunification to accommodate the United
States. Taiwan is a matter of national unity, and therefore of political legitimacy, and Beijing would undoubtedly go to extreme measures to protect its interest in forestalling a permanent separation of the island from
the mainland—regardless of the impact on relations with the United
States, its global image, or even on its own economy. Managing Taiwan's
aspirations under a second Chen Shui-bian administration will likely
test the much-improved U.S.-China relationship.

Washington should hold realistic expectations about China. Economic development, regime survival, and reunification with Taiwan remain Beijing's top priorities, not the war on terrorism, and there are
limits as to how much China will do in support of U.S.-led efforts. China
will continue to cooperate actively with the United States only where
U.S. and Chinese interests intersect. When China disagrees with U.S.
policies, it will refrain from aggressively opposing Washington only if
Chinese interests are not directly at stake. Such was the case with the U.S.
invasion of Iraq. However, a U.S. surgical strike on North Korean nuclear facilities would likely evoke a tougher response and reverberate
through other areas of bilateral cooperation.

Chinese cooperation is also constrained by wariness about American
global preeminence and the apparent willingness of the United States to
use military force preemptively. Moreover, China is dissatisfied with the
prevailing global power structure and its second-class role in it. It is uncomfortable with the United States as the sole superpower and the
world's self-appointed policeman. Beijing favors a global arrangement
with several major powers simultaneously exerting influence and checking each other, although it recognizes that such a multipolar world is not
achievable in the near term.

Chinese cooperation with the United States is limited as well by the persisting deep suspicions that the Chinese leadership and elite harbor about U.S. intentions toward China. Despite notable improvement in Sino-U.S. ties, the Chinese continue to worry that the United States will seek to inhibit China's rise as a great power and prevent the reunification of Taiwan with the mainland. In addition, concern about preserving domestic stability and regime survival require Chinese leaders to pay attention to criticism of the government for being too soft on the United States, especially with regard to Taiwan.

Unease about American power has prompted China to look for opportunities to balance U.S. power, but only when it can do so without harming ties with Washington. Recent efforts to cozy up to the European Union provide a good example of how China is seeking to counterbalance U.S. power and mitigate the negative consequences of U.S. unilateralism. Chinese leaders have forged particularly close relations with France and Germany, the two largest European nations that have demonstrated a willingness to challenge the United States.

China's acquiescence to American force presence in Asia is primarily a function of its pragmatic recognition that challenging the United States at this juncture would be counterproductive. Beijing looks forward to a time, however, when it can hold sway in its own backyard. Steps to promote economic and security cooperation with its neighbors while rhetorically assuring them that China's rise will be peaceful are only some of the measures that China is taking to lay the foundation in the region for a more defined leadership position. Over time, the Chinese anticipate that the countries on its periphery will accommodate China's rising power. Although Beijing likely has no coherent strategy to expel U.S. forces from East Asia, it hopes, and increasingly expects, that the situation in the region will evolve so that its neighbors conclude that hosting American troops no longer serves their interests.

Chinese wariness is matched by U.S. uncertainty about China's future aims. How will China use its new wealth, assuming that its economy continues to grow at a rapid pace? What kind of influence will China exert on its increasingly dependent neighbors? What will closer Chinese ties with both Europe and East Asia mean for U.S. alliances? Will China's rise in fact be peaceful? Will China reconcile itself to the rise of a separate Taiwan identity and the desire of its people to participate meaningfully in the global community or employ military force to compel the Taiwanese to become part of "one China"? The United States continues to hedge against the possibility that China's rise will threaten U.S. interests just as Beijing hedges against a possible U.S. strategy of containing China.

Ongoing misgivings about each side's intentions underscores the main challenge in Sino-U.S. relations: although bilateral ties have improved in breadth and depth over the past three years, the relationship remains fragile. An unexpected crisis could arrest cooperation across all areas and trigger a substantial deterioration of the relationship overnight. The lesson of the 1999 accidental bombing of the Chinese embassy in Belgrade and the 2001 plane collision incident is that U.S.-China relations can sour very quickly. China lacks effective crisis management mechanisms and has weak decisionmaking institutions. Its leadership's response to a crisis is invariably driven by domestic political considerations. Anti-American sentiment in China simmers below the surface, just as anti-China sentiment remains a latent, but potent factor in U.S. domestic politics.

What lies ahead? Beijing will continue to pursue a constructive, cooperative relationship with the United States, while quietly working to address its own domestic economic and security challenges, to shift the balance in the Asia-Pacific region in China's favor, and to strengthen its capabilities to reclaim Taiwan. If Sino-U.S. ties remain amicable, differences over Taiwan are carefully managed, and the United States does not overtly challenge China's rise to great power status, then Beijing may continue along its current path of accommodation and adaptation to prevailing international norms. If, on the other hand, the United States blocks China from achieving its national objectives, Beijing will have positioned itself regionally and globally to more effectively counter the United States.

Notes

[1] Speech by George W. Bush, "A Distinctly American Internationalism," delivered at the Ronald Reagan Presidential Library in Simi Valley, California, November 19, 1999.

[2] Ibid.

[3] Although President Clinton pursued a policy of engagement with China, U.S.-China relations were not without tensions during his two terms in office. Early fights over the linkage of human rights and trade, the 1995–1996 crisis in the Taiwan Strait, and the 1999 bombing of the Chinese embassy in Belgrade all tested Sino-American relations.

[4] Colin Powell, "A Strategy of Partnership," *Foreign Affairs* 83, no. 1 (January/February 2004).

[5] David Shambaugh, "The New Stability in U.S.-China Relations: Causes and Consequences," paper prepared for conference, *The United States and China in a Global Strategic Context,* sponsored by the China Policy Program of the Elliott School of International Affairs, The George Washington University, and the China Institute of International Studies (CIIS), November 14–15, 2002, Washington, D.C.

[6] David M. Finkelstein, "China's 'New Concept of Security': Restrospective and Prospects," paper prepared for the National Defense University conference, *The Evolving Role of the People's Liberation Army in Chinese Politics,* Fort Lesley J. McNair, Washington, D.C., October 30–31, 2001.

[7] China's new security concept is, according to a 2002 government position paper, based on "mutual trust, mutual benefit, quality and coordination at its core. . . . The new security concept is, in essence, to rise above one-sided security and seek common security through mutually beneficial cooperation. It is a concept established on the basis of common interests and is conducive to social progress" (http://www.fmprc.gov.cn/eng/wjb/zzjg/gjs/gjzzyhy/2612/2614/t15319.htm).

[8] Wang Jisi, "China's Changing Role in Asia," paper prepared for the Atlantic Council, January 2004 (http://www.acus.org/Publications/occasionalpapers/Asia/WangJisi_Jan_04.pdf).

[9] October 19, 2001 (http://www.whitehouse.gov/news/releases/2001/10/20011019-4.html).

[10] Shambaugh, "New Stability in the U.S.-China Relations: Causes and Consequences."

[11] See Jiang Zemin, Report to 16th Party Congress, November 2002 (http://english.peopledaily.com.cn/200211/18/eng20021118_106983.shtml).

[12] Resolution on CPC Central Committee Report, November 14, 2002 (http://www.chinatoday.com.cn/English/y200211/16da9/1115/1115f3.htm).

[13] Zheng is now chairman of the forward-thinking China Reform Forum, a Beijing-based think tank, and is a senior adviser to some of China's senior leaders.

[14] Wang Jisi, "China's Changing Role in Asia."

[15] Zheng Bijian, "New Path for China's Peaceful Rise and the Future of Asia," speech presented at Boao Conference, November 3, 2003.

[16] Jiang Zemin, speech to China's 16th Party Congress, November 8, 2002. See Resolution on CPC Central Committee Report, November 14, 2002, paragraph 2.

[17] China's domestic challenges are great and include job creation, banking, and state-owned enterprise reform, the creation of a social safety net, an effective crackdown on corruption, environmental degradation, HIV/AIDS, and other health cri-

ses, and some sort of political reform and internal democratization (with Chinese characteristics), and Taiwanese reunification, to name just a few.

[18] Wang Jisi, "China's Changing Role in Asia."

[19] The Six Party Talks, hosted by China, also include the United States, North Korea, South Korea, Russia, and Japan.

[20] Robert Sutter, "China's Rise in Asia—Are U.S. Interests in Jeopardy?" *PacNet*, March 7, 2003 (http://www.csis.org/pacfor/pacnet.cfm).

[21] Interview by Bonnie Glaser, December 6, 2001.

[22] Michael Swaine, "Reverse Course? The Fragile Turnaround in U.S.-China Relations," Carnegie Endowment Policy Brief, February 22, 2003.

[23] Ibid.

[24] Quadrennial Defense Review, September 30, 2001.

[25] One Chinese scholar who focuses on Russia and Central Asia commented that "the Chinese government thinks the Bush administration is the most hardline U.S. administration among all previous governments. . . . What is the meaning of the Defense Department's QDR? The report says that the U.S. will put emphasis on the Western Pacific to guard against a big power. China's vital national interests are touched upon in these very areas." Interview by Bonnie Glaser, December 6, 2001.

[26] President George W. Bush's comment to Charles Gibson, ABC News, "Good Morning America," in an interview about his first 100 days in office, April 25, 2001.

[27] Testimony before the Senate Foreign Relations Committee, Subcommittee on East Asian and Pacific Affairs, May 1, 2001.

[28] CCTV interview, July 28, 2001 (http://www.state.gov/secretary/rm/2001/4330.htm).

[29] Remarks to the press en route to Canberra, Australia, July 29, 2001 (http://www.state.gov/secretary/rm/2001/4347pf.htm).

[30] Remarks by President Bush and President Jiang Zemin in Press Availability, APEC Leaders Meeting, Shanghai, China, October 19, 2001 (http://usinfo.org/wf-archive/2001/011019/epf501.htm).

[31] These exchanges were suspended after the EP-3 incident.

[32] Bush gave his word to Jiang that these talks would be restarted and reportedly had to push Secretary of Defense Donald Rumsfeld into making it happen. Apparently little, if anything, was achieved at the meeting. Interestingly, reports from U.S. officials who participated in the December 2002 talks indicated that it was the Chinese who came to the table with a specific agenda, while the Americans had little to offer.

[33] The National Security Strategy of the United States of America (http://www.whitehouse.gov/nsc/nss.html).

[34] Perhaps only a Republican administration could have achieved the de facto silencing of the Blue Team, as perhaps only a strident anti-Communist, Richard Nixon, could have opened the door to Communist China. July 2002 Report to Congress of the U.S.-China Security Review Commission, *National Security Implications of the Economic Relationship between the United States and China* (http://www.uscc.gov/researchreports/annualreport.htm). For another example of a Blue Team perspective, see Dan Blumenthal, "Unhelpful China," *Washington Post,* December 6, 2004, p. A21.

The term "Blue Team" is used to describe an amorphous circle of U.S. policymakers and commentators who view China as fundamentally working against the interests of the United States and who thus take a hard-line position on U.S. China policy. The phrase became popularized in a February 22, 2000, *Washington Post* article by Robert G. Kaiser and Steven Mufson, "'Blue Team' Draws a Hard Line on Beijing: Action of Hill Reflects Informal Group's Clout," and refers to the term applied to the U.S. side of a wargame (the opponent is traditionally termed the "Red Team").

[35] Interview by Bonnie Glaser, November 2001.

[36] Interview by Bonnie Glaser, January 2004.

[37] World Bank, *World Development Indicators Database,* August 2004 (http://devdata.worldbank.org/external/CPProfile.asp?SelectedCountry=CHN&CCODE=CHN&CNAME=China&PTYPE=CP).

[38] Morris Goldstein and Nick Lardy, "What Kind of Landing for the Chinese Economy?" Policy Briefs in International Economics (November 2004), Institute for International Economics (http://www.iie.com/publications/pb/pb04-7.pdf).

[39] Andy Xie and Denise Lam, "Greater China: More Growth Now, Less Later," Morgan Stanley Global Economic Forum (December 2004) (http://www.morganstanley.com/GEFdata/digests/20041207-tue.html#anchor0) and World Bank, *East Asia Update* (November 2004), p. 36 (http://lnweb18.worldbank.org/eap/eap.nsf/Attachments/EAP+Regional+Overview+Oct+2004+Nov+5-04+FINAL/$File/EAP+Regional+Overview+Nov04.pdf).

[40] Aaron L. Freidberg, "11 September and the Future of Sino-American Relations," *Survival* 44, no. 1 (Spring 2002).

[41] A Chinese scholar stated that "people in China believe that China has more leverage over the U.S. on Taiwan and some other issues because we are supporting you in your counterterrorism campaign. Cooperation in fighting terrorism is will be more beneficial to you than to us. Taiwan remains our first priority." Interviews by Bonnie Glaser, December 3–11, 2001.

[42] Beijing has taken a number of actions to try to cut off these international ties. For example, there were rumors that, before September 11, Beijing had been reaching out to the Taliban in an effort to secure the border and keep terrorists based in Afghanistan from developing ties with Chinese separatists. In addition, China

founded the SCO in large part to try to stop the infiltration into China of terrorists (and their resources) based in Central Asia.

[43] It took the United States almost a year after September 11 to declare any of the Xinjiang groups as terrorists, and it is unclear why ETIM was selected over other groups.

[44] China claims not to have made a connection between its support for the U.S.-led war on terrorism and its request for support for its efforts to crack down in Xinjiang, but the connection is clear. One Beijing-based scholar noted that "after September 11, we can't have double standards. You can't claim that activities against you are terrorist activities, but against others is not. If you adopt this approach, then you can't sustain a coalition against terrorism. I think there is no direct connection between China's support for counterterrorism in Xinjiang, however." Interview by Bonnie Glaser, December 4, 2001.

[45] Human rights groups are deeply concerned about this revitalized crackdown, arguing that the central government is using the ETIM designation as an excuse for human rights abuses and that the United States has undermined human rights in China in its enthusiasm for the war on terror. President Bush also cautioned that "the war on terrorism should never be an excuse to persecute minorities." Joint press conference with President Bush and President Jiang, October 19, 2002.

[46] Bonnie Glaser, "Sino-American Relations: A Work in Progress," prepared for the conference, *U.S.-China Relations and Regional Security,* cosponsored by the Center for American Studies at Fudan University, Asia-Pacific Center for Security Studies, and Pacific Forum CSIS, Honolulu, Hawaii, April 27–29, 2003. Article published in *American Foreign Policy Interests* 25 (2003): 417–424 (http://www.ncafp.org/projects/oct03glaser.pdf).

[47] David M. Lampton and Richard Daniel Ewing, *The U.S.-China Relationship Facing International Security Crises: Three Case Studies in Post–September 11 Bilateral Relations* (Washington, D.C.: The Nixon Center, 2003).

[48] Powerpoint presentation by Bates Gill, CSIS Freeman Chair in Chinese Studies, April 2003.

[49] China usually abstains on such votes.

[50] CSI involves intelligence sharing, use of advanced technology to secure and screen shipping containers, and the stationing of American customs agents in foreign ports to screen cargo, among other components. This latter requirement might have, under different circumstances, been particularly problematic for Beijing, seen as a breach of sovereignty. Instead Jiang Zemin enthusiastically signaled his commitment to joining the initiative just days after meeting with President Bush at his Crawford, Texas, ranch in October 2002.

[51] Powerpoint presentation by Bates Gill, CSIS Freeman Chair in Chinese Studies, April 2003.

[52] Interview with a Chinese scholar by Bonnie Glaser, February 21, 2003.

[53] According to Lampton and Ewing, enforcement is a significant problem, and the United States has sanctioned a number of Chinese firms for proliferation violations. In May 2003, for example, the State Department charged North China Industries (NORINCO) with selling missile technology to Iran and imposed $200 million in sanctions. Beijing did not issue sanctions.

[54] The government reportedly bused Chinese students and workers to the U.S. embassy in Beijing to stage protests, which turned violent when protestors threw rocks at the building and U.S. personnel.

[55] Zhang Youxia, a Chinese major general, reflected a commonly held view when he wrote, "This Iraq war…was fought for oil." "The Iraq War: Effects on the International Strategic Situation and the Security Environment of Our Country," *Shanghai Guoji Zhanwang*, July 15, 2003.

[56] Public opinion in China was strongly—80 percent according to one informal poll—against the war in Iraq. China kept a tight hold on media reporting on the issue so that the Chinese people would not overreact to Beijing's lack of outright opposition to U.S.-led efforts in the United Nations.

[57] In 2002, the Beijing-based Chinese Academy of Social Sciences (CASS) launched a study on the history of China's northeastern provinces. Based on this study, Chinese scholars claimed in early 2004 that the ancient kingdom of Koguryo, which once ruled much of Korea and Manchuria until it vanished 1,300 years ago, was historically part of China. This sparked a diplomatic row with Seoul, which rejected the claim as a distortion of history.

[58] Interestingly, the United States has not been overly critical of China's unwillingness to join PSI. During a recent visit to China, Undersecretary of State John Bolton stated, "PSI is an activity, not an organization" that one joins, and despite not being a signatory, "China shares the objectives with the nations participating in the PSI." In the U.S. view, China's ongoing cooperation on counterproliferation is more important than signing onto PSI, though Bolton also indicated that there may be room for negotiation on that front as well.

[59] Foreign ministry press conference, February 12, 2004, cited in Wade Boese, "Proliferation Security Initiative Advances," *Arms Control Today*, March 2004 (http://www.armscontrol.org/act/2004_03/PSI.asp).

[60] China National Petroleum Corporation has a 40 percent share in the international consortium extracting oil in Sudan, and China relies on Sudan for almost a quarter of its oil imports.

CHAPTER TWO

SHAKING UP THE SYSTEM: GEORGIA AND THE WAR ON TERROR

Cory Welt

Since the late 1990s, Georgia's foreign relations have been as tumultuous as its politics. After consolidating power in Russia's shadow, Georgian president Eduard Shevardnadze began seeking ways to balance against Russian influence in the Caucasus, restore Georgia's territorial integrity, and erect strong central state institutions. The promise of a newly pro-Western and successful Georgia captured the attention of the United States and its European allies.

By the fall of 2001, however, it was evident that Shevardnadze was not going to be able to fulfill his ambitions or his promises. Beset by weak domestic leadership and the persistence of politics for personal gain, Georgia was unable to cope with new Russian pressures—linked to the arrival of Chechen militants on Georgian territory—or satisfy the expectations of its potential Western partners. Georgia instead appeared headed toward the fate of a failed state with little hope of becoming much more than a Russian dependency.

The September 11 attacks offered Georgia a rare opportunity to reverse course. First, the war on terror gave Georgia the chance to deepen its strategic partnership with the United States. Georgia hastened to pledge "full cooperation" in the war on terror, including overflight rights for coalition forces en route to Central Asia, in exchange receiving a prominent package of counterterrorism assistance. At the same time, Georgia was compelled to start taking its state-building endeavors more seriously by establishing control over the lawless Pankisi Gorge occupied by Chechen and foreign militants. Together, these developments suggested that Georgia might be able to start defending itself more effectively against Russian pressures and even launch the country toward NATO membership—for Georgia, the ultimate balancer against Russia and a potential tool for restoring lost territories. In the war on terror, Georgia was a classic bandwagoner: granting the United States what it wanted while promoting its own strategic goals.

The Georgian government never anticipated, however, that bandwagoning with the United States would entail greater obligations than merely establishing control over the Pankisi Gorge. After September 11, the Georgian government's domestic legitimacy and effectiveness of rule continued to decline. As Georgia prepared for November 2003 parliamentary elections, the ruling party had become a shell of its former self, with state officials and parliamentary representatives departing en masse to form new opposition parties. Georgia's competence as a state—and as a reliable partner of the West—was on the line. In the end, Shevardnadze refused to bow to the pressure for change stemming from his own people and the United States. Instead, he futilely threw in his lot with those who preferred the existing dysfunctional system of rule.

After the November 2003 "Rose Revolution," the administration of President Mikheil Saakashvili adopted an ambitious state-building strategy seeking to bandwagon onto both U.S. *and* Russian power. In 2004, the government did not entirely master this agenda. It remained, however, in a better position to succeed than the government that originally led Georgia into the post–September 11 world.

This chapter first details Georgian grand strategy at the end of the 1990s. It then discusses the "new" threat to Georgia posed by the resurgence of the Russian-Chechen war in 1999 and Georgia's limited response to that threat. The next sections explain how events after September 11 compelled Georgia to take the tasks of state building more seriously and—with American assistance—provided it with an opportunity to balance against Russian power. The penultimate section discusses Georgia's subsequent support of the United States in the war on Iraq and why that support did not translate into further U.S. support for the faltering Georgian government. The chapter concludes by considering how the November 2003 "Rose Revolution" put Georgia back on track but by no means guaranteed its future success.

BALANCING HEGEMONY, RESTORING INTEGRITY, KEEPING TOGETHER

By 1999, Georgian grand strategy centered on three goals. The first was to balance against Russian hegemony. Georgians defined their prime security threat as a Russian effort to establish Georgia as a neocolonial dependency, with military, economic, and foreign policies tailored to suit Russian needs and desires. Battered by civil war and separatist conflict, Georgia joined the Russian-led Commonwealth of Independent States (CIS) in 1993 and subsequently signed an agreement with Russia (never ratified by parliament) that permitted Moscow to retain four Soviet-era military bases in Georgia for 25 years.

In 1999, however, Shevardnadze made moves to strategically distance his country from Russia. Together with Azerbaijan and Uzbekistan, Georgia refused to renew membership in the CIS Collective Security Treaty. It also retracted its invitation to host Russian military bases. Russia agreed to withdraw from two of the bases—near Tbilisi and in the breakaway region of Abkhazia—but delayed a commitment to withdraw from two others near the Turkish border.

Georgia also began to more actively pursue security and energy relationships with the United States and its European allies. Although Georgian leaders called for Georgia's integration into NATO as soon as the USSR fell apart, they became serious about this appeal only eight years later, after Georgia withdrew from the CIS Collective Security Treaty. Georgia supported U.S. policy on the construction of the Baku-Tbilisi-Ceyhan energy corridor by which Caspian oil and gas was to transit directly through the South Caucasus (the gas pipeline, in particular, promised to lessen Georgia's dependence on Russian energy supplies). The Georgians also sold a majority share of their main energy company Telasi to a U.S. firm in a bid to provide at least the capital city of Tbilisi with a steady supply of electricity as well as further reduce Georgia's reliance on Russian energy sources.

In addition to balancing against Russian hegemony, a second component of Georgian grand strategy was to restore the country's territorial integrity. Georgia lost de facto control over two formerly autonomous territories, Abkhazia and South Ossetia, during and shortly after its struggle for independence from the Soviet Union. The war over Abkhazia resulted in the departure of virtually the entire Georgian community of the region—nearly half Abkhazia's population. The recovery of the lost territories, especially Abkhazia, was a goal the Shevardnadze government stressed almost as much as establishing a bulwark against Russian hegemony. These goals were, moreover, linked: Georgians blamed Russia for supporting separatism in the breakaway regions and allowing them to remain apart from Georgia.

The third component of Georgian grand strategy was to keep the rest of the country together. Shevardnadze was careful not to alienate Aslan Abashidze, the feudal-like head of autonomous Ajara, home to one of the Russian bases. He also appointed presidential representatives to all the country's regions and incorporated the leadership structures of Georgia's ethnic Armenian and Azerbaijani communities into an overall system of patronage rule.

Although Georgia's strategic goals may not have been that contentious, by 1999 President Shevardnadze's rule had become highly controversial domestically. Shevardnadze was no dictator: he allowed his people political and civil freedoms. But if Georgia was a democracy, it was only with a generous understanding of the term. Elections were routinely marred by violations significant enough to affect outcomes. Legislative and judicial bodies had no real power.

Most important, Shevardnadze had done little to pull the country out of economic stagnation. Despite the achievement of stability and the appointment of a number of reform-minded officials, Georgia continued to operate by the rules of a heavily corrupt clan system in which government posts were used for personal gain. Most Georgians remained impoverished, even lacking elementary supplies of gas and electricity. By the end of the 1990s, Shevardnadze's government had lost whatever popular legitimacy it may have had.

Initially, none of this was a significant barrier to cultivating relations with the West. In 1999, Georgia was the first South Caucasus state to join the Council of Europe. The next year, it became a member of the World Trade Organization. Under Shevardnadze's rule, Georgia was also a heavy recipient of American aid—more than $1 billion in U.S. assistance. Dwelling on Shevardnadze's role in ending the Cold War—as well as on the stability, civil society, and new generation of pro-Western politicians he promoted—foreign supporters of Georgia remained hopeful that the country would yet flourish.

The Georgian government was, of course, glad to divert the attention of foreign supporters away from internal misrule to the threat from Russia, the country's separatist problems, and the "stability" Shevardnadze had restored to the formerly war-torn state without resorting to authoritarian rule. By the end of the decade, however, it had become highly doubtful that Shevardnadze was going to be able to cultivate an image of partnership and success if he continued to squander the assistance of his potential Western allies and was unable to fundamentally transform the nature of his fragmented, corrupt state.[1]

PANKISI: THE GATHERING STORM

The resurgence of the Russian-Chechen conflict in the autumn of 1999 posed a severe challenge to the precariously positioned Georgia. In the months that followed the Russian Army's reentry into Chechnya, an esti-mated several hundred Chechen fighters made their way across the Cau-casus, together with several thousand refugees, to seek refuge in Georgia's Pankisi Gorge, home of Chechen kin that had settled there in the nine-teenth century.

Consequently, Georgia experienced a barrage of verbal assaults from Moscow. Disregarding their own responsibility for letting armed fighters cross the border, Russian authorities accused Georgia of harboring "in-ternational terrorists" who "regularly hold negotiations with their for-eign patrons and supporters." Expressing hope that the Georgians would "step off [this] dangerous path," the Russians demanded that they either apprehend the militants or let Russian troops in to do the job for them.[2] The Georgian highlands also became the target of an occasional Russian missile, raising the specter that Moscow would eventually engage in a more thorough effort to reestablish control over Georgia.

If Georgia were to cave to Russian demands, however, the country's strategic goals would have been shattered. With control over the Pankisi Gorge tenuous as it was, Shevardnadze was reluctant to alienate the local population through an armed effort to capture militants. Even if he had been willing to take the risk, Georgian officials insist that their armed forces—long neglected and suffering exceedingly low morale—would not have been able to succeed in apprehending battle-hardened Chech-en militants.[3]

That said, the Georgians were also unwilling to let Russian troops go after the militants. This would have enabled Russia to prominently dis-play its military power inside the country, just as Georgia had departed the CIS collective security zone and was trying to distance itself more from the Russian sphere of influence. It would also have meant granting Russia the implicit right to use lethal force—against militants or, worse, refugees and Pankisi residents who could get caught in the crossfire. Al-lowing this, Georgia would have directly contributed to yet another vio-lent regional conflict on its soil.[4]

BEFORE SEPTEMBER 11: A MISSING STRATEGY

Confronting a problem they resented having to deal with and did not believe they *could* deal with in any way that accommodated their strategic goals, the Georgians did nothing. Their opening tactic was simply to counter Russia's propaganda campaign with one of their own. For months, state officials contended that they were "in control of the situation as never before." Georgian officials denied they were "letting Chechen fighters through" and insisted they were fully capable of guarding Georgia's northern border.[5]

Mounting evidence that Chechen gunmen were sheltering in the Pankisi Gorge, however, soon compelled the government to tone down its denials. In April 2000, the Georgian government began denying the number of militants the Russians alleged were in Pankisi, not their presence altogether. After Georgian forces encircled tens of fighters that had crossed the border, Shevardnadze gave up all pretenses: "There really is a group of the so-called fighters [in Pankisi]," he said. Although he sought to moderate this statement by noting that among them were Kists (i.e., Georgian citizens, not Russian), he conceded he could not "rule out the possibility of ethnic Chechen citizens of Russia, that is the so-called Chechen fighters, hiding in the Pankisi [G]orge." A few months before September 11, Shevardnadze again acknowledged that Chechen militants were in Georgia, although he claimed that "the total number of these persons is not larger than 200 to 300."[6]

These admissions did not mean the Georgians were prepared to accommodate Russian demands. After Shevardnadze first acknowledged the presence of Chechen militants, the government reiterated it would "under no circumstances" allow "Russian armed units [to] be involved in any operations on Georgian territory."[7] In March 2001, Shevardnadze pointedly derided the Russians' claims that foreign mercenaries and "terrorists" had joined the Chechen militants in Pankisi.[8] The Georgians also rejected Russia's claim that Ruslan Gelaev, one of the Chechen militants' leading field commanders, was in Georgia.

Besides increasing the military pressure from Russia and raising the specter of internal conflict, the situation in Pankisi had an additional negative effect: it sent the government's domestic legitimacy crashing to new lows. Exemplifying one of the sorrier aspects of the Georgian state, some officials began taking criminal advantage of the government's reluctance to impose order in the Pankisi Gorge. Employees of the Interior and Security Ministries were widely accused of involvement in a string of Pankisi-based kidnappings of locals and foreigners as well as the drug trade passing through the area.[9] In December 2000, Georgian villagers picketed roads into Pankisi, threatening to take matters into their own hands if the authorities did not crack down on criminal elements in the gorge, an act repeated the summer of 2001 when "defense volunteers" protested that their relatives had been kidnapped and that the government had "done nothing to eradicate camps of the Chechen fighters and foreign mercenaries."[10]

Eventually, this criminal complicity threatened to slide into a bizarre national security partnership. In August 2001, a group of armed Chechens—rumored to be led by Ruslan Gelaev himself—made their way across Georgian territory unimpeded and, joined by Georgian guerrilla fighters, appeared to be preparing to fight their way into Abkhazia. Although no conflict erupted, Shevardnadze eventually issued the mysterious admission that "an attempt to invade Abkhazia" had been "halted by our troops."[11] By so blatantly allowing the militants to cross Georgia, Shevardnadze (or others in his entourage) greatly risked weakening Georgia's position vis-à-vis Russia.

By September 11, Georgia's grand strategy was largely bankrupt. The Georgian leadership had acknowledged a militant presence in the Pankisi Gorge but was doing very little to deflect Russian pressure. Worse, it had permitted Pankisi to become a haven for criminals, providing them with official associates and patrons. Finally, it had permitted militants to go adventuring across the country to the border with Abkhazia.

This was certainly a novel approach for achieving Georgian state security. In 1999, when the Russians first began to accuse Georgia of harboring terrorists, Shevardnadze announced that Georgia would be "knocking very hard on the door" of NATO—the Georgians' favored guarantor of security and internal order—within five years.[12] By 2001, Shevardnadze certainly was not presiding over a state that stood a chance of entering NATO or acquiring any other guarantees of national security so soon.

TOWARD A SECURE STATE: THE WAR ON TERROR

The September 11 attacks on New York and Washington had the local consequence of forcing Georgians to adopt a more coherent approach to national security. In the new global environment, and with the United States rallying support for its war on terror, Georgia could not afford to tolerate the militants' presence any longer. Russia had gained considerable leverage against Georgia, including the threat of direct attack—following the example of the United States in Afghanistan—if the Georgian "host state" did not agree to evict its "terrorist" guests.

Three days after the Al Qaeda attacks on the United States, a leading centrist, Russian parliamentarian Boris Nemtsov, remarked that "Russia will have to resort to military action" if the Georgian authorities do not surrender the "terrorists" on their soil. A few days later, the Russian Federal Security Service announced that the prime suspects in the 1999 apartment-building bombings in Moscow, which had killed more than 200 people, were sheltering in the Pankisi Gorge and that they had links to foreign terrorists. The Russian Foreign Ministry issued a note demanding that Georgia immediately extradite suspected terrorists and "take tough measures against the bandits [who are] planning fresh acts of terrorism. . . . It is time for Georgia in deed and not in word to join the common front of civilized states in eliminating the threat of international terrorism."[13] Such rhetoric from the Russians suggested a qualitatively new level of threat.

At the start of December 2001, a former foreign policy adviser to the president, Archil Gegeshidze, revealed just how September 11 had altered the context of the Russian threat. Before September 11, Gegeshidze suggested, Georgia might have been able to count on the United States to help support Georgia against Russian advances. Now, however, "major" U.S. foreign policy shifts had "made traditional national goals subordinate to combating international terrorism." The implication was clear: if Georgia did not clean out the Pankisi Gorge, the United States was not going to be able to offer Georgia very much protection. Russia would be given "a free hand" in its dealings with Georgia.[14]

A STRATEGY TAKES SHAPE

Immediately after September 11, the Georgian government acknowledged the shift in context that the attacks on the United States had precipitated. At first, Georgia seemed to have no choice but to succumb to Russian demands—in other words, bandwagon with, not balance against, Russian power. An unusually accommodating Foreign Ministry declared that "given the tragic events in the U.S." as well as recent terrorist acts in Chechnya, "the Georgian side understands the increased sensitivity of

Russian colleagues to the problems of terrorism." Shevardnadze declared a willingness to discuss plans with Russia for a "joint fight" against terrorism "at the top government level, to say nothing of the level of special services . . . the ethnic or the social origin of the terrorists notwithstanding." The president subsequently acknowledged "dangerous trends which propagate terrorism in Georgia."[15]

These words were matched by deeds. A few weeks after September 11, there was a second act to the August "Abkhazian affair": Chechen fighters crudely invaded Abkhazia only to be repulsed by local troops. Several commentators in the Russian media, normally skeptical of Shevardnadze's sincerity, held that this failed attack reflected a government effort not to capture Abkhazia but to move the militants out of Georgia.[16] At the end of September, relatives of Ruslan Gelaev's associates indicated that Shevardnadze had recently told Gelaev it was time that he and his men left Georgia. Later, two Dagestanis who said they had been in Pankisi with Gelaev affirmed that Georgian authorities had resolved to remove Gelaev after September 11, since "he posed problems for both Shevardnadze and foreign states."[17]

At the end of October, an indirectly related scandal freed the government to consider more open methods to resolve the Pankisi problem. Security forces raided the offices of a popular independent television station, Rustavi-2, known for its reporting on state corruption. The raid provoked large demonstrations calling for the government's resignation; the crisis was resolved only when the security and interior ministers resigned.[18] Presumably, Shevardnadze did not orchestrate the entire affair to have an excuse to remove these ministers who were major obstacles to getting anything done in the Pankisi Gorge.[19] Given the new context, however, it is not surprising that Shevardnadze let them go without a fight.

As if in confirmation of these ministers' opposition to resolving the Pankisi problem, new revelations came to light. Days before his forced resignation, then interior minister Kakha Targamadze was still insisting that Gelaev was not in Georgia. After his removal, Shevardnadze soon announced that Gelaev had been in Georgia, though he claimed no knowledge of his current location.[20] After further protests in January 2002 involving the relatives of a kidnapped monk and members of the Soviet-Afghan War Veterans Union, the new security and interior ministers revealed that some 600 "criminals" were in Pankisi and announced the start of an "anticrime" operation to "free hostages, remove firearms, and eliminate drug trafficking."[21] Although it is unclear what the mission actually accomplished, the declaration was at least a step forward in dealing with the Pankisi problem. Security Minister Valery Khaburdzania admitted that several dozen Chechen fighters had been crossing the Russian-Georgian frontier regularly and that "Gelaev and his group are hardly infrequent visitors to Pankisi."[22]

THE "VIRTUAL OPERATION": GTEP AND THE RESOLUTION OF PANKISI

In addition to increasing the need to clear out the Pankisi Gorge, the war on terror ultimately provided the Georgians with a new occasion to do so, and in a way that would enable them to balance against Russian influence. This opportunity came in the form of a $64 million U.S. military assistance program called the Georgian Train and Equip Program (GTEP), announced in February 2002.

GTEP was the product of a number of U.S. interests. A strong program of military assistance to Georgia—a potential ally in a strategic, energy-rich region—had been developing since 1998, including the training of border and coast guards and a grant of ten used combat helicopters. After September 11, a ramping up of that program made sense. With Russian pressure against Georgia stronger than ever before, Georgia had pledged firm support for the war on terror. As the United States could establish at least some connection between the militants in the Pankisi Gorge and global terrorist networks (see below),[23] it thus had an interest in helping Georgia clean up its act. Although it may not have been prepared to directly go after militants in the Pankisi Gorge, it was at least interested in providing cover for the Georgians to take care of the problem themselves and, in so doing, provide a buffer against Russian threats.

GTEP was justified precisely on the premise that militants in the Pankisi Gorge had links to Al Qaeda. On February 11, 2002—the fifth-month anniversary of the Al Qaeda attacks—U.S. charge d'affairs in Georgia, Philip Remler, remarked in a local media interview that several dozen "mujahideen" from Afghanistan were in the Pankisi Gorge and that the United States was prepared to assist Georgia in establishing anti-terrorist units.[24] Later that month, the U.S. State Department indicated that the United States was prepared to "assist Georgia in developing the capability to control its own borders, and to conduct limited counter-insurgency operations against terrorist elements." In his March 2002 speech on the sixth-month anniversary of September 11, President Bush cited Georgia as the third recipient of U.S. antiterror assistance, after Yemen and the Philippines, and noted that "terrorists working closely with Al Qaeda operate in the Pankisi Gorge."[25]

With the announcement of GTEP, Georgians' depiction of the Pankisi problem underwent a radical shift. Two days before Remler made his comments about the mujahideen, Khaburdzania noted that the government had arrested two "Arabs," accusing them of trying "to form an illegal armed unit in the Pankisi Gorge with the aim of carrying out sabotage and terrorist acts in Russia." He also revealed that foreigners were distributing money in the region to spread Wahhabism and construct mosques. Some days later, Khaburdzania admitted that "suspicious people" of many different nationalities could be in Pankisi, noting that five Afghans and seven Iranians—illegal migrants seeking to reach Europe—were recently arrested.[26]

The government's disclosures did not stop there. In March, a week after returning from discussions in the United States and on the same day the defense minister reported that U.S. military instructors would be arriving in Georgia, Khaburdzania reported that some individuals in the Pankisi Gorge had been "previously connected" with Al Qaeda. In May, as these instructors were arriving in Georgia, he declared there were "some one hundred Arabs" in Pankisi, many of whom had fought in Chechnya but also some who were posing as "representatives of humanitarian and religious organizations, or masquerading as teachers."[27] The next day he raised the official count of militants in the gorge to three times the Georgians' pre–September 11 estimate—800 Chechen fighters plus 100 foreign mercenaries, "mainly ethnic Arabs."[28]

The Georgians were reluctant, however, to push the Al Qaeda connection too far. In April, Defense Minister Davit Tevzadze indicated that the American suggestion of an Al Qaeda connection "[had come] as something of a surprise." At the end of that month, Khaburdzania offered a similarly hesitant position, noting that there are some in Pankisi "who are connected, maybe not directly, but indirectly with terrorist organizations like Al Qaeda." Khaburdzania explicitly denied that mujahideen had come to Georgia from Afghanistan after September 11. In May, Tevzadze told an American audience that "personally, it is very difficult to believe" that fighters from Afghanistan had recently fled to Georgia.[29]

These inconsistencies were not failures of Georgian strategy but rather indicative of Georgia's interest in U.S. military assistance. The Georgians never perceived a clear and present danger of Al Qaeda–linked terrorism against their country. However, they understood that they now had to clean out the gorge and that GTEP provided them with a way to do so without bending to Russian pressure. Furthermore, it established a bulwark against further Russian advances. Alexander Rondeli, the head of a government-linked policy foundation, best expressed the peculiarity of the twin pressure and opportunity the United States was providing. On the one hand, Rondeli admitted, "Georgia is in the limelight and has to perform better." At the same time, "the day I heard the Americans were coming I was the happiest man on earth."[30]

The American offer was especially fortunate because it provided the Georgians a way to solve the Pankisi problem without a single shot being fired. GTEP did not transform Georgia's beleaguered armed forces into a lethal antiterrorist machine overnight. What it did was signal to the militants that the Georgians were at last serious about denying them shelter. Before September 11, the Georgians had no hope of credibly sending this signal, given the state of the armed forces, Georgia's desire to avoid conflict with the militants, and state officials' own criminal interests. Now, as partners in the war on terror, Georgians could make a convincing case that their hands were tied, that they had U.S. military support, and that the militants were going to have to leave the gorge or risk conflict.[31]

Georgia clearly used GTEP to send this signal. At the start of March, the deputy defense minister noted that "a small group of rebels have [already] left Pankisi" in light of the announcement that the United States was sending troops to Georgia. In a May press conference in the United States, Defense Minister Tevzadze asserted that "the situation in Pankisi dramatically improved [after] the . . . train-and-equip program was loudly announced." Shevardnadze himself declared that the authorities were "trying to suggest" to the fighters "that they make their way out of here as quickly as possible because the noose is gradually tightening . . . . We still want to part with them in a friendly way, and I believe that we will be able to do it." He was careful to note that "Russia has a special interest in [the militants], and so does the USA."[32]

Although the first stage of this "virtual operation" in Pankisi involved the eviction of foreign mercenaries alone, Georgia later pressured the Chechen militants to leave as well. These efforts coincided with the start of actual GTEP training and were prodded by the United States.[33] As the initial stage of training—a 70-day course for 200 officers—was taking place in the summer of 2002, Georgian officials began to report an exodus of Chechen fighters. In mid-July, the police chief responsible for the Pankisi Gorge reported that there were only 300 fighters left in Pankisi, that some two-dozen fighters had departed for the border a few days before, and that "several more groups" were planning to leave for Chechnya. Later that month, Shevardnadze declared that the Chechen fighters understood that "this is their last summer in Georgia and that they will have to leave Georgian territory by the fall."[34] Shortly after, the head of the Russian border guard confirmed that up to 60 fighters had recently crossed the border and, though at least 200 fighters were left in Pankisi, that most of these were planning to cross over soon.[35]

In late August 2002, the Georgian government engaged in heavily publicized operations to demonstrate Georgia's reassertion of control over the Pankisi Gorge. To make sure the gorge was reasonably free of militants beforehand, officials publicly discussed the impending operation in advance and conveyed messages to the remaining militants that it was time for them to depart.[36] During the operation, 1,000 Interior Ministry troops were dispatched to the gorge. The Defense Ministry held preannounced exercises south of Pankisi, with the participation of some 1,500 troops. Only after this operation did the first of five sessions of actual GTEP field training begin.

BALANCING AGAINST THE "NEW" RUSSIAN THREAT

GTEP enabled Georgia to undermine Russia's main coercive pressure against them. At the same time, it provided the Georgians with appropriate cover to avoid Russia's wrath. Russian officials expressed great frustration that Georgia was sending militants back to Russia rather than allowing Russian troops to go in after them. As a Kremlin spokesman declared that Moscow was "tired" of the Georgians' "flat-out lies," Russian aircraft bombed (unofficially) the Georgian side of the border days after Russian troops clashed with a group of fighters returning from Georgia, and again a few days later when survivors from that battle tried to cross back into Georgia.[37] The Russian defense minister indicated that the only way to solve the problem was to deploy Russian special forces in Georgia, while the chair of the Russian parliament's international affairs committee insisted that Russia had the right "to conduct targeted retaliatory actions against rebel bases outside its borders."[38] On August 23, as Georgia prepared its clean-up operation in the Pankisi Gorge, Russia again bombed Georgian territory, this time killing one.

With its newly elevated partnership with the United States, however, the Georgians received support against Russian coercion. The first bombing in July resulted in a State Department declaration that the United States "strongly supports the sovereignty and territorial integrity of Georgia" and "would . . . be seriously concerned to learn of any violations of that sovereignty." After the third, fatal attack, Secretary of State Colin Powell called the Russian foreign minister to express his concerns, and the State Department publicly urged Russia to "cooperate with Georgia" and allow it to "deal with the question of international terrorists and Chechen fighters" on its own. The White House issued its own statement that "the U.S. regrets this loss of life and deplores the violation of Georgia's sovereignty."[39]

The U.S commitment to Georgia was tested shortly thereafter. On September 11, 2002, Russian president Vladimir Putin observed the anniversary of the Al Qaeda attacks with a stunning broadside against the Georgians. In a televised speech, Putin declared his objection to the way the Georgians had addressed the problem of the militants by allowing them to head back across the border into Russia. He rejected the claim that the bulk of the militants had left Georgia already, insisting that they had merely "scattered in other regions . . . along the borders" and were "preparing to perpetrate new crimes." If Georgia "is unable to create a zone of security" on the Georgian-Russian border and "fails to put an end" to cross-border attacks, Russia reserved the right to invoke Article 51 of the UN Charter, the same article the United States invoked to attack Afghanistan. Consequently, Putin instructed his power ministries to prepare proposals "on the possibility and practicability of delivering strikes" on terrorist bases across the border.[40]

Although preparing to make its case for preemptive war in Iraq when Putin issued his statement, the Bush administration rejected what appeared to be—and was interpreted by many as—an attempt to trade Georgia for Russian support on Iraq. The State Department again stated its "strong exception to statements . . . threatening unilateral action against Chechen targets on Georgian territory." President Bush himself indicated that the administration had "made it very clear to the Georgian government that we expected them to rout out the Al Qaeda–type terrorists" but that the Russians had to "give the Georgians a chance to achieve a common objective . . . and that is to get the Al Qaeda killers and bring them to justice."[41]

Georgian officials actively disavowed speculation that the United States had forsaken them. Parliamentary chairwoman Nino Burjanadze considered President Bush's statement to be "very significant" and argued that it confirmed there was no deal. Shevardnadze himself "never doubted that Washington would react firmly and directly . . . in defense of Georgia's rights." His national security adviser Tedo Japaridze expressed confidence that Georgia "is the red line that President Putin and his people cannot trespass." Later, Japaridze flew to the United States to hold further talks with administration officials. These talks produced a letter from President Bush affirming U.S. support for Georgia. Shevardnadze's office noted that the letter was particularly important "in light of the unprecedented anti-Georgian campaign unleashed by Russia."[42]

Nonetheless, Georgia hastened to clean out the gorge and outlying environs. A few days after Putin's speech, Japaridze reiterated that "[s]ome members of Al Qaeda and persons affiliated to that organization are staying in the Pankisi Gorge" and that "the most active phase of the anti-terror and anti-crime operation . . . will start today or tomorrow." When Shevardnadze announced this new phase, he noted that the situation in Pankisi would be resolved in a matter of weeks. To the militants, the president conveyed the message that "resistance is senseless" and, for the first time, warned that "armed clashes cannot be ruled out."[43] The government also agreed to one of Putin's key demands—to extradite a number of militants the Georgians had been holding in custody—and to hand over any new prisoners they captured.

By the end of the month, the saga was basically over. Russian troops clashed with a group of approximately 180 militants that had recently crossed the border, killing some 50 to 60 and hunting down the rest.[44] In January 2003, the Security Ministry acknowledged that some militants might still be in Pankisi but noted that authorities were working to root them out. With this, Georgian officials largely considered the Pankisi problem to be solved.[45]

At the same time, the Georgians found it a propitious time to move forward on their basic goal of NATO membership. Georgia had more or less solved the Pankisi problem and had begun to build a security relationship with the United States. In early August, as the Russians were threatening them with words and bombs, Shevardnadze announced Georgia's intention to draft a program guiding the country into NATO. Parliament passed a resolution approving of this move on September 14, three days after Putin issued his threat. At the November NATO summit in Prague, President Shevardnadze presented Georgia's official request to join the Euro-Atlantic organization. Commenting on the summit a few days later, Shevardnadze declared: "Never before has Georgia had [such a] good ... chance to join NATO .... [N]ever before ... has Georgia had such guarantees of future security [like the ones] we will gain once we join NATO."[46]

WHAT WENT WRONG: FROM IRAQ TO REGIME CHANGE

As the United States shifted its attention from the war on terror to the war on Iraq, the Georgian government continued offering the Bush administration its firm support. Even before Secretary of State Colin Powell made the case for war to the United Nations, Shevardnadze indicated he approved of the use of military force in Iraq.[47] Subsequently, Georgian officials and politicians affirmed that they would allow the United States to use Georgian military bases if requested. After some debate, the parliament also passed an agreement granting U.S. military and civilian personnel visa-free transit and the right to carry weapons in Georgia. After the fall of Saddam Hussein, Shevardnadze offered to send Georgian specialists to assist in postwar reconstruction, and in August, a contingent of 70 special-purpose forces, medics, and engineers were sent.[48] Defense Minister Tevzadze and U.S. ambassador to Georgia Richard Miles indicated that GTEP-trained personnel might later serve in Iraq (something that came to pass in 2004 after Shevardnadze left power).[49]

Explaining Georgian support for the United States in Iraq, Georgian officials noted, first of all, that it was a consequence of past obligations. "Since 1992," Shevardnadze declared, "the U.S. has been providing considerable aid to Georgia; in our turn, we must support the [United States]." He also noted that "not a single country has rendered as much valuable assistance to Georgia as has the United States. I sometimes say that we would not have survived without it." His foreign minister agreed that the Georgian position was "based exclusively on our commitments as an ally and the people's attitude towards the United States, which has done a lot for Georgia."[50]

At the same time, Georgian support was predicated on the hope of keeping the United States engaged and of further deepening the U.S.-Georgian alliance. Shevardnadze noted that "Georgia is a small country and the United States supports Georgia's many efforts in many fields. Georgia will therefore always support the United States." He indicated that Georgia's "position will benefit the country in the future." After the first Georgian units departed for Iraq, Tevzadze argued that their deployment "confirms Georgia's reliability as an ally. Its participation in the counterterrorism coalition is not an empty phrase."[51]

The Georgian government faced little overt opposition to its position on the war in Iraq. The Georgian Orthodox Church spoke out against the government's position and called for restraint "to prevent the threat of war." Several members of (mostly marginal) political movements and parties also expressed criticism of the government's support for military action as well as fear that Georgia would face its own terrorist threat if it were to join the war. Still, one media poll found that residents in Tbilisi were equally divided on the question of Georgian support for the war.[52] A Georgian commentator, writing for the Western press, noted that two antiwar demonstrations in March attracted fewer than 100 participants. She concluded "the verdict is unanimous: Georgia is wholeheartedly and unconditionally with the United States."[53] Whether or not this was completely true, government support of the U.S. position was at least not a source of public discontent.

Unfortunately for Shevardnadze, tacit public approval of his foreign policy was not nearly enough to rally the population to his side. The economy remained in the doldrums, corruption flourished at every level, and most Georgians had to struggle to meet even the most basic needs. As Georgia approached the November 2003 parliamentary elections, the ruling party and its allies had little public support. New opposition parties—mostly made up of former government members—were bound to be victorious if free and fair elections were actually held.

More surprisingly, Shevardnadze's support of the United States was also not enough for him to receive the American blessing. Regardless of Georgia's success in cleaning out the Pankisi Gorge and its support for the Iraq War, the Bush administration viewed Shevardnadze's government as hopelessly compromised and believed that only a transfer of power away from the ruling party could enable Georgia to avoid the fate of a failed state.[54] Rather than turn a blind eye to Georgia's potential slide into authoritarianism and decay, the United States resolved to lend its active support to a democratic process that would bring new parties to power and pave the way for presidential elections in 2005 and the "post-Shevardnadze" era.

Indeed, several indicators in 2003 suggested that Georgia had not yet veered from the road to failure it had been on since 1999. In the summer, the Georgians were unable to find a way to purchase a controlling share of the power company the financially strapped American firm AES was now trying to sell. This led to its purchase by the Russian United Energy Systems. This deal was, admittedly, a challenging one for the Georgians to avoid, given AES's own determination to sell, but both Georgian politicians and U.S. officials have indicated the government could have received the foreign aid and assistance needed to retain control of the power company if it had truly tried.[55] Shevardnadze's consent to signing a *secret* 25-year agreement with the Russian company Gazprom to surrender control of Georgia's gas distribution network in exchange for subsidized imports was even more indicative of the way Georgia was planning to do business in the future. In October, the global nongovernmental organization Transparency International ranked Georgia as one of the three most corrupt countries in the CIS (Azerbaijan and Tajikistan were the other two), listing only five out of 133 countries in a worse position. Unable to get the Georgians to implement their recommendations, the International Monetary Fund (IMF) declared it was suspending assistance to Georgia. The United States also announced a reduction in foreign aid. Georgian support for the United States in Iraq—appreciated but hardly critical—was not going to be enough to maintain U.S. support for the Georgian administration. Shevardnadze would have to demonstrate a commitment to his own political end.

Not surprisingly, Shevardnadze failed to deliver. Feeling a sense of betrayal from the United States, Shevardnadze permitted himself to be swayed by a segment of the ruling elite that was determined to thwart the elections and was apparently not opposed to the transformation of Georgia into a Russian dependency if it meant personal gain. Shevardnadze also continued to be overly cautious of the possibility of further territorial disintegration. He accommodated the efforts of his nominal (and pro-Russian) ally, Ajaran leader Aslan Abashidze, to thwart both a preelection compromise with the opposition regarding the composition of the Central Election Commission (the so-called Baker Plan, which former U.S. secretary of state James Baker helped broker) and, in the end, an honest vote count in November.[56] Believing that the opposition would not be able to sustain mass demonstrations and that the United States would ultimately give fraudulent elections a pass, Shevardnadze stood firm. However, government efforts to bargain their way out of the crisis failed, and members of Shevardnadze's government shed their support. The opposition refused to give the newly elected legislature a chance to convene and stormed the parliament building. Declining to risk either bloodshed or the disobedience of security organs, Shevardnadze resigned. The "Rose Revolution" had occurred.

AFTER SHEVARDNADZE: A WAY FORWARD?

The "Rose Revolution" did not alter Georgia's three fundamental security goals. Georgia still seeks to balance against Russian hegemony. It still seeks to restore territorial integrity, and it still wishes to construct a strong central state.

Regime change in Georgia, however, enabled the country to develop a more coherent strategy for achieving these goals. First of all, it gave Georgia a second chance at integration with the West. Both the United States and the European Union promised firm engagement to Georgia, pledging increased levels of aid. In March, Georgia was a late addition to a list of 16 countries eligible for increased levels of development assistance via the newly established U.S. Millennium Challenge Account. Although the Department of Defense's Train and Equip Program concluded in April, U.S. and Georgian officials agreed to establish a new Sustainment and Stability Operations Program (SSOP) in 2005 to provide training for Georgian troops to serve in peacekeeping missions abroad. Motivated by the "Rose Revolution," the European Union added Georgia (and its two South Caucasus neighbors) to its European Neighborhood Policy, which previously included only Ukraine, Moldova, and Belarus from CIS states, and established a Rule of Law Mission in Georgia, the first of its kind. The consent of France to permit its active-duty ambassador to Georgia Salome Zourabichvili—herself of Georgian origin—to serve as Georgia's foreign minister was another striking sign of European support. Finally, in October, NATO approved Georgia's Individual Partnership Action Plan, increasing prospects for NATO membership. Accordingly, Georgia engaged in a number of necessary military reforms—appointing a civilian as defense minister, increasing defense expenditures, reducing the military's size, and merging the Soviet-era "internal troops" with the conventional army.

As for the war on terror, Georgia substantially increased its coalition role. In April 2004, Georgia replaced its 70 peacekeepers in Iraq with 159 GTEP-trained troops. It replaced these troops with another 300 in November and pledged to deploy 550 more soldiers in 2005 to provide security for the United Nations mission in Baghdad. Georgian peacekeepers also served a 100-day deployment in Afghanistan in the fall. Back home, Georgia's new government sought to become far more effective in modernizing the country's defense and security forces and establishing control over state borders. At the start of his term, President Mikheil Saakashvili asserted that the Pankisi Gorge was clean of

Chechen fighters and that the "new" Georgia would not permit militants to enter the country or extremists to set down roots.

Regime change in Georgia also initially promised to lead to a transformation in Georgian-Russian relations. While affirming Georgia's goal of NATO membership, Saakashvili made it clear that establishing close economic and security relations with Russia was a top priority. Although asserting that Russian military bases had to be withdrawn from Georgia, Georgia did not push for an immediate agreement on withdrawal, agreed to establish coordinated patrols on the Russian-Georgian border to prevent infiltration of Chechen militants, and proposed to set up a joint counterterrorism center. Georgia also sought to encourage Russian investment, hosting a Russian business conference in May 2004 and appointing the Russian-based tycoon Kakha Bendukidze as minister of economy. When the Georgian government forced the leader of autonomous Ajara, the pro-Russian Aslan Abashidze, to resign in May, Moscow facilitated his departure. By the start of the summer, Saakashvili's efforts to reconcile with Russia appeared to be bearing fruit.

Unfortunately, Georgia's attempt to restore control over breakaway South Ossetia after its victory in Ajara halted the warming of relations with Russia. Determined not to be sidelined in South Ossetia—and later in Abkhazia—Russia staunchly resisted Georgia's initiation of an "anti-smuggling" operation in the region, frequently consulted with South Ossetia's leadership, threatened intervention, and allowed weapons and armed volunteers from the North Caucasus to cross the border into South Ossetia. A threat by Georgia to open fire on Russian ships seeking to dock in Abkhazia increased Russia's ire. In August, Russian president Vladimir Putin cancelled an official visit to Georgia, postponing development of a new Georgian-Russian treaty. The tragic terrorist attack at a school in Beslan, North Ossetia, the next month prompted Russia to reassert the right to conduct preventive attacks against militant bases abroad, the Pankisi Gorge included. Despite its claims that Chechen fighters were still operating from Georgia, however, Moscow refused to allow the consensus-based Organization for Security and Cooperation in Europe (OSCE) to renew a successful monitoring mission on the Georgian side of the Georgian-Russian border.

Simultaneously building effective state institutions, restoring territorial integrity, maintaining a trajectory toward Euro-Atlantic integration, and establishing a productive partnership with Russia remains a tall order for Georgia. By 2005, corruption, disorganization, and personalistic rule continued to put a drag on Georgian state-building reforms, and no breakthrough in conflict resolution efforts was in sight. Maintaining the attention of the United States and the European Union while cultivating civil relations with Russia also proved more of a challenge than Georgia expected.

Considering where the country was headed from 1999 until 2001, however, the developments that grew out of September 11 assuredly provided a net gain for Georgia. The impetus for post–September 11 reform in Georgia stemmed from an unexpected set of external pressures. Prospects for fundamental change now hinge on a new set of external developments. Whether these involve new NATO and EU commitments to the South Caucasus or a radical rethinking of Russian foreign policy objectives, Georgia will have the best chance to succeed if it knows this success will be rewarded.

Notes

[1] For an early observation of Georgia's troubles, see Cory Welt, "Georgia Annual Report 1999: A Return to Eurasia?" *Transitions On-Line*, May 2000 (http://www.tol.cz). Also see Charles King, "Potemkin Democracy: Four Myths about Post-Soviet Georgia," *National Interest* 64 (Summer 2001): 93–104.

[2] Interfax (Moscow), December 21, 1999.

[3] Valeri Khaburdzania, "Pankisi, Abkhazia and the Problem of International Terrorism," *In the National Interest*, February 5, 2003 (http://www.inthenationalinterest.com); author's interview with a senior Georgian government official, October 17, 2003, and with a U.S. Defense Department official, October 23, 2003.

[4] Regarding this latter threat, see Shevardnadze's comments on Georgian Radio (Tbilisi), December 18, 2000, trans. by BBC Summary of World Broadcasts, December 20, 2000.

[5] Georgian Television (Tbilisi), December 29, 1999, trans. BBC, December 31, 1999; Agence France Presse, October 8, 1999; ITAR-TASS, October 25, 1999.

[6] Prime News Agency (Tbilisi), April 25, 2000; Georgian Radio, December 18, 2000, trans. BBC, December 20, 2000; Caucasus Press (Tbilisi), June 25, 2001.

[7] Interfax, February 20, 2001.

[8] As Shevardnadze put it: "You know that I went to the Pankisi [G]orge and visited all villages there, but could not find a single terrorist." Georgian Television, March 13, 2001, trans. BBC, March 15, 2001.

⁹ Georgian officials openly acknowledged the drug trade in the region at the time and now admit that former officials were involved in Pankisi-based criminal activity. Revealingly, just weeks after the appointment of new Security and Internal Affairs ministers in the fall of 2001, two Spanish businessmen that had been taken hostage in a highly publicized kidnapping a year before were "rescued" from Pankisi. When they returned home to Spain, the former hostages explicitly accused former state officials of involvement. On the drug trade, RIA-Novosti, October 24, 2001, and ITAR-TASS, November 30, 2001. On government complicity, ITAR-TASS, December 19, 2001; Jaba Devdariani, "Georgia's Pankisi Dilemma," *Institute for War & Peace Reporting*, January 25, 2002; Thomas de Waal, "Into the Georgian Quagmire," *Moscow Times* (Moscow), May 24, 2002; Rustavi-2 TV (Tbilisi), July 21, 2002, trans. BBC, July 22, 2002; author's interview with senior Georgian government official, November 7, 2003.

¹⁰ Prime News Agency, December 3, 2000; Deutsche-Presse Agentur, July 18, 2001.

¹¹ Agence France Presse, August 27, 2001.

¹² *Financial Times*, October 25, 1999.

¹³ *Daily Telegraph* (London), September 25, 2001; ITAR-TASS, September 18, 2001; Interfax, September 18, 2001.

¹⁴ Archil Gegeshidze, "Remarks to the AGBC Fourth Annual Conference," Washington, D.C., December 6, 2001 (http://www.agbdc.com/Gegeshidze.doc). This logic was reiterated in author's interviews with senior Georgian and U.S. government officials, November 7, 2003, and February 13, 2004.

¹⁵ ITAR-TASS, September 19, 2001; Georgian Radio, September 24, 2001; Agence France Presse, September 26, 2001.

¹⁶ Three such theories are that Gelaev was made to understand that he had no future in Georgia and thus initiated the fight into Abkhazia on his own; that the Georgian government colluded with the Chechens to move them out of Pankisi and into Abkhazia; and that Shevardnadze duped Gelaev into thinking that the government supported the operation when, instead, he collaborated with the Abkhazians to deliver the militants a decisive blow. *Moscow News*, October 10, 2001; *Rossiiskaya Gazeta* (Moscow), November 10, 2001; *Moscow Times*, November 16, 2001.

¹⁷ ITAR-TASS, September 28, 2001; Glasnost–North Caucasus, April 8, 2002, cited in RFE/RL Caucasus Report, December 4, 2002. Some commentators hold to the interpretation that this affair was an effort to use the militants from Pankisi to seize Abkhazia. See, for example, RFE/RL Caucasus Report, October 12, 22, 2001; de Waal, "Into the Georgian Quagmire"; and Mark Irkali, "Georgia: Welcome to America's New El Salvador," *Diacritica.com* (http://www.diacritica.com/sobaka/2003/ salvador.html), March 12, 2003.

[18] This occurred with a political deal in which the entire government, including parliamentary speaker Zurab Zhvania, resigned (although many ministers were subsequently reappointed to their posts).

[19] In an interview with the author, a senior Georgian government official affirmed that the removal of the interior and security ministers was a consequence of domestic politics, not of international pressure to clean up the Pankisi Gorge. November 7, 2003.

[20] ITAR-TASS, October 24, 2001; Agence France Presse, November 9, 2001.

[21] Giorgi Sepashvili, "Pankisi Gorge—A Criminal Enclave," *Civil Georgia*, January 17, 2002 (http://www.civil.ge).

[22] Interfax, February 6, 2002.

[23] *Washington Post*, February 27, 2002; author's interview with a U.S. Defense Department official, October 23, 2003.

[24] *Akhali versia* (Tbilisi), February 11, 2002, cited in RFE/RL Newsline, February 14, 2002; *Guardian* (London), February 15, 2002; *New York Times*, February 28, 2002.

[25] U.S. Department of State Daily Press Briefing, February 27, 2002; "President Bush's Remarks at the White House Ceremony to Honor Victims of the September 11 Terrorist Attacks," March 11, 2002 (usinfo.state.gov/products/pubs/sixmonths/bushremarks.htm); "Georgia 'Train and Equip' Program Begins," April 29, 2002 (http://www.defenselink.mil/ news/Apr2002/b04292002_bt217-02.html).

[26] ITAR-TASS, February 9, 2002; Prime News Agency, February 15, 2002.

[27] ITAR-TASS, March 21, 2002, May 20, 2002.

[28] Georgian Television, May 21, 2002, trans. BBC, May 21, 2002. Khaburdzania later indicated that Chechen Wahhabis in Pankisi had been receiving financial assistance from abroad, including one instance of a $600,000 bank transfer prior to September 11. This money, he said, was partially for refugee aid and partially to support the fighters. He also noted that some foreigners had maintained contact with Al Qaeda officials. A Security Ministry spokesman noted that one Chechen field commander had been "receiving funds directly from Al Qaeda." Caucasus Press, August 16, 2002; RIA *Oreanda* (Moscow), December 31, 2002; Giorgi Sepashvili, "Security Ministry Unveils Classified Details on Pankisi," *Civil Georgia*, January 20, 2003 (http://www.civil.ge).

[29] *Time*, April 1, 2002; *Washington Post*, April 28, 2002; "Media Availability with Rumsfeld and Georgian Defense Minister," May 7, 2002 (http://www.defenselink.mil/ transcripts/2002/t05072002_t0507ma.html).

The Georgian reluctance to embrace the Al Qaeda connection has led a number of observers to question the sincerity of the U.S. "war on terror" justification for the train and equip program. See Gary Leupp, "'Train and Equip' for What?

Georgia and the 'War on Terrorism,'" *Counterpunch*, May 29, 2002 (http://www.counterpunch.org/ leupp0529.html); Christopher Deliso, "A Georgian Gaffe and the War on Terror," Antiwar.com, June 18, 2002 (http://www.antiwar.com/orig/deliso45.html); Mark Irkali, "Guess Who Stole the Silverware? Invisible Terrorists and Disappearing Bombs," Diacritica.com, June 23, 2002 (http://www.diacritica.com/sobaka/archive/ diary0623.html); and Irkali, "Georgia: Welcome to America's New El Salvador."

[30] *Washington Post*, April 28, 2002; *Boston Globe*, March 19, 2002.

[31] Such logic has been confirmed by senior Georgian government officials in interviews with the author, October 17, 2003 and November 7, 2003. Also see the account by Security Minister Valeri Khaburdzania in "Pankisi, Abkhazia and the Problem of International Terrorism."

[32] Khaburdzania also noted later that month that Georgian authorities are "working to ensure that these armed persons lay down their arms or leave the territory of Georgia." Associated Press, March 7, 2002; "Media Availability with Rumsfeld and Georgian Defense Minister," May 7, 2002; Georgian TV, May 22, 2002; ITAR-TASS, May 20, 2002.

[33] Author's interview with senior U.S. government official, February 13, 2004.

[34] Interfax, July 16, 2002; Prime News Agency, July 31, 2002; Agence France Presse, August 1, 2002.

[35] ITAR-TASS, August 2, 2002.

[36] Author's interviews with a senior Georgian government official, October 17, 2003, and with a U.S. Defense Department official, October 23, 2003. Also Khaburdzania, "Pankisi, Abkhazia and the Problem of International Terrorism"; TASS, August 23, 2002; *Moscow Times*, August 26, 2002; Agence France Presse, August 28, 2002.

[37] Agence France Presse, July 29, 2002.

[38] *New York Times*, August 15, 2002; Interfax, July 30, 2002.

[39] U.S. Department of State Daily Press Briefings, July 31, 2002, and August 28, 2002; "Statement by the Press Secretary," August 24, 2002 (http://www.whitehouse.gov/news/releases/2002/08/ 20020824-2.html); *New York Times*, August 15, 2002.

[40] Official Kremlin International News Broadcast, September 12, 2002.

[41] *New York Times*, September 13, 2002; "Remarks by the President and Prime Minister Berlusconi of Italy," September 14, 2002 (http://www.whitehouse.gov/news/releases/2002/09/ 20020914-2.html).

[42] RIA *Oreanda*, September 13, 2002; Agence France Presse, September 13, 2002; *Washington Post*, September 14, 2002; Caucasus Press, September 21, 2002.

[43] ITAR-TASS, September 17, 2002; Georgian Radio, September 16, 2002, trans. BBC, September 16, 2002.

[44] Deutsche Press-Agentur, September 27, 2002; Interfax, September 26, 2002.

[45] Sepashvili, "Security Ministry Unveils Classified Details on Pankisi." In June 2003, officials estimated that there were fewer than 50 militants in the gorge. In August, Georgian media indicated that 40 militants had been detained. By the start of October 2003, the deputy interior minister reported that there were no militants left in the Pankisi Gorge. See *New York Times*, June 15, 2003; ITAR-TASS, August 25, 2003, October 1, 2003.

[46] Georgian Radio, November 25, 2002.

[47] Interfax, February 3, 2003.

[48] Caucasus Press, August 2, 2003.

[49] Caucasus Press, May 10, 2003; Agence France Presse, May 11, 2003.

[50] ITAR-TASS, February 10, 2003; Georgian Radio, March 24, 2003, trans. BBC, March 24, 2003; Prime News Agency, March 18, 2003.

[51] Natalia Antelava, "No War Blues Here," *Transitions Online*, March 22, 2003; ITAR-TASS, March 17, 2003; *Nezavisimaia Gazeta* (Moscow), August 6, 2003.

[52] ITAR-TASS, February 10, 2003, February 13, 2003.

[53] Antelava, "No War Blues Here."

[54] Author's interview with senior U.S. government official, February 13, 2004.

[55] Rustavi-2 TV (Tbilisi), August 6, 2003, trans. BBC, August 7, 2003; author's interview with senior U.S. government official, February 13, 2004.

[56] For more on the November 2003 parliamentary elections, see Jean-Christophe Peuch, "Georgia's Parliamentary Elections: Democracy in the Making?" *Caucasus Election Watch*, Center for Strategic and International Studies (CSIS), October 27, 2003 (http://www.csis.org/ruseura/caucasus/pubs), and Cory Welt, "Georgia: A Post-Election Crossroads," *Caucasus Election Watch*, CSIS, November 18, 2003.

CHAPTER THREE

GERMANY: A QUESTIONABLE ALLY?

Daniel Benjamin

INTRODUCTION

For all its indisputable successes, the history of the Atlantic Alliance has been one of recurrent crisis punctuated by intermittent moments of calm. Yet even against this backdrop of fractious friendship, the events of the period following September 11, 2001, stand apart. Henry Kissinger's judgment that disagreement over the global war on terror posed "the gravest crisis" in postwar history is correct. Never has the alliance come so close to crumbling; never has such transoceanic acrimony spilled out so dramatically.

A key distinction between this episode and previous ones was the role played by Germany. It is hardly novel for France to seek to balance against the United States in international politicking—to carve out an independent role for itself and, if possible, to bring other Europeans along. Often, however, France has used this stratagem to extract concessions from the United States as a prelude to common action. Germany, by contrast, has historically shown great reluctance to differ openly with the United States over major issues. In the run up to the invasion of Iraq, this pattern was shattered. A German chancellor broke with all precedent and made his opposition to U.S. policy a centerpiece of his reelection campaign. With the election won, he did not, as some expected, quietly retreat from this position. Instead, he rushed into France's embrace, joining Paris in an effort to throw further roadblocks into Washington's path. Later, these two partners would work together to frustrate U.S. efforts to gain international legitimacy for the invasion of Iraq in the UN Security Council.

Germany, at least temporarily, appeared to abandon its traditional role as America's anchor on the continent and mediator between Europe and the superpower. This shift was accompanied by an explosion of public rancor on both sides of the Atlantic. It has often been remarked that America's true "special relationship" during the postwar period was not with Great Britain but rather the Federal Republic of Germany, which it had nurtured from the ashes of World War II.[1] Some interpreted the events of 2002–2003 as heralding the end of an epoch that had been defined, at least in part, by that relationship.

For all the unseemly spectacle, there are strong reasons to question whether this description of events suffices. Have we witnessed a fundamental, structural change in the nature of the U.S.-German relationship or something more epiphenomenal in character? Undoubtedly, a dynamic process of change was already under way in the bilateral relationship, and the sudden arrival of the global war on terror accelerated—and quite possibly, distorted—this development. On closer examination, it appears that Germany has balanced against the United States less than the headlines would indicate. Moreover, such critical factors as Germany's evolving threat perception, attitudes within the political class, public opinion, and some recent policy initiatives point toward the potential of a long-term revitalization of the U.S.-German relationship.

Over the last few years, many of Germany's decisions have been reactive, reflecting the novelty of the situation and personalities of key individuals. Although some factors, such as the country's demographic trajectory and its role in a united Europe, will affect the relationship— and in a way that American leaders may not welcome—Germany has not taken any irreversible steps that would foreclose the possibility of a partnership comparable to that of the past. Germany, like the United States, *is* moving farther from the historic experience of the postwar period, in which a relationship of closeness and deference to Washington was established. But Germans are not agitating for a significantly changed posture vis-à-vis America. Unsurprisingly, future relations will depend at least as much on how the United States navigates its course in a new security environment as on Germans' understanding of their own strategic situation.

A MATTER OF TIMING

German-American relations were already in transition before September 11, reflecting changes both within the individual nations and across the international landscape. During what in retrospect looks like the false spring of the 1990s, Germany was preoccupied with the aftermath of its own "9/11"—November 9, 1989, the fall of the Berlin Wall and the consuming project of German reunification. For years, Germans were saddled with annual costs in the vicinity of $100 billion, a perpetually sluggish economy, and a plethora of cultural and emotional burdens that came with the "growing together of what belongs together," to paraphrase the famous words of Willy Brandt. The monetary union of 1990 may have been a political necessity, but it was an economic disaster, and the dismal state of the eastern economy offered no solace.

When they were not focused on domestic matters, Germans focused on the realities of a new, undivided Europe. The government navigated by two stars: the project of "widening and deepening" the European Union and relations with the United States. There were, to be sure, some irritants in the latter, such as persistent disagreements over defense burden sharing. Still, the United States was pleased by Germany's slow but determined effort to play a larger global role. This was seen as a key U.S. ambition from the time of President George H.W. Bush, who spoke of Germany as a "partner in leadership."

Although that phrase made Germans squirm, the vision dovetailed at least partially with Helmut Kohl's goal of creating a "normal" German role in foreign policy. At times, the conduct of this policy resulted in re-grettable outcomes, such as the hasty and ill-advised recognition of Slovenia and Croatia in 1991. In security policy, though, excessive speed was not the problem: Kohl's dispatch of military medics to Cambodia in 1991 and the "out-of-area" deployment in the Adriatic in 1994 were landmarks from the legal and historical perspectives, but small steps when considered in any international comparison.

With the election of Social Democrat Gerhard Schroeder and his Green foreign minister Joschka Fischer in 1998, two politicians with left-wing, pacifist credentials came to power. They were thus well placed on the political spectrum to bring a skeptical public to a greater embrace of international engagement, and the development that had begun under Kohl began to accelerate. Schroeder was viewed in the Clinton White House as something of a cipher and failed to establish anything like the rapport that Kohl had enjoyed with the American president. Fischer, however, became a favorite in Washington, esteemed for his vision and cooperativeness. The experience during the Kosovo campaign was seen on both sides as something of a success story, particularly against the context of intra-alliance wrangling over military operations.

Despite the positive outcome of the Kosovo operation and the generally close ties, the nature of the long-term relationship was a subject of perpetual discussion among German and American strategic thinkers and policymakers. The disappearance of the Soviet threat and the declining number of U.S. troops stationed in Germany had changed the essential security situation. With the heavy hand of necessity withdrawn, some of the glue that bound the allies together began to weaken. American disappointment over German defense spending was a constant throughout the period. Both sides—especially Germany—fretted that the evolving strategic landscape, particularly the rise of China, would inevitably turn American interest away from Europe and toward Asia. European policymakers complained that the United States was becoming poorer at consultation and increasingly unilateral in its actions. Consciousness of cultural differences was growing, with issues such as the environment, gun control, genetically modified food, the social safety net, and the death penalty becoming points of increasingly strident disagreement.

Until 2001, though, none of these issues reached a boil, and most observers characterized German-American relations as still essentially healthy. However, with the inauguration of George W. Bush, a rapid series of events set off tremors in Germany. Most revolved around international agreements: two days before Bush's first meeting with Schroeder in March 2001, Christie Todd Whitman, head of the Environmental Protection Agency, declared the Kyoto Treaty on climate change dead, shocking Germans, among the world's most environmentally conscious people. Germans were also dismayed by the administration's avowed intention of abolishing the Anti-Ballistic Missile Treaty, its withdrawal from the work on the draft protocol of the Biological Weapons Convention, and the sharp turn away from its predecessor's policy regarding North Korea. Similarly, the Bush administration's powerful and undisguised hostility toward the International Criminal Court (ICC)—which ultimately led to the unprecedented May 2002 "rescinding" of the U.S. signature on the treaty establishing the court—was profoundly unpopular in a nation that viewed the creation of the court as a hallowed goal, supported as a matter of conscience because of the catastrophe of the Third Reich. Although the initial meeting of Bush and Schroeder was uneventful, any belief that the new administration would pursue the same kind of highly coordinated diplomacy that the new president's father had was quickly dashed. Thoughts of a close working partnership with the new administration were replaced by a desire to limit damage.[2]

If there was a storm brewing in the summer of 2001, the attacks on the World Trade Center and the Pentagon deflected it off course. Ordinary Germans, like most Europeans, reacted to the carnage with an outpouring of support. Before a vast crowd of Berliners, President Johannes Rau declared, "No one knows better than the people here in Berlin what America has done for freedom and democracy in Germany. . . . We would not be standing next to the Brandenburg Gate tonight without America's contributions over long years and in difficult times."[3] Gerhard Schroeder spoke of Germany's "unlimited solidarity" with the United States.[4]

These remarks, like many such reactions in Europe, were strong reminders of the bonds that have united Americans and Europeans over the last five decades. German officials quietly hoped that the brief era of the untrammeled hegemon had come to an end and that the imperative of building a global coalition to confront a global menace would be decisive. "It is safe to say that Germans after 9/11 expected that the attacks would lead to greater multilateralism," reflected one German diplomat.[5]

The most telling demonstration of solidarity came the day after the attacks: Germany and its NATO partners unanimously invoked Article V of the NATO Charter, thus defining the attack against America as an attack against all the allies. Yet Washington's response suggested that this expression of unity was less than welcome. From the outset, the Defense Department was concerned that any road to action through NATO would be too slow and difficult for the operations it contemplated in Afghanistan. With Kosovo still fresh in its collective mind, the Pentagon sought to dampen enthusiasm for an allied response. Working with the allies, it was felt, would again constrain the flexibility of U.S. forces, entail bureaucratic tussles for which the Defense Department had no appetite, and add little or nothing in capabilities. Although Washington ultimately welcomed the invocation as a gesture, the lack of interest was immediately evident. At meetings in Brussels two weeks after the attacks, Deputy Secretary of Defense Paul Wolfowitz announced, "If we need collective action, we will ask for it; we don't anticipate that at the moment."[6]

As Washington turned to plan its campaign to topple the Taliban in Afghanistan and destroy Al Qaeda, Berlin, like many other American allies and friends, offered military support. How specific the offer was remains a subject of some debate. Some U.S. officials, without identifying Germany, argue that many allies' offers were designed to be turned down.[7] Whatever the case, German diplomats maintain that they were shocked that their support was rejected. The surprise no doubt increased after Gerhard Schroeder insisted on—and won—a vote to dispatch 3,900 Bundeswehr troops to Afghanistan in November, which could have ended his government. This would mark the first time in postwar history that German combat troops were to be deployed outside Europe.

Secretary of Defense Donald Rumsfeld's maxim—"The mission determines the coalition. The coalition does not determine the mission"—summarized the prevailing approach and a departure from decades in which the United States had placed a high premium on coalition building as a way of legitimacy building. German AWACs began patrolling American airspace in October 2001, and a naval task force joined other NATO forces deployed in the Horn of Africa. But substantial use of non-American forces on the ground in Afghanistan began in earnest only after the fighting was done, and Germans were dispatched to participate in stabilization through the International Security Assistance Force, or ISAF.

In other areas, Germany also behaved as a dutiful ally, both out of loyalty to a wounded partner and self-interest in the face of newly manifest threat. German officialdom had been dismissive of the threat from Al Qaeda prior to September 11. To those within the government—as well as in the press—the American fixation on jihadists could be explained only as the need for a new *Feindbild* after the passing of the Soviet threat.[8] The attacks and the consequent revelations about the Hamburg cell left Germans deeply embarrassed. Berlin responded by quickly detailing hundreds of intelligence and law enforcement personnel to deal with counterterrorism issues overnight, a turnaround that left FBI officials delighted.

To enhance prosecutorial powers, Interior Minister Otto Schily introduced two new sets of legislation, which for their capaciousness were soon nicknamed the "Otto Catalogues," a reference to Hamburg-based Otto Versand, the world's largest mail order firm. The first passed the Bundestag less than 12 weeks after the New York and Washington attacks, the second in 2002. An additional raft of legislation that strengthened the legal authority for conducting surveillance, obtaining bank records, and investigating religious groups also was enacted. Revisions were introduced that helped in the effort to stop money laundering and allowed the state to prosecute individuals for supporting international terror groups such as Al Qaeda.[9] In Washington, intelligence and law enforcement officials spoke approvingly of their newly galvanized German partners.

THE END OF SOMETHING

Any thought that Germany's course correction to address the jihadist threat or its expressions of solidarity would lead to a new comity at the political level was soon put to rest. President Bush's State of the Union Address on January 29, 2002, provided a seminal moment for Europeans trying to understand how the United States would confront the terrorist menace. Many aspects of the speech stood out: the unambiguous denunciation of the "axis of evil," the deeply religious tone, the Manichean vision that had been a stock part of presidential rhetoric since Bush had declared on September 20, 2001—"Every nation, in every region, now has a decision to make. Either you are with us, or you are with the terrorists."[10]

The speech was unsettling, even shocking for many Europeans—especially the naming of the axis of evil. Moreover, as Simon Serfaty has pointed out, the failure to mention NATO, the European Union, or the UN further disturbed European listeners. As Serfaty observed, "The speech deepened the allies' apprehension that, as had been shown in Afghanistan, they were being moved to a secondary role even for the treatment of issues with which they were directly concerned and which they had explicitly committed to defeat in coordination with their senior partner across the Atlantic."[11]

With its heavy emphasis on the danger posed by rogue states, the State of the Union was the first step in preparing the way for toppling the Iraqi regime of Saddam Hussein. As the administration began assembling the case it would put to the nation and the international community, it resolved on a style for doing so as well. A central element of that approach would be what James Mann has called "the follower hypothesis. . . . The theory was that if America led, its friends and allies would inevitably follow." Mann cites a 1997 article by Paul Wolfowitz that states, "A willingness to act unilaterally can be the most effective way of securing effective collective action" and concludes that the entire Bush team embraced the approach.[12] As a result, there was an unwillingness to take on board the counsel or criticism of longtime allies, guaranteeing that the eventual collision of interests would be that much more violent.

Accounts of how Gerhard Schroeder came to oppose the U.S. decision to invade Iraq vary, but the essentials of the story remain constant.[13] The first milestone came during Bush's May 2002 visit to Berlin. During their meetings, the two leaders touched on the issue of Iraq and thought they had an understanding: Schroeder would not make Iraq an issue in the fall election, and Bush would keep the chancellor apprised of U.S. decisionmaking. The Germans came away believing that no military action was imminent.[14]

In Washington, however, the wheels of policy were already turning fast. The following month, Bush spoke at West Point and previewed the doctrine of preemption that would later be canonized in the *National Security Strategy* released by the White House in September. About deterrence and containment, he said:

> In some cases, those strategies still apply. But new threats also require new thinking. Deterrence—the promise of massive retaliation against nations— means nothing against shadowy terrorist networks with no nation or citizens to defend. Containment is not possible when unbalanced dictators with weapons of mass destruction can deliver those weapons on missiles or secretly provide them to terrorist allies.
>
> We cannot defend America and our friends by hoping for the best. We cannot put our faith in the word of tyrants, who solemnly sign nonproliferation treaties, and then systemically break them. If we wait for threats to fully materialize, we will have waited too long.[15]

For Europeans, as for others paying close attention, this line of argument pointed to the conclusion that action against Iraq—and perhaps others—was inevitable.

In Germany, Gerhard Schroeder's reelection campaign, which pitted him against Bavarian minister-president Edmund Stoiber, was going poorly. He had lagged in the polls consistently, at times by as much as 10 percent. Schroeder is the most political of men—the embodiment of what highbrow Germans disdain in the career apparatchik. He concluded, probably correctly, that he had no other card to play except that of opposition to America's impending war. With a chronically mediocre national economic performance—which contrasted with the long run of prosperity and growth in Stoiber's Bavaria—the chancellor turned his election into a referendum on the conduct of the global war on terror. In the face of a possible career-ending defeat, he was not a man to blanch before the taboo of attacking a core U.S. policy.

For Schroeder, the position had numerous virtues. Opposing military action in Iraq would allow him both to appeal to the deeply ingrained German inclination toward pacifism and also to advance his goal of a more normal German role in the world. Schroeder, in short, could at once represent German values and be the champion of a Germany that could say no. This posture contrasted with the one Helmut

Kohl's government had taken in 1990–1991, when Bonn professed its *Betroffenheit*—a nearly untranslatable word that signifies being deeply affected in a sober, sorry, and almost melancholy manner—and took out its checkbook to contribute to the coalition effort to dislodge Saddam from Kuwait. But strong declarations of support were mostly absent, and Kohl (and to a lesser extent) Foreign Minister Hans-Dietrich Genscher confined themselves to chiding demonstrators for excessive anti-Americanism.

Moreover, taking an antiwar position would also enable Schroeder, who had demonstrated little enduring interest in foreign affairs, to achieve something that Social Democrats had been yearning to do since unification: squeeze the Party of Democratic Socialism (PDS), the successor party of the former ruling East German Communist Party, to the margins in eastern Germany. Easterners were more inclined to pacifism, and despite the affinities of the northern, Protestant, and industrial Social Democratic Party (SPD) with the citizens of the five new Länder, the PDS had managed to survive and hold onto roughly a quarter of the vote in the region. An appeal to this pacifism might peel off enough voters to block the PDS from winning the 5 percent of the national vote required to gain entry into the Bundestag.

Schroeder reckoned correctly. During his campaign rallies, he railed against foreign "adventures" with the same vehemence that Konrad Adenauer had inveighed against any "experiments" in social or foreign policy advocated by the SPD. He managed to do so while underscoring a German exceptionalism based on moral objections to war. "We will go our special German way," he told approving crowds.[16] There was a high-wire quality to this rhetoric. The language of a "special German way" (*Sonderweg*) was historically charged—Germany was now supposed to be embedded in alliances, both transatlantic and European. By stirring up anti-Americanism in the public, the chancellor was breaking a taboo that none of his predecessors had dared—not during Vietnam and not when Ronald Reagan began raising Cold War tensions with anti-Soviet rhetoric.

The strategy worked. Schroeder scored repeatedly, flat-footing his opponent. Stoiber tried to one-up Schroeder by saying that if he were chancellor, he would deny the United States the right to stage to the Persian Gulf from Germany, a position from which he was forced to walk back a day later.[17]

During the final phase of the campaign, Washington unintentionally handed Schroeder another, larger stick with which to beat his drum of opposition. On August 26, Vice President Dick Cheney spoke before the Veterans of Foreign Wars and left no doubt that the United States was moving beyond containment and deterrence in dealing with Iraq. Cheney announced that Saddam had resumed work on nuclear weapons and questioned the utility of weapons inspections. "Deliverable weapons of mass destruction in the hands of a terror network, or a murderous dictator, or the two working together, constitutes as grave a threat as can be imagined. The risks of inaction are far greater than the risk of action."[18] With this virtual declaration of the inevitability of conflict, Schroeder was emboldened to complain not only about the substance of the U.S. policy but the process as well. There had been nothing like the kind of consultations he expected, and he believed that Washington had discarded an effort to disarm Saddam for one to topple him. Schroeder spoke vehemently against this American high-handedness.[19]

His line of argument played well with Germans. Although two-thirds or more of Americans were convinced that Iraq had played a role in the September 11 attacks, Germans did not see the connection. Their leaders were looking at some of the same intelligence as their American counterparts, and they did not see the relationship either. (It did not help that U.S. diplomats quietly told them that there was no connection between Iraq and Al Qaeda.)[20] Yes, Saddam had chemical and biological weapons, the Germans believed. But they were not persuaded he was mad enough to use them and elicit certain, overwhelming retaliation. The drumbeat of argument in the United States that all rogue states and terrorists were in cahoots found little echo in Germany, and Germans fell back on a central postwar belief: wars usually turn out badly.

Gerhard Schroeder was reelected on September 22 by a hairbreadth margin. The new Red-Green coalition had only a nine-seat majority, and the PDS failed to make it back into the Bundestag.

THE ANIMUS RUNS WILD

In surveying the period from the German elections through the invasion of Iraq, it is difficult to recall any other episode in which personal pique played such a prominent role in driving the course of nations. That it did so underscores how the climacteric of September 11 swept away all the usual bureaucratic levees and dikes that regulate international relations.

That is not to say there was not ample reason for irritation. Two days before the election, a provincial newspaper reported that the German justice minister, Herta Dauebler-Gmelin, had commented that the American president was pressing for war to "distract attention from his domestic political problems." She added, "That's a favorite method. Hitler did that too."[21] The White House reacted with outrage. Dauebler-Gmelin denied she had made the offensive remark. Although she was eventually forced out of the cabinet, Schroeder compounded matters with a poorly worded note of apology.

The event crystallized the White House's antipathy for the German leader. National Security Adviser Condoleezza Rice spoke of a poisoned relationship and the president's lack of trust for the chancellor—a reference to Bush's belief that Schroeder had promised not to make Iraq a campaign issue. In the months that followed, the White House made it a policy to isolate and ignore Schroeder. The president declined to make the traditional phone call to congratulate Schroeder after his election victory and maintained the silent treatment, barely acknowledging Schroeder when they met in St. Petersburg in late May 2003 and forgoing a one-on-one meeting at the G-8 summit in Evian.

The cold shoulder policy was adopted by Secretary of Defense Donald Rumsfeld as well. Only Secretary of State Colin Powell conducted regular business with his counterpart Fischer, though relations were hardly warm. There was remarkably little shyness about publicly displaying the president's aversion to the German leader. An administration official recounted to a *New York Times* reporter an exchange between the president and his national security adviser:

> "I can't do it with Schroeder," Mr. Bush told Ms. Rice. . . . who had not directly suggested that Mr. Bush meet with Mr. Schroeder [and therefore] rushed to reassure. "No, no, no, we won't make you do it with Schroeder," she said. But Mr. Bush seemed to know what Ms. Rice had in mind. "Wait a minute, you'll get me back with Schroeder, I know what you're trying to do," the president said, the official recounted.[22]

Because Schroeder had run his campaign on opposition to an invasion of Iraq even if there were a Security Council mandate—a position that appalled both independent foreign policy analysts and leading members of Schroeder's party, such as Hans-Ulrich Klose—there was no turning back. At the same time, he must have felt an increasing sense of the peril of his *Alleingang* (going it alone), another taboo in postwar German foreign policy. When the opportunity afforded itself, he found a new ally in French president Jacques Chirac, who only months earlier had been known to favor a Stoiber victory. Celebrating the 40th anniversary of the Elysee Treaty in Versailles in late January, the two publicly avowed their opposition to an early war and their insistence on a Security Council mandate.

The occasion triggered a response in Washington that brought an already tattered relationship to a new low. During a press briefing the same day, Rumsfeld dismissed the position of continental Europe's two greatest powers by calling them "old Europe" and argued that the center of gravity in NATO had moved to the east and the more pro-American new members. The remark reverberated across the Atlantic, suggesting that a senior U.S. official was driving a wedge among Europeans—that the United States was, as one commentator has suggested, "counter-counterbalancing." A few days later, Rumsfeld struck again. When reviewing international support for the United States, he said, "There are three or four countries that have said they won't do anything; I believe Libya, Cuba and Germany are the ones that I have indicated won't help in any respect."[23]

Already deeply divided over Iraq, Europe began to tear itself apart, with rows breaking out between the French and Germans on the one hand and, on the other, the more pro-American/Atlanticist camp that included the British, Spanish, Italians, and the Vilnius Ten, a group of candidates for NATO membership. At the level of high politics, it appeared that a period of reflexive balancing and counterbalancing had begun between the two continental heavyweights and the United States. Soon NATO was embroiled in a dispute over military support for Turkey. Later, still, another spat exploded into public view as the French and the Germans declared that the EU's European Security and Defense Policy required its own military planning cell. As one senior American diplomat bemoaned, "Four and a half years of meetings on the planning cell were undermined in a matter of days."[24] There was much drama still to come, especially at the UN, in the debate over Iraq and a second Security Council resolution to authorize the use of force. But the story, in the sense of the further development of the characters involved, ended there. The Germans and the French were as determined in their opposition to the use of force as the United States was to topple Saddam.[25] There was little to do but watch the wreckage.

TEXT AND SUBTEXT

It would be easy to write this story as one of a classic case of balancing against the hegemon, of the continental duo trying to lash down the American Gulliver. The story line became hard to resist when France and

Germany found other partners, such the Russians, to join them for the showdown. At the level of the highest politics, the Franco-German camp *did* want to limit the power of the hegemon. The individual players' reasons undoubtedly differed, but for the Germans, there were calculations of both power and principle involved. If the United States succeeded in its grand goals, thus becoming vastly more influential in the Middle East and the Persian Gulf, it could well have threatened German and other European interests. (It is at least as likely that German leaders worried that the U.S. invasion would make a great mess of the region, also undermining German and European equities.) Furthermore, the principle that the use of force had to be legitimated, especially in a case of preventive war, by the international community acting through the Security Council, was also a serious matter for the Germans. (This was especially pertinent for Joschka Fischer, who had been alarmed by Schroeder's actions during the campaign, but still found a strong basis for opposing the contemplated U.S. action.) In Kosovo, at least, there had been the legitimacy conferred by NATO and a broader union of democracies. But on grounds of principle, Iraq was a different case entirely.

Behind the harsh rhetoric, however, the state of affairs was considerably more complicated. While Washington was aggressively ignoring Germany, Berlin pursued a strategy of damage limitation. It sought to cordon off the dispute over Iraq from other matters and avoided conflict with the Americans over other issues. In taking the measure of this part of the "gravest crisis," what did *not* happen is remarkable. For example, there was no recourse to economic instruments such as trade to show disfavor with the United States. One can argue that this was the case because EU involvement would have been required, which was out of the question, and it would not have had much effect. Still, the subject was not even mentioned because of the desire to contain the disagreement.

Moreover, Germany went to considerable lengths to soften the blow of its opposition to the U.S. invasion and, where possible, to provide a kind of compensation. First, it undertook quiet measures that made the U.S. deployment to the Gulf easier. For example, 2,500 Bundeswehr troops were assigned to provide security for American bases in Germany that were facing a manpower shortage at a time of heightened tension. Despite Schroeder's earlier threats about withdrawing the detachment of the chemical and biological weapons–detecting Fuchs vehicles stationed in Kuwait, these *Spuerpanzer* were left in theater. Despite the conflict over military support for Turkey, German Patriot missile systems were shipped there before the invasion, and Germans manned AWACs flights over the region.[26] The presence of nearly 8,000 Bundeswehr troops in the Balkans further eased pressure on American forces. And there was, of course, no further question about allowing the American forces to stage from Germany.

Above all, though, Berlin sought to underscore its commitment to the war on terror, which it distinguished from the war in Iraq. The German navy maintained its presence in the Horn of Africa as part of Operation Enduring Freedom and took command for a six-month period in 2002—with 1,400 personnel, it was the largest such deployment since World War II. Most notably, though, the Germans took on burdens in Afghanistan that would have been difficult to imagine only a few years earlier. They deployed forces to participate in ISAF and, in February 2003, assumed joint command of the mission with the Netherlands. The total number of personnel rose to 2,500, and the Bundeswehr extended its reach outside of Kabul with the stationing of forces in a Provincial Reconstruction Team in Kunduz—over the objections of CDU parliamentarians who feared that Germans were being put in harm's way to salve a wounded transatlantic relationship.[27] American military experts may not have viewed these as terribly robust moves, but in the German context, they were nonetheless remarkable. By one reckoning, Germany had the second most forces deployed in the world in 2003 after the United States, which suggests that Rumsfeld's remarks putting Germany in the same class as Cuba and Libya were wildly off the mark.[28] Germany also played a critical role in supporting the Petersberg Process for restoring political stability in Afghanistan, including hosting the conference that prepared the way for the Loya Jirga—the national assembly of Afghan leaders that met in June 2002 to select a transitional government. As one German diplomat put it, in the global war on terror, "For us, Afghanistan has been a way of demonstrating our commitment."[29]

The argument that this kind of support has been a band-aid on the larger transatlantic disagreement about the military capabilities is belied by other, longer-term steps Germany has taken. For years, Germany has come in for relentless criticism because of its low level of defense spending, which had been hovering around 1.5 percent of GDP, its continued reliance on conscription, its continued emphasis on territorial defense, and its difficulties in raising the number of deployable troops. Yet well before the transatlantic sniping over Iraq had ended, German defense minister Peter Struck unveiled a new set of guidelines that put his country's military on a new course.

Struck, who had been personally snubbed by Rumsfeld, produced a policy that aims at preventing the widely predicted decoupling of the German military from the United States. With its assertions that German security begins in the Hindu Kush and that "security policy situation requires that the prevention and stemming of crises and conflicts must be the goals of security and defense policy,"[30] it sounded a harmonic note with the *U.S. National Security Strategy.* The German Defense Ministry is bound by fiscal constraints that will prevent an increase in spending before 2007, but Struck has undertaken an initiative to cancel unneeded weapons systems and close bases to save money. German efforts in this direction have not always panned out in the past. But Struck's emphasis on shifting from territorial defense to mobile operations appears to be moving forward as indicated, for example, by the Bundestag's approval of EUR 8.3 billion to buy 60 Airbus A-400 military transport aircraft by 2012.[31] It is noteworthy that even after their initial differences, Rumsfeld and Struck appear to be developing a better personal relationship. Rumsfeld has reportedly even spoken positively of Struck's reforms.[32]

The desire to maintain a close partnership in prosecuting the war on terror has been manifest in other areas as well. Perhaps the most notable example is the relationship that formed between German Interior Minister Otto Schily and Secretary for Homeland Defense Tom Ridge and, in particular, Attorney General John Ashcroft. As one American analyst noted of the tie between the two nations' top law enforcement officials, one a former attorney for the members of the Baader-Meinhof terrorist group and the other a lifelong conservative, "This is truly the odd couple of the German-American relationship. Schily may be visiting here more often than Fischer."[33]

The relationship became sufficiently well known in Washington that even the *Weekly Standard,* the house journal of neoconservatism and no friend of continental Europe, wrote approvingly. It quoted Ashcroft as saying that the fight against terror is

> "what unites us . . . . Otto takes the threat of terrorism seriously, and he addresses the threat with a very complete willingness to devote whatever it takes to win this battle."
>
> . . . In doing whatever it takes, Schily has become a major proponent of biometric identifiers: microchips in passports and visas, fingerprinting, facial recognition technology at airports, and retinal scans—the kinds of

things that probably would have appalled the old Schily. And Ashcroft is fully on board: "When it comes to who you're letting in and out of your country, and who you're letting on and off your airplanes, you need to have reliable information and information of integrity, and [biometric identifiers] are a way of doing it. I think [Schily] has been a leader in saying when we do these things, we ought to do them in a rational way."[34]

The passage is indicative but not exhaustive. With either direct government support or involvement, Germans are working together with Americans on homeland security issues ranging from port security to biodefense. There are undoubtedly plenty of points of disagreement—particularly on matters having to do with data protection and, as has been much discussed, the use of intelligence in trial proceedings. But so much is to be expected in a cooperative venture of this breadth.

Josef Joffe has termed the strategy of America's European critics in the run-up to Iraq as "soft balancing," an effort to restrain "no. 1 by enmeshing him in the ropes of institutional dependence" through appeals to international law and the UN Security Council.[35] This is true up to a point; Germany, at least, was "soft balancing"—but at the same time Berlin was trying to preserve and strengthen ties to the United States to deal with the perceived common threats.

WHICH WAY DO WE GO?

Joffe's diagnosis of soft balancing, incomplete though it may be now, could prove prophetic about the future. If the United States carries forward a global war on terror that emphasizes regime change in rogue states and preventive war and refuses to take on board the counsel of longtime allies, then this is a likely outcome. The result will be the shredding of the multilateral institutions that bind America and its European partners as well as those that include larger parts of the international community. At least in Germany's case, such U.S. unilateralism will be deeply distressing but is not likely to lead to truly "hard" balancing. It is simply impossible to imagine Germans paying for significant amounts of hard power any time in the near future. This is, after all, a populace that wants to emulate Switzerland more than any other nation, as polling data has shown.

It is also improbable that Germany will join France in a sustained effort to create the multipolar world that Jacques Chirac and others have envisioned, with the EU as the main counterweight to America. Although Germans may want a stronger EU to increase their influence in Washington, they will be wary of attempts to build the institution in opposition to the United States. Before the Iraq War, Berlin had followed a deft course of championing smaller members of the EU and especially new candidates for membership. Germany's ability to shape the EU into the federal entity it envisions and to strengthen its own influence within the EU will be better served by returning to this course, which most policymakers seem to recognize. That requires making common cause with states whose "definition of Europe does not include anti-Americanism," as one U.S. official put it.[36] Germans were stung by criticism of the Schroeder-Chirac common front that came from much of the rest of Europe. A permanent Franco-German bloc, most Germans recognize, would open deep rifts in Europe and likely take them in a direction they do not want to go.

The key variable in the near to mid term will be U.S. policy. To German government officials and foreign policy analysts, this is the great unknown before them. Asked if they expect the bilateral relationship to return to what it was before Iraq, they uniformly express uncertainty and ambivalence. "We hope [the relationship] will snap back and sometimes we let ourselves believe it will. But when we think it through, we don't really believe," explained one senior German diplomat.[37] "We want to go back, but there is a sense that things will not be the same," said a foreign policy adviser in the CDU.[38]

It is important to emphasize the range of options available to the United States; if Washington revises its approach to the war on terror and other global issues, Germans are likely to respond positively and rapidly—and perhaps even to give America a wider berth on issues that had been irritants. Already, as Iraq begins to recede as an issue in the bilateral relationship, American officials are reporting strong signals that Berlin wishes to improve the relationship.

As early as February 2004, in the view of some analysts, Germany began to mend fences when Joschka Fischer spoke at the annual *Wehrkunde* conference in Munich and, while reiterating his belief that the reasons for going to war in Iraq were not valid, adopted a conciliatory tone that contrasted with his remarks a year before. Another sign of a nascent rapprochement came in late fall of the same year, when Germany— along with the Paris Club—wrote off 80 percent of Iraqi debt, a move long sought by the Bush administration. Reciprocation came in the form of the White House's decision to schedule a visit to Germany in

February 2005. That turn of events signaled, at a minimum, that Bush was eager to put behind him the rancor of the past. The question that hung over the impending trip was whether the new tack demonstrated a desire merely to present a better image of the bilateral relationship or to achieve genuinely improved cooperation. The absence of any announcement of major policy initiatives in the runup to the trip left the matter open to debate. Nonetheless, several factors suggest that a substantive revitalization of ties is within reach.

A Potential Common Agenda

In discussing the jihadist threat, German diplomats, intelligence, and military officials express considerable unease. There is surprisingly little understanding in the public about the nature of the new terrorism, but within the bureaucracy, an acute awareness of the challenge exists alongside a sense of foreboding. German officials recognize the danger Islamist terror poses and are alarmed at the spread of the ideology behind it. Although the German public—at least prior to the Madrid bombings—may have answered pollsters' questions by putting terrorism at the top of their fears, there is little of the anxiety one finds in the United States or even Britain. Instead, as German officials concede, there has been a sense that the big targets are elsewhere. The discrepancy between public perceptions and actual threats worries many of them, who believe Germany's attractiveness as a target is underappreciated. Asked why there has not been more of an effort to educate the public, officials say that, after Iraq, the political will is not there.

If Washington refocuses the war on terror on the jihadist threat, Germany could prove a strong partner. Building on the already strong law enforcement, intelligence, and homeland security cooperation, Germany would be inclined to join an effort that addresses issues related to "root causes." Issues of education, democratization, rule of law, and the like are ones that would elicit a positive German response. Given the generally toxic view of the United States in the Muslim world today, such an endeavor would need the appearance of being a broad-based effort involving numerous partners. It goes almost without saying that a sustained reengagement in the Middle East peace process, especially after the death of Yasser Arafat and the election of Mahmoud Abbas as president of the Palestinian Authority, would vastly increase the ease of joining together behind such an effort to address the underlying causes of terror.

A Constituency for Partnership

Unlike in France, business interests in Germany remain enormously influential, regardless of who is in power. The country's identity as an exporter remains as strong as ever. Such organizations as the BDI (the German Federation of Industry) and the *Arbeitgeberverband* (Association of German Employers) were deeply concerned during the period when the brickbats were flying and did their best to smooth matters over, placing statements of solidarity in American newspapers and holding meetings with American businesses. They are also said to have weighed in forcefully with the chancellory and the Foreign Ministry on the need to improve ties. German business is acutely mindful of the enormous trade flows and high levels of foreign direct investment going in both directions across the Atlantic. In outlook, it tends to be pro-American and would likely seek to influence opinion if there was a perception that Germans and Americans were reviving their partnership.

Public Opinion

The permanence of the antipathies of 2002–2003 has been much overstated. The quarrel was a public one, and the media campaigns of mutual vilification were ugly.[39] Yet anti-Americanism is not a permanent aspect of German public opinion. On the contrary, as is often pointed out, Germany is Europe's most Americanized country—so much so that even its anti-Americanism is reflective of American left-wing criticism of U.S. policies. One need only recall the large 1990–1991 demonstrations against the first Gulf War to be reminded that anti-Americanism is not necessarily growing and that it is triggered by a very specific kind of event—the use of force. It is not news that Germans have distinctly different ideas about military force in world affairs. The question is which way those attitudes are developing. Given all the extraneous issues that came into play in the war against Iraq—from the power struggle within Europe to the personal tension between George Bush and Gerhard Schroeder—it is difficult to say with assurance that they are headed in a way inimical to American interests.

As Michael Mertes, a former senior chancellory official during the Kohl years has pointed out, there has been a rough stability in pro-American sentiment, with temporary peaks and troughs right after the September 11 attacks and before the invasion of Iraq. Germans were less likely than Britons or the French to want the Iraqis to show strong resistance. And although in the spring of 2003, a remarkable 80 percent of Germans opposed the war in Iraq, in May, a poll found that 71 percent of

Germans said they liked Americans.[40] As Mertes and others point out, distinguishing anti-Bush from anti-American sentiment is essential; he strongly suggests that the former has been the driver in the recent trough in support for America. There is also an increasing preference for the EU as opposed to America, but this a transition period for the EU, and attitudes may not be as fixed as they appear. The years 2002–2003 were an aberration, he contends, and there is, at least now, no reason to believe in a sea change in German opinion.[41] Additional polling data support Mertes's contention. Writing in the *Frankfurter Allgemeine Zeitung* in July 2002, Elisabeth Noelle of the well-regarded Allensbach Institute said that the president's "extreme unpopularity in Germany could very well be poisoning . . . overall attitudes toward the United States." At this point, 66 percent of those polled had a poor opinion of Bush, down from 80 percent two months earlier. Noelle notes that those questioned overwhelmingly attributed current anti-American feelings to the division over Iraq.[42]

IMPONDERABLES

At the level of high politics, it is certainly premature to predict enduring, significant changes in the essentials of German foreign policy. The transatlantic debacle of 2002–2003 is hard to imagine without the intervening distortion provided by the German national election. One can hardly conceive a more potent collision of personalities than that of Bush and Schroeder—one a leader for whom personal loyalty is the paramount virtue, the other, a tactician with few, if any, red lines. Personalities, we should be grateful, rarely leave the most lasting imprints on the ties between nations.

Many factors will play a role in determining whether Germany bandwagons its way into the future together with the American colossus. Gerhard Schroeder acted in 2002–2003 out of dire political exigency, and this is unlikely to happen again anytime soon if the signals coming out of Berlin are true indicators. Could there be another such rift in several years? Given the sense expressed by many Germans in influential positions that the country's interests were damaged by the events of 2002–2003, it seems unlikely. German leaders will not be inclined to endorse military action against another rogue state, particularly given the widespread belief that their original objections to invading Iraq have been borne out. For this reason, the handling of the issue of Iran's nuclear program poses the greatest challenge for those trying to strengthen bilateral ties. Exogenous factors such as elections could, of course, again play an important role in driving events.

Over the longer term, prognostication becomes, naturally, more speculative. For decades, the appearance of a new generation of Germans has been heralded, a generation that feels no burden of the past and that wishes to see Germany take a new, more determined role in world affairs. It has not happened yet, but there is no certainty that in 15 years, things will not change. Indeed, it seems likely that some alterations in the strategic understanding of Germans will occur. But what direction this will take is difficult to say. If one looks deeper into the ranks of the political class and asks how rising politicians might behave, there are also few clues. Among those currently building their careers in the junior ranks of government and in the backbenches of the Bundestag, there is little indication of a desire to challenge the United States. Equally, however, there may be less of the deep sense of transatlantic kinship that many in earlier generations exhibited. One can ask whether Germany is producing politicians who think strategically about their country's place on the world stage. Perhaps it is a reach to draw any conclusion from the recent, bizarre choice of a new federal president, which resulted in the selection of Horst Koehler, former head of the International Monetary Fund, but it does raise questions about whether Germany's parties view their work with appropriate seriousness. Overall trends in political engagement certainly do not indicate that they are getting much pressure from the grassroots to do so. According to one leading opinion analyst, to the extent that Germans have become more politically active, there chief concerns have been at the local level—it is the politics of the kindergarten and *Spielplatz* (playground).[43] Whether the transatlantic split over Iraq has resulted in a more enduring mobilization of opinion to deal with international issues seems unlikely.

The ties between the German democracy and the American one are undergirded by strong cultural affinities that are not so quickly undone, as pollsters' interpretations of the temporary quality of the recent antipathies suggest. Yet one assertion that will hold up is that Germany is a graying country with shrinking youth cohorts. That may well dampen the country's interest in playing a more assertive international role. Germany's own chronic inability to achieve vigorous economic growth is a further concern that will affect the national desire to spend on the military. As mentioned, Germany is extremely unlikely to press ahead with military programs to balance against the United States, but the lack of resolve on these matters may also undermine efforts such as Peter Struck's to strengthen Germany's role as an ally to America. If Berlin cannot enhance its influence over U.S.-led military action in the long term, Germany could enter a long, secular drift into a relationship that is solely focused on economics and shared culture—exactly what some critics, especially on the right, allege has already begun.

In light of Germany's seemingly perpetual difficulties in dealing with the aging of its population and the related issue of loosening its restrictions on immigration, this is a genuine possibility that could undermine even strong resolve to revitalize the partnership for the future. At a minimum, the demographic outlook for Germany argues for a revitalization of the relationship before there is further erosion of political will. As has been seen, the elements necessary for a strong U.S.-German partnership are at hand. The question is whether the leadership and vision exists on the two sides of the Atlantic to make that partnership a durable reality.

Notes

[1] "From the final resignation of Winston Churchill to the arrival of Margaret Thatcher, German leaders and diplomats were consistently more respected and frequently more listened to in Washington than their (admittedly mostly mediocre) British counterparts." Walter Russell Mead, "Goodbye to Berlin," *National Interest,* Spring 2004.

[2] For a prescient early account of transatlantic relations, see Hugo Young, "We've Lost That Allied Feeling," *Washington Post,* April 1, 2001, p. B1.

[3] David Rising, "200,000 Berliners gather at Brandenburg Gate in Show of Solidarity with Americans," Associated Press, September 14, 2001.

[4] Agence France Presse, "Schroeder Says US Attacks Were War Declaration against Civilized World," September 11, 2001.

[5] Author's interview with German diplomat, January 8, 2004.

[6] "The reaction in Washington was quick and decisive—NATO could not be allowed to reign in any U.S. response. According to a senior State Department official speaking to reporters after the first emergency meeting on 12 September, the United States was pushing for a resolution that would mention that the article could be invoked, without actually voting on the measure itself. A senior Administration official said that it was the Europeans who were 'desperately trying to give us political cover and the Pentagon was resisting it.' Eventually, Secretary of Defense Rumsfeld relented and agreed to accept the clause." Rebecca Johnson and Micah Zenko, "All Dressed Up and No Place to Go: Why NATO Should Be on the Front

Lines in the War on Terror," *Parameters* 32, no. 4 (Winter 2002–2003): 48–63. For an early critique of this approach, see Daniel Benjamin, "Get Those Allies into the Tent," *Time International*, December 3, 2001, p. 40.

[7] Author's interview with Bush administration official, October 29, 2003.

[8] Daniel Benjamin and Steven Simon, *The Age of Sacred Terror* (New York: Random House, 2002), p. 315.

[9] Tessa Szszkowitz, "Germany," in *Europe Confronts Terrorism*, ed. Karin von Hippel (New York: Palgrave Macmillan, 2005). The author is indebted to Dr. von Hippel for sharing this chapter prior to publication.

[10] Address to a Joint Session of Congress and the American People (http://www.whitehouse.gov/news/releases/2001/09/20010920-8.html).

[11] Simon Serfaty, *Renewing the Transatlantic Partnership* (Washington, D.C.: CSIS with support of the DaimlerChrysler Corporation Fund, 2003), p. 5 (http://www.nato.int/docu/conf/2003/030718_bxl/ serfati-transatlpart.pdf).

[12] James Mann, "Bush Wanted His Doctrine and the Allies, Too," *Washington Post*, March 16, 2003, p. B1.

[13] Three accounts of these events stand out: Elizabeth Pond's *Friendly Fire: The Near-Death of the Transatlantic Alliance* (Washington, D.C.: Brookings Institution/European Union Studies Association, 2004), Philip Gordon and Jeremy Shapiro, *Allies at War* (Washington, D.C.: Brookings Institution, 2004), and Stephen Szabo's *Parting Ways: The Crisis in German-American Relations* (Washington, D.C.: Brookings Institution, 2004). The author is indebted to Messrs. Gordon, Shapiro, and Szabo for sharing their manuscripts.

[14] Pond, *Friendly Fire*, p. 57. "The American view of the thrust of both this meeting and the earlier one in Washington in February was that the Chancellor had told the President explicitly, that he would support a war so long as it was quick and civilian causalities were kept to a minimum. The sense of what Schroeder said was, 'If you lead I will not get in your way, but be decisive, move quickly and win.' One American present at the discussions stated that Schroeder said he did not have a problem with Iraq so long as it did not interfere with the election. Bush assured him that nothing would happen before the election and that he would consult with the Chancellor. Schroeder responded, 'That's all I need to know.' The President had the clear sense that Schroeder was with him. The problem was that no one at the time knew what would happen and what being with the U.S. meant." Szabo, *Parting Ways*, p. 20.

[15] Remarks by the President at 2002 Graduation Exercise of the United States Military Academy, West Point, New York (http://www.whitehouse.gov/news/releases/2002/06/20020601-3.html).

[16] Stefan Theil and Michael Meyer, "The German Problem," *Newsweek* (Atlantic edition), September 30, 2002, p. 34.

[17] Pond, *Friendly Fire,* p. 57.

[18] Remarks by the Vice President to the Veterans of Foreign Wars 103rd National Convention (http://www.whitehouse.gov/news/releases/2002/08/20020826.html).

[19] "At campaign rallies, the unpopular German chancellor began to find that his only effective applause line was when he denounced the idea of war on Iraq. On August 30, Schroeder announced that Germany would withdraw its biological and chemical detection equipment from Kuwait if the Americans attacked Iraq. Earlier in the year, Schroeder had told a German journalist that he knew that any German chancellor who withdrew such equipment would 'not be welcome in the United States in the next twenty or thirty years.' But now, with his political back against the wall, he was proposing to do just that." Gordon and Shapiro, *Allies at War,* p. 100.

Evidently, the lack of consultation was not an issue that troubled Washington. Szabo writes, "A close confidant of Cheney's, when asked by the author as to whether the impact of the speech in Germany was considered, replied, 'Why should he care about the reaction in Germany?'" Szabo, *Parting Ways,* p. 28.

[20] Author's interview with German diplomat, September 10, 2003.

[21] Carol J. Williams, "Germany Apologizes for Comment; Europe: Chancellor expresses his regret amid an official's insistence that her Hitler reference in remarks about Bush was misrepresented," *Los Angeles Times,* September 21, 2002, p. 3.

[22] Elisabeth Bumiller, "A Partner in Shaping an Assertive Foreign Policy," *New York Times,* January 7, 2004, p. 1.

[23] Robert Burns, "Rumsfeld Travels to Meet with Europeans amid Tensions over Iraq Policy," Associated Press, February 6, 2003.

[24] Author's interview with American diplomat, January 9, 2004.

[25] The importance of the character of relations at the time should not be underestimated as an irritant. As Christoph Bertram, distinguished foreign affairs commentator and research director of the German Institute for International and Security Affairs, noted, "The Americans are pushing their weight around and doing it with rhetoric that may go down well in some parts of the U.S. but rubs us the wrong way all of the time." "And the fact we're aware of our continuing dependence on the U.S. doesn't help. It's American power, but also the *rhetoric* of American power that has exacerbated the sense of weakness, alienation and uneasiness that we see all over Europe." [Italics mine.] Quoted in Glenn Frankel, "Sneers from Across the Atlantic; Anti-Americanism Moves to W. Europe's Political Mainstream," *Washington Post,* February 11, 2003, p.1.

[26] Richard Bernstein, "Berlin Hopes Bruises Will Heal," *International Herald Tribune,* March 14, 2003, p. 1.

[27] Author's interview with German parliamentarians, September 12, 2003.

[28] Pond, *Friendly Fire,* p. 53.

[29] Author's interview with German diplomat, January 8, 2004.

[30] BBC Monitoring International Reports, "German Armed Forces to Prioritize Global Crisis Prevention," March 6, 2004.

[31] Roland Eggleston, "Berlin Discarding Outdated Arms, Moving to Professional Military," Radio Free Europe/Radio Liberty (http://www.globalsecurity.org/military/library/news/2003/05/mil-030523-rfel-163410.htm).

[32] BBC Monitoring International Reports, "German Defence Minister Says 'All Problems' with US 'Solved,'" February 6, 2004.

[33] Author's interview with former State Department official, February 7, 2004.

[34] Victorino Matus, "Schily Season: John Ashcroft's Favorite German," *Weekly Standard,* March 29, 2004.

[35] Josef Joffe, "Gulliver Unbound: Can America Rule the World?" (http://www.cis.org.au/Events/JBL/JBL03.htm).

[36] Author's interview with Bush administration official, October 29, 2003.

[37] Author's interview with German diplomat, September 10, 2003.

[38] Author's interview with senior CDU official, September 12, 2003.

[39] See, for example, Timothy Garton Ash, "Anti-Europeanism in America," *New York Review of Books,* February 13, 2003.

[40] Poll conducted by Forschungsgruppe Wahlen in May 2003, cited in Michael Mertes, "German Anti-Americanism? Forget it!" *Internationale Politik* 4 (2003).

[41] Ibid., pp. 18–22.

[42] Elisabeth Noelle, "Iraq Takes Its Toll on German-U.S. Ties," *Frankfurter Allgemeine Zeitung,* July 25, 2002.

[43] Author's interview with former German chancellory official, September 8, 2004.

CHAPTER FOUR

INDONESIA: RESENTMENT, SUSPICION, AND DOMESTIC POLITICS ON THE "SECOND FRONT"

Derek Mitchell

In the years following the September 11 attacks, Indonesia has reluctantly been placed at the epicenter of counterterrorism initiatives in Southeast Asia, a region that has been termed the "second front" in the war on terrorism. As the world's fourth largest country, and the largest majority Muslim nation in the world, with about 90 percent of its 220+ million people adhering to Islam, Indonesia has traditionally been viewed as a moderate, tolerant, and highly pragmatic nation, where economic development and social stability are paramount values and violence is disdained. Indeed, this image is so ingrained—both in the Indonesian population and in long-time observers of the country—that the idea of Al Qaeda–style radicalism on Indonesian soil was dismissed as unlikely even in the aftermath of September 11.

Nonetheless, it has become increasingly apparent that a regional network of jihadists affiliated with Al Qaeda is not only active but also reliant on spiritual and operational leadership from clerics and functionaries based in Indonesia. The Bali and Jakarta bombings of 2002–2003 provided brutal confirmation of this reality. Indonesia has struggled not only with how to respond to this challenge on its soil but also with an increasingly insistent and proactive United States that has pressured Indonesia for a more rapid and decisive action in the war on terrorism.

Since emerging from the 1997 Asian financial crisis and the end of Suharto's authoritarian rule in 1998, Indonesia has endured a difficult economic, political, and social transition. Weakened border and territorial controls, massive corruption, and the sprawling geography of a nation of 16,000 islands have made Indonesia an ideal setting for illicit groups to operate. Social unrest and economic decline over the past several years have altered Indonesia's international standing and its perspective on the world. No longer one of the region's economic "tigers," Indonesia has focused inward in its current struggle to maintain domestic stability. In the process, it has relinquished its traditional leadership role in the region, particularly in the Association of Southeast Asian Nations (ASEAN).

At the same time, because of the turmoil of transition and the dissolving of the authoritarian glue that held them together, Indonesians are turning to their Muslim identity for a sense of nationhood and unity, albeit more in a cultural than religious sense. In addition, with the help of Indonesia's now unfettered media, they are acquiring a greater sense of Muslim solidarity with others outside Indonesia, with particular attraction to those seen as being victimized by external powers.

As a result, Indonesians have become notably uncomfortable with U.S. foreign policy since September 11. They have resented the intense focus the United States has maintained on Southeast Asian links to terrorism, to the perceived detriment of other critical regional interests. U.S. actions since September 11, particularly the invasion and occupation of Iraq, perceived disdain for international institutions and norms, and continued pressure on Indonesia to conform to U.S. counterterrorism priorities have spurred increasing resentment within the Indonesian public. This development increased the constraints on the Indonesian leadership's options in working with the United States, particularly as legislative and presidential elections approached in 2004. The elite and broader population alike recognize the need for U.S. engagement in Indonesia, particularly on the economic front, but many instinctively resent interference in what they deem internal affairs, whether Indonesia's handling of separatism in its western province of Aceh, human rights abuses by the military, or combating of homegrown Muslim extremists.

In response to concerns about trends in U.S. foreign policy, a leading Indonesian analyst recently wrote, "At the moment, everyone worries about U.S. hegemony," and as a result "an old traditional balancing act is called for."[1] Others have characterized relations between Indonesia and the United States as being at their lowest point in more than 40 years.[2] Given the crosscurrents in Indonesian perspectives toward the United States, it is reasonable to ask: How has Indonesia viewed the U.S. "war on terrorism," and in what way has U.S. prosecution of this campaign affected Indonesia's perspective on international relations? Has Indonesia responded with changes in its own overall international strategic outlook, particularly in relation to the United States? What are the prospects for future U.S.-Indonesia relations? Will Indonesia be a cooperative member on the "bandwagon," or will it seek to "balance" and block U.S. counterterrorism efforts?

PRINCIPLES OF INDONESIAN FOREIGN POLICY: INDEPENDENT, ACTIVE, AND MULTILATERAL

Indonesia's colonial experience, first under the Portuguese and later under the Dutch, continues to inform its traditional "independent and active" foreign policy. Indonesia harbors a deep and instinctive antipathy toward the involvement of other nations in its internal affairs. Indeed, Indonesia's status as a founding member of the Non-Aligned Movement during the Cold War remains a point of pride for members of the Indonesian elite. Its external relations have served more as a vehicle to resist outside interference in what it views as domestic matters than to promote a particular ideology or strategic worldview. The most notable exception to Indonesia's allergy to external influence, however, is in its economy, which at one time helped Indonesia achieve status as one of the region's leading economic "tigers."

Today, Indonesia's foreign policy is based both on this traditional "non-aligned" mentality and on what Indonesian analysts refer to as a "concentric circle" approach—that is, attention to relations with closest neighbors first, then moving steadily outward. ASEAN, and relations with ASEAN members, are therefore foremost in Indonesia's strategic calculations. Indonesia's commitment to ASEAN also reflects its broader commitment to multilateralism as the preferred method of international engagement, for itself and others, to embed nations in a constraining web of rules and consultative procedure. Indeed, as enshrined in the organization's Treaty of Amity and Cooperation, ASEAN enables Indonesia to better promote and protect notions of territorial integrity, noninterference in its internal affairs, and strict sovereignty.

Through ASEAN, Indonesia is also able to engage on a more equal basis with other powers in more distant concentric circles, such as China, Japan, and Korea, both individually and through the ASEAN + 3 process; the European Union through ASEAN–European Union Meeting (ASEM); and the United States and India, through the

ASEAN Regional Forum process. APEC similarly provides a useful forum for engaging its neighbors and the United States in regional—especially economic—affairs. However, the perception that the United States is attempting to turn the group away from its founding principle as an economic forum and into a venue for security discussions, particularly counterterrorism, has irritated Indonesians. As a result, some suggest, attention to "bilateral" relations between ASEAN/Indonesia and individual Northeast Asian states, excluding the United States, may become more prevalent as time progresses.[3]

RESENTMENT AND SUSPICION: TRENDS AGAINST COOPERATION WITH THE UNITED STATES

The September 11 attacks elicited both sympathy and suspicion within Indonesian society. Shortly thereafter, President Megawati paid a previously scheduled visit to the United States, where she vigorously denounced the attacks and pledged support for the United States in the antiterrorism effort.[4] However, the political constraints from within her own society, and even her governing coalition, were evident from the start. While she visited the United States, small but radical elements back home staged angry demonstrations in front of the U.S. and British embassies to protest impending U.S. action against Afghanistan. Her vice president, Hamrah Haz, said September 11 would "cleanse" the United States of its "sins" and called the United States the "king of terrorists."[5] As opposition parties began to see an opportunity in criticizing U.S. foreign policy to further their domestic political positions, Megawati followed with her own vocal condemnation of U.S. international policies in Afghanistan and elsewhere and moved only slowly to acknowledge and act upon the increasingly apparent presence of jihadist elements at home.

Several additional trends in Indonesian views of the United States after September 11 continue to inform Indonesia's official and unofficial perspectives on the relationship. First, one can hardly talk to an Indonesian or read a newspaper in Indonesia without hearing about the "arrogance" of the United States and the misapplication of U.S. power internationally. Although the government has never officially addressed the issue, conversations with Indonesians reveal deep and fundamental opposition to the U.S. "preemption" doctrine set forth in the 2002 National Security Strategy. Such a doctrine strikes at the heart of Indonesians' concerns about sovereignty and nonintervention in their internal affairs. Many Indonesians apparently even disapproved of U.S. involvement against the Abu Sayyaf Group in the Philippines. The presence of the United States on foreign soil to prosecute the war on terror caused some to fear that Indonesian territory might be the next theater for U.S. involvement.[6]

Similarly, the general sense persists that what the United States calls a "war on terror" is actually a "war on Islam." Indonesians remember Suharto playing the "radical Muslim" card in defending his oppressive policies at home. This memory informs how Indonesians today view U.S. rhetoric and actions against radical Islam both globally and toward Indonesia itself. It also affects how the Indonesian people view the actions of their government and thus constrains the leadership's ability to take decisive action against suspected jihadists. President Bush's reference shortly after September 11 to the war on terror as a "crusade" is widely seen in Indonesia as reflecting Bush's true mind-set.[7]

The Iraq War crystallized in Indonesian minds this pervasive sense of Islam as being under siege from the United States. Many Indonesians construed U.S. motives in Bosnia, Kosovo, and Afghanistan to have been cynical at best; intervention in Bosnia was seen as "too little, too late" and Afghanistan, at least initially, as an attack on Muslim innocents. However, the Iraq War placed these past interventions into a perceived pattern of U.S. activity that appeared fundamentally hostile toward the Muslim world. As one commentator put it, "the Iraq War played into Indonesian conspiracy fears about a war on Islam. They don't like Osama or Saddam, but they cannot countenance a unilateral invasion or killing of innocent Muslims."[8]

Israel, Palestine, and Conspiracy Theories

The Israel-Palestine impasse also lies at the heart of Indonesian negative perceptions of U.S. foreign policy that constrain strategic bandwagoning. "Double standard" is the term most often heard from Indonesians as they try to reconcile what they view as unconditional support for Israeli actions in the Palestinian territories against a seeming lack of appreciation for suffering and destitution of Palestinians under Israeli occupation.[9] The Palestinian cause, which is in the headlines of Indonesia's media daily, has been an emotional issue for Indonesians since the Suharto years, when the media was controlled. How the United States handles the Middle East stand-off remains a critical component of how

Indonesians view U.S. actions toward the Muslim world and will continue to color their support for U.S. actions.

Furthermore, Indonesians, like others, are very susceptible to conspiracy theories, and these abound in the current environment to constrain cooperation with the United States. "No Jews in the World Trade Center" and its corollary "Mossad was behind September 11" represent widespread beliefs perpetuated through specific sensationalist media and community leaders. One hears the suspicion that "international terrorism is the result of Western and Israeli intelligence agencies out to undermine Islam," with the related explanation that "the United States created Al Qaeda through its assistance to Afghanistan in the 1980s" in order to have a convenient excuse for attacking Islam. The result is not only a pervasive popular attitude of resentment toward the United States but also an attitude that terrorism, though a problem in the aftermath of Bali and the Marriott bombing, is in large part a product of U.S. policy itself. In the minds of many Indonesians, even within the elite, the United States is thus associated with the very evil it is trying to gain cooperation to suppress.

The Indonesian masses likewise have a related tendency toward scapegoating and paranoia, Indonesian observers note, particularly in the wake of their travails since 1998. As in many other Muslim countries, popular opinion casts domestic problems as a "foreign conspiracy to prevent Indonesia from becoming a strong international player."[10] When bombings such as those in Bali or Jakarta force attention to the problem of extremism at home, Indonesian citizens often will assert that they are victims of "external forces," that the persons who create the problem are actually Malaysian or Filipino. Indonesian elites explain that their countrymen's conspiracy theories are a product of their experience under Suharto: "in a non-transparent environment, conspiracy theories proliferate," as one put it.[11] However, conspiracy theories also have real roots in Indonesia's understanding of U.S. involvement in its modern history. For instance, Indonesians will readily remind an observer about CIA involvement in the 1958 separatist movement in Sumatra, which colors perceptions of U.S. intervention in the matters of Aceh and Papua.[12] They will also point to an alleged assassination plot against Sukarno in the early 1960s—purportedly with U.S. backing.[13] Perceived current patterns and accepted notions of past U.S. actions in Indonesia combine to shape lasting suspicions of U.S international policies and prevent strategic bandwagoning.

Irritants in Bilateral Relations

Indonesians point to other irritants in bilateral relations in recent years that are complicating official assistance to U.S. foreign policy generally, and the counterterrorism campaign specifically:

Anti-Muslim Profiling. Indonesians express deep resentment, bordering on anger, over a perceived increase in anti-Muslim profiling in the United States. For instance, increasing obstacles to receiving travel visas to enter the United States, and the requirement to be fingerprinted and photographed upon entry, are considered to be highly humiliating, and leading to fewer Indonesians who desire to travel to the United States.

Terrorist Labeling. The term "Jemaah Islamiyah" (JI) means "Islamic Community" and is a generic phrase in the Koran referring to the desired end state among the faithful. Use of the term to represent a terrorist organization confuses and often offends the Indonesian population, thus constraining the government's ability to crack down and formally ban the organization. Many in Indonesia, including the new president Bambang Yudhoyono, have suggested that the United States has not done enough to present publicly its case on the actual existence of the organization, or perhaps more importantly, to provide Indonesian authorities themselves the means to present the case to their people to add credibility to the counterterrorism mission. Others have faulted the Megawati government for political cowardice for failing to present the compelling case it had against the organization for fear of popular reaction. The trial in late 2004 of suspects in the Bali bombing may have helped to turn the corner on this problem, as individuals have been convicted for their connections to JI. Nonetheless, Yudhoyono still refuses to acknowledge publicly the existence of the organization, perhaps a continued reflection of the sensitivity over the group's nomenclature.

Detention of Hambali. The United States has consistently rejected Indonesian access to Hambali (Riduan Isamuddin), the notorious Jemaah Islamiyah operations chief in U.S. custody, explaining that Indonesian authorities failed to deal with Hambali when he resided on Indonesian soil and thus have little standing to protest lack of access, particularly since the United States finally captured him in Thailand. (The United States has agreed to allow Indonesians to submit written questions and receive written answers from the detainee.) Indonesian authorities and media bristle over this perceived affront to Indonesian pride and sovereignty given that Hambali is an Indonesian citizen. They have threatened to limit cooperation with the United States as a result: "Unless you [the United States] hand over Hambali, we cannot help more [with counterterrorism],"[14] one official warned, although the practical effect of this warning on actual CT cooperation is unclear.

Aceh. Indonesians resent what they see as a double standard over U.S. condemnation of their aggressive handling of unrest in Aceh province while seeming to provide a free pass to Israeli actions in the Palestinian territories. Indonesians also detect a double standard as they compare Aceh with Iraq, commenting that they have more of a right to subdue a rebellious province than the United States does to invade another country. Indeed, Indonesian officials have cited U.S. tactics when they embed journalists with Indonesian military operating in Aceh, or hold Acehnese suspects incommunicado without charge like U.S. detentions in Guantanamo Bay. They note wryly that their actions in Aceh are now called an "integrated operation"—humanitarian, military, and social—to echo U.S. rhetoric of "nation building." Jakarta has also sought to tag the Acehnese rebellion as a form of "Islamic terrorism" to cloak its actions in U.S. garb. The United States, according to an Indonesian senior official, has lost its moral standing to challenge Indonesia over such tactics.

Military-to-Military Sanctions. Continued U.S. sanctions prohibiting bilateral defense engagement with Indonesia's military, which rose from a lack of accountability for atrocities committed by Indonesia's armed forces (TNI) in East Timor and a suspicion that the military was responsible for the August 2002 murder of two Americans in Timika (Papua), have caused great anger toward the United States within the Indonesian military. One Indonesian official close to the United States explained the detrimental psychological effort sanctions continue to have on the overall relationship; from an Indonesian perspective, sanctions "are not what friends do to one another."[15] Thus the issue has attracted a nationalist response even from those sympathetic to U.S. aims.

Indonesian officials have complained that cooperation seems to be a one-way street in which the United States makes demands and provides nothing in return. They believe that even if they complied completely with U.S. desires in the war on terror, they would still be sanctioned over human rights and military abuses. Given current U.S. law and sentiment within the U.S. Congress, they would indeed be correct concerning military-to-military assistance; however, the United States does provide substantial police training, democracy aid, educational support, and other forms of aid to benefit the development of Indonesian society, although such assistance may not receive the public notice that military sanctions have garnered.

Megawati

Perhaps the final constraint on Indonesia's cooperation with the United States in recent years was President Megawati herself. Despite continuing to benefit politically from the strength of the Sukarno name, by all accounts Megawati was a timid and indecisive president on a range of issues critical to Indonesians. Her weak Islamic credentials also constrained her during a period of increasing Islamic identity and limited her flexibility to cooperate with the United States. Although many urged patience with Megawati given such constraints, her leadership deficiencies ultimately led to her defeat in the 2004 presidential election, when Indonesians clearly preferred a stronger hand to fight corruption, curtail crime, and drive economic reform. More courageous and dynamic leadership could boost Indonesia's efforts to cooperate with the United States on counterterrorism and other issues, a proposition that will be tested in the new presidency of Bambang Yudhoyono, who, as Megawati's security minister, was a leading advocate of stronger action against domestic violence. Indeed, the personal qualities that had prevented Megawati from more active and visionary cooperation with the United States had also prevented her from adopting the kind of proactive policies that might have shifted Indonesia into a strategic balance against the United States.

Australia

An interesting corollary to tensions in Indonesia-U.S. relations is the chill in Indonesia-Australia relations in recent years. This came despite great appreciation within the Indonesian government for Australia's quiet but effective police-training assistance to enable Indonesia to maintain domestic stability and investigate suspected militant radicals on its soil. Nonetheless, a continued sense of coolness in the relationship is apparently a product both of bilateral issues of the past—such as Australia's role in the independence of East Timor—and, in the minds of some Indonesians, of Australia's strong ties with U.S. foreign policy and international activities.[16]

When Megawati snubbed Australian prime minister John Howard at a memorial service to mark the one-year anniversary of the Bali bombing, it was explained as reflecting her concerns that Australia is "positioning itself too closely with the United States. . . . [She] cannot be seen to be too close to Australia, especially since she plans to run in the 2004 elections."[17] An Australian analyst commented, "The longer term relationship is going to become increasingly strained as Australia gets uncritically aligned with the United States and gets involved in their adventures around the world."[18] When Australia announced in December 2003 its intention to cooperate with the United States in research and development on missile defense, Indonesia's initial sharp reaction—in contrast to China's relatively muted response—was viewed as an expression of sensitivity to potential U.S. domination in the region and a nod to Indonesian popular sentiment toward the U.S. ally. There is no evidence, and indeed it is almost inconceivable, that Indonesia and China coordinated their public positions on the matter. However, any decision by Indonesia to balance against the United States may be apparent first in Indonesian relations with Australia.

IMPLICATIONS FOR INDONESIAN FOREIGN POLICY

Despite sensitivities over perceived U.S. violations of national sovereignty, double standards, and "war on Islam," there is nonetheless no real sense among the Indonesian public that the United States has aggressive intent toward Indonesia in particular. What does pervade Indonesian sentiment is a sense that the United States is not interested in the concerns of Indonesia, but instead sees the country as an instrument for its own ends worldwide—ends that are unhelpful to Muslims. For instance, Indonesians resent U.S. suggestions that the country is a haven for terrorists, which inevitably works to the detriment of Indonesia's economic prospects and national pride.

More concretely, Indonesians increasingly feel that their country has relied too much on the United States and needs to diversify its bilateral foreign relations, if only to send a signal that Indonesia has options. This is particularly true for defense relations and military sales. In September 2002, Megawati visited Africa (Algeria, Egypt, South Africa) and Eastern Europe (Hungary, Bosnia-Herzegovina, Croatia) to consult on economic, political and military affairs. In April 2003, she took part in a high-profile summit with Russian president Putin that led to dramatic statements of a new era in bilateral relations and of Indonesian intent to procure Russian warplanes and helicopters.[19] By late 2004, despite limited funds and the Indonesian military's reported unhappiness with the quality of non-Western weapons, Jakarta had "all but completed" an agreement with Russia to buy eight advanced fighter aircraft (six SU-27SKs and two SU-30MKs) to add to four other such aircraft acquired in 2003; procured helicopters, armored personnel carriers, and small arms; and displayed serious interest in acquiring long- and medium-range air-defense systems from Russia.[20] Indonesia hosted an arms show in Jakarta in December 2004 that included potential suppliers not only from Russia but also Canada, France, Germany, Malaysia, the Netherlands, Singapore, and South Korea. Another meeting on Indonesia's future military needs was held in Bali in January 2005 that included a similar array of nations.[21] Defense cooperation has even been discussed between Indonesia and China. A visit by Chinese state councillor and former foreign minister Tang Jiaxuan in November 2004 apparently included discussions on the issue and led Indonesian Minister of Foreign Affairs Hassan Wirayuda to express his hope that China might "provide ways to help [Indonesia] to rejuvenate our weaponry."[22]

Nonetheless, there is little evidence of any real continuity or fundamental strategic realignment reflected in such episodic developments in Indonesia's diplomatic and military relationships. Indonesia's engagement with these nations is consistent with its long-standing practical and nonaligned orientation, although Indonesia is likely also to be using diversification of its defense contacts, including with China, as leverage to induce the United States to revisit its military-to-military curbs. Indonesia may also be sending a signal to the United States that Russia, China, and others could serve at least as tactical allies for Indonesia to register displeasure with Washington in the future should current trends continue.

THE CHINA FACTOR

As reflected in the talk of potential defense cooperation between Indonesia and China, questions have arisen over the trajectory of Jakarta's relations with Beijing in recent years, particularly whether interaction has warmed to a degree that the two countries may join in a strategic balance against growing U.S. power and perceived unilateralism. Indonesia's relations with China indeed have undergone substantial changes in recent years. During the Cold War, particularly beginning in the

1960s, Indonesia was deeply concerned with China's support for communist insurgencies in Indonesia and elsewhere in Southeast Asia. In 1967, after Suharto's rise to power and following an abortive coup in Indonesia in which Chinese involvement was suspected, Indonesia broke off relations with its communist neighbor, only resuming official ties in 1990.

Although the sense of China as a potential threat remained in the Indonesian mind even after reestablishment of diplomatic ties, President Abdurrahman Wahid began to view China as a potential counter to the United States as relations with Washington soured in the aftermath of the 1997 financial crisis.[23] Attitudes toward China further moderated under Megawati in the face of China's ineluctable rise as a regional political and economic power. Chinese investment in Indonesia exploded 2500 percent between 1999 and 2003 to $6.8 billion,[24] as China became Indonesia's third largest investor since 1998.[25] China today ranks officially as Indonesia's fourth largest trading partner with projected bilateral trade to total more than $10 billion by the end of the 2004, an increase of 25 percent over 2003.[26] Megawati traveled to China, and two PRC premiers, Zhu Rongji (2001) and Wen Jiabao (2003), visited Indonesia to conclude a variety of cooperative assistance and investment deals focused not only in the energy sector, but also in agriculture, banking, tourism, and general infrastructure development.

For its part, China has subtly reengaged with Southeast Asia through a consistent charm offensive, signing the region's Treaty of Amity and Cooperation, promoting a free trade agreement with ASEAN, offering a China-ASEAN "Strategic Partnership" agreement in October 2003, and promoting in late 2004 the establishment of an East Asian Community and an annual East Asian Summit. In contrast to the United States' laser-like concern about terrorism in its conduct of regional affairs, China has understood Indonesia's preference for multilateralism and economic development and has been taking a softer line that by almost all accounts is resonating well in the region.

Nonetheless, Indonesian observers suggest that warming ties between the two sides have not overcome a strong residue of mistrust that continues to pervade Indonesia's views of China. Jakarta, uncertain about what course a rising China may take, desires, like the rest of the region, a hedge against China's growing power. In addition, Indonesian prejudice against ethnic Chinese persists, a prejudice that led to anti-Chinese riots in Jakarta as recently as 1998. China's investment in

Indonesia and its overall economic strength could also fuel jealousy and sour relations in the future as they have in the past.

Most fundamentally, despite the warmth in the relationship, Indonesia's war-gaming continues to be based on the prospect of a "big power" coming down from the north; indeed, the Indonesian military reportedly continues to view China as the most likely threat to its strategic interests in the long term.[27] Despite positive rhetoric and agreements to intensify cooperation, relax tensions, and provide an atmosphere of good will, analysts ask "where's the beef" and note that the relationship is "polite but empty" and "without an agenda."[28] The prospect of Indonesia's strategic realignment toward China is therefore relatively far-fetched in the absence of more concrete and fundamental changes in Indonesia's popular and elite attitudes toward China.

TRENDS TOWARD COOPERATION

For all the tensions, many trends in Indonesian society and U.S.-Indonesian relations favor future cooperation, if not bandwagoning, with the United States. Foremost among these, in fact, were the terrorist acts committed in Bali and at the Jakarta Marriott in 2002 and 2003 respectively. After Bali, the Indonesian people could no longer ignore the threat in their midst. Although they have tended to consider these acts domestic violence rather than terrorism, many Indonesians have welcomed U.S., Australian, and others' assistance in police training and investigative work to curb the effectiveness of extremist groups.

The support of the leading moderate Islamic social organizations in Indonesia, specifically the Nadhlatul Ulama (NU) and Muhamadiyah, has been crucial to the leadership's ability to enhance counterterrorism cooperation with the United States. NU claims 40 million members, and Muhamadiyah rolls number 30 million. NU has said publicly that an Al Qaeda affiliate is responsible for Indonesian terrorism, and Muhamadiyah openly calls for surveillance of such radicals. Given the prevalence of these social organizations throughout the Indonesian Muslim community, and the political weight they carry as a result, the support of these organizations for the fight against terror remains essential.

Moreover, Indonesians continue to believe that the United States is the critical power with which their country must engage for reasons of both economics and national security. The United States is Indonesia's second-largest export market. U.S. companies have invested more than

$10 billion in the country; annual bilateral trade totals about $12 billion. Washington provided Indonesia with $160 million in economic assistance in 2004, making Indonesia among the top 10 recipients of U.S. bilateral aid. Without U.S. economic engagement and a commitment to safeguarding regional security, Indonesians understand that their economy cannot regain its strength, and investment will not flow back into the country.

Even Amien Rais, a leading politician from an avowedly traditionalist Islamic political party, has commented that Indonesia must hold back its anti-U.S. rhetoric for the sake of its economic interests. As one senior Indonesian official commented, "Indonesia needs the United States more than the United States needs Indonesia—in economics, investment, finance—as a matter of pure national interest. Most see the United States as indispensable as a critical investment and trade partner."[29]

Indonesia's cultural preferences for the United States also apparently remain strong. To many Indonesians, despite resentment toward U.S. international policies and activities, the United States remains a model of democracy, openness, and tolerance, though the prevailing domestic environment prevents open expression of such positive sentiment. "Many do not like Americans because they have never met one," one Indonesian observer optimistically noted. "Once they meet Americans, they can change."[30] Particular dislike is directed at President George W. Bush, however, who is widely considered a "warmonger," suggesting that Indonesian anti-Americanism may be not only situational but also highly personalized.[31]

U.S. humanitarian assistance to Aceh following the tragic tsunami on Christmas Day 2004 may also help reverse the negative trend in popular opinion regarding the United States, and particularly the U.S. military, which took the lead in transporting and distributing aid in the early days following the disaster. The actual impact of the tsunami relief effort is difficult to predict as of this writing. Nonetheless, though views of the United States may moderate to a degree in the short run, longer-term impressions will likely continue to hinge more on the U.S. approach to the many issues of particular sensitivity to Indonesians noted above—such as the perception that the war on terror is a war on Islam, treatment of Indonesian sovereignty and territorial integrity, Israel/Palestine, and Iraq—than on any individual episode in the relationship.

ISLAMIC IDENTITY AND INDONESIAN FOREIGN POLICY

Indonesian analysts note that although the rise of Islamic sentiment at home is leading the government to be more sensitive to how certain foreign policy issues play to the masses, Indonesia does not yet think in terms of Islamic identity or solidarity in its foreign policy. One scholar offered as illustration a policy discussion between his international affairs institute and a Pakistani delegation during which Indonesian participants addressed concerns over human rights in Tibet and Palestine while, to the dismay of the Pakistanis, evincing little concern over the situation in Kashmir when raised. Indonesians actually take little interest in most such "Islamic" matters worldwide, the analyst suggested, except in specific cases like Iraq and Israel/Palestine.[32] While active in the Organization of the Islamic Conference (OIC), Indonesia is not yet moving to exercise leadership in that forum or on specific international Islamic interests.

Given the growth of an active and diverse media culture that may try to cater to a growing Islamic identity within the citizenry, this dynamic may change in the future. Nonetheless, there is no indication yet that Indonesia's concern for particular Muslim causes around the world is fundamentally influencing its foreign policy or its strategic choices. Instead, practical considerations of economic development and domestic security remain paramount. A senior Indonesian official did suggest, however, that the United States increase its attention to the OIC, adding that if something becomes acceptable to the organization, it becomes easier for the Indonesian government to sell at home.[33]

THE IMPACT OF THE 2004 ELECTION SEASON[34]

Indonesian observers note that foreign policy has never been a factor in Indonesian elections since the first elections in 1955. Local concerns and "money politics" traditionally dominate, as do narrow religious, ethnic, or personalized sentiment toward a particular leader (such as popular attraction to Megawati because of her father). One scholar explained that "the making of Indonesia is not completed yet…. The Indonesian nation only exists because of the Indonesian state, not the other way around," and thus notions of elections as vehicles for consideration of national interest are not yet mature.[35] He calls this mind-set a relic of the colonial era.

Indeed, these traditional domestic concerns were ultimately determinative in the 2004 elections. Foreign policy, including relations with the United States, was not an issue on the voters' agenda; rather predictably it was "the economy, stupid." Jobs, economic development, the need to battle corruption, and desire for a stronger hand at the top to take care of domestic security were the issues that resonated most deeply, while relations with the United States, Iraq, Palestine, and international terrorism *per se* seemed of relatively minimal electoral importance. Many observers had worried early in the campaign period that U.S. missteps could lead opportunistic political parties to appeal emotionally to voters' anti-American instincts to gain electoral advantage. However, this never happened, perhaps because the United States was aware of this sensitive dynamic and acted accordingly.

Although the election did not hinge on foreign policy, Indonesian candidates did attend to their Islamic credentials. No candidate could afford to be viewed as insufficiently "Islamic" in background, lifestyle, or international outlook. For these reasons, for instance, Megawati, whose Muslim credentials were seen as weak, was especially careful to shore up her standing. An early indication of her sensitivity on this issue came in a surprisingly pointed speech at the UN General Assembly in September 2003 in which she attacked Western policies in the Middle East—particularly toward the Israel-Palestine conflict—as a critical reason for the rise of extremism and terrorism around the world.[36] Indeed, some observers were stunned to hear Megawati take such a strong public position on the region and to so publicly fault U.S. policy toward the Islamic world for being a root cause of international terrorism. Megawati clearly sought to give voice to general popular attitudes of Indonesians toward the United States and to create some political distance from her Western friends for public consumption.

Nonetheless, although a candidate's Muslim bona fides may have been relevant to voters, Islamic issues proved not only secondary in electoral importance to secular ones, but in fact were viewed by parties as detrimental to their electoral prospects. An Australian observer noted that conservative Islamic parties chose to downplay Islamic issues during the campaign after internal polls showed they turned off voters, quoting Islamic political leaders as telling him "our branch leaders tell us no one will come to rallies" if religious issues are raised.[37] In the end, the aggregate vote total for Islamic political parties rose slightly over 1999,[38] helped by the surprising success of one particular party, the

Prosperous Justice Party, but "Islamism" was considered a nonfactor in this result.[39] Islamic parties remained deeply divided among themselves, making the prospect of a future unified governing coalition among them unlikely. Their showing demonstrated the Indonesian citizen's continued strong commitment to the nation's secular foundation.

Of the various contenders in the presidential contest, domestic and international observers had considered the ticket of Bambang Yud- hoyono and Jusuf Kalla the most promising for addressing the radical Islamist threat at home because of their personal popularity, experi- ence, pragmatism, and credibility within the Islamic community. In fact, the victory of Yudhoyono in the presidential contest presents both an opportunity and a challenge for U.S.-Indonesia relations and counterterrorism cooperation. Called the most Western-friendly leader in Indonesian history,[40] Yudhoyono has close and affectionate ties to the United States from his many years living and training as a military officer in the United States. He has said publicly that he views the United States (despite "all its faults") as his second home.[41] Both as security minister and immediately after assuming the presidency, Yudhoyono has been outspoken in denouncing the terrorist threat in Indonesia.[42] His victory in the country's first direct presidential elec- tion thus provides Yudhoyono a clear popular mandate for leadership on this issue.

However, Yudhoyono will confront several limitations to his au- thority in coming years. He is unproven as a chief executive and has been faulted in the past for indecisiveness. He has no base of support in the legislature: his political party, the Democratic Party, is extremely small, accounting for only 10 percent of parliamentary seats.[43] He will thus be highly constrained by popular opinion, which will require him to focus first on the economy, corruption, and internal security and to avoid any reflexively pro-American statements or actions. Indeed, Yudhoyono has reiterated the longstanding Indonesian demand for access to the terrorist Hambali and for better legal evidence of the ex- istence of JI. In his initial presidential statements, he has character- ized terrorism not in international or ideological terms, as the United States would do, but in terms the region, and Indonesians, accept more readily—that is, in terms of domestic stability and economic develop- ment. This suggests at least Yudhoyono's recognition of the limits on how he may frame the terrorism issue to the Indonesian public, and the potential for a continued disconnect between the United States and Indonesia over the definition and scope of the terrorism the two sides seek to counter.

CONCLUSION

Indonesia's response to the post–September 11 era can be condensed to "three D's"—denial (pre-Bali), defensiveness (after Bali/Jakarta), and domestic politics (particularly as the 2004 election season approached). The initial response after September 11 was mixed as Indonesia struggled—and the United States begged it—to recognize the danger in its midst. Megawati's strong rhetorical support for U.S. counterterrorism efforts immediately after September 11 soon gave way to domestic pressure against U.S. action in Afghanistan and denial of an Al Qaeda connection at home. The Bali and Jakarta bombings put that issue to rest, as Indonesians turned with anger to domestic extremists and as cooperation with the United States on investigations and intelligence-sharing intensified. Nonetheless, resentment grew over U.S. heavy-handedness in bilateral and international affairs, and traditional suspicions of the United States prevented full acceptance of a U.S. partnership. In an election year, such dynamics further constrained the leadership's ability and desire to act on U.S. terrorism concerns.

Under President Megawati, Indonesia took no fundamental decisions to seek strategic alignments against the United States. Bambang Yudhoyono, who harbors keen pro-American instincts, is unlikely to change this approach, absent a dramatic deterioration in the relationship. More likely, Indonesia will maintain its traditional pragmatism, a hedging, non-aligned strategy that may send signals to one or the other of the major powers while seeking their continued economic engagement to provoke the country's development. If anything, Yudhoyono may have to take care not to appear too pro-American, instead ensuring that Indonesia's wariness about undue major power influence in the region and in Muslim affairs globally is given adequate voice, lest he lose credibility with his domestic constituency.

President Megawati's handling of the Iraq War—dutifully expressing her country's opposition to U.S. action, while ensuring U.S. assets in Indonesia were secure and stating her view that the Iraq War was not part of a general U.S. war on Islam—was emblematic of Indonesia's balancing act. Indonesian elites recognize the country's need to stay on the good side of the United States in order to promote national recovery. At the same time, any Indonesian leader must heed the growing popular mistrust and concerns over U.S. international policies. So far, a good personal relationship between key members of the two elites, including the two presidents, has helped keep the official relationship relatively stable and positive.

An Indonesian specialist based in Jakarta noted that Indonesia today has no clear blueprint for its foreign policy, describing it as "ad hoc," "messy," and devoid of strategy beyond supporting domestic economic development.[44] But is Indonesia bandwagoning with or balancing against the United States in the aftermath of September 11? The answer, so far, is neither. Given Indonesia's principles and tradition of independent, non-aligned foreign policy, it is certainly not bandwagoning. Its active antiterrorism cooperation with the United States is based on Indonesia's own experience with domestic violence rather than the desire to join the United States in its international war on terrorism. The U.S. policy of preemption, allergy to international institutions and agreements, and military action in Afghanistan and Iraq are all at odds with Indonesia's central foreign policy tenets of nonintervention, multilateralism, and strict commitment to the principle of national sovereignty. Indeed, Indonesia has opposed most recent U.S. international actions and policies.

To the degree that Indonesia may seek to balance against the United States, it is a subtle balancing. In recent years, largely in response to lingering U.S. sanctions, Indonesia has sought to diversify its international relationships, reaching out to Eastern Europe, Africa, Russia, and China. As indicated above, in the face of perceived U.S. unilateralism and following some years of national retreat since 1998, Indonesia has sought to reengage actively in multilateral forums such as ASEAN and the OIC. However, Indonesia's outreach so far seems as much a matter of reestablishing Indonesian pride, hedging against too much reliance on the United States, and signaling to the United States that it has other options.

Even if the Islamic parties had gained electoral strength in the 2004 elections, most expected that pragmatism would have prevailed in their attitudes toward the United States, given the substantial economic and security interests in maintaining a sound bilateral relationship. Should a more radical Islamic figure ascend to power in the future, China, Russia, and the ASEAN nations would be unlikely to choose to balance with Indonesia against the United States, especially if such a leader espoused a strong Islamist agenda. Indonesia could decide to take a more assertive role within the OIC, particularly at a time when Indonesians' anger toward the United States may be rising and their sense of Islamic identity is growing. However, Indonesia currently offers little indication of such an inclination. Furthermore, the OIC is hardly cohesive, and the damage to Indonesian interests of antagonizing the United States would likely mitigate any attempts to use the organization to promote an anti-U.S. agenda.

The wild card in future U.S.-Indonesia relations exists not within the Indonesian elite but within the population at large, whose democratic muscles are increasingly being exercised after several decades of atrophy. If one theme permeated this author's conversations with Indonesians, it was their recommendation that the United States do better in engaging with the Indonesian populace to prevent further deterioration in popular attitudes, particularly with the Indonesian parliament, whose influence and assertiveness in national policymaking is increasing.

Despite resentment over specific U.S. actions, the majority of Indonesian people continue to admire U.S. culture and society and instinctively understand that no other country may provide the benefits that a positive relationship with the United States can bring. As one Indonesian commented, Indonesian political sentiment is ultimately based not on ideology—even Islam—but on "what you can do for me" and vice versa.[45] And Indonesians apparently sense that they need the United States more than the United States needs them.

Members of the Indonesian elite also recognize that the counterterrorism fight is as much their fight as America's, though they perhaps define it somewhat more narrowly and prefer different means to address the problem. Following the Bali and Jakarta bombings, bilateral and multilateral cooperation—within and among members of ASEAN—has intensified dramatically. Indonesian authorities understand that the extremists mean to take down the regime and create instability, so however they define the issue, cooperation with the United States will be important to their ultimate success.

Perhaps the brightest redline in Indonesia's relationship with the United States would be an action in violation of Indonesia's sovereignty and territorial integrity, or a new violation of sovereignty elsewhere in the manner of Iraq, which would instill fear in Indonesia that it may be next. China felt the brunt of Indonesia's sensitivity on this point for almost 25 years following the suspension of diplomatic relations in the mid-1960s over apparent Chinese support for communist insurgencies.

Should the United States endure another major attack and Indonesia prove unable to effectively manage its home-grown terrorists, the United States may be tempted to consider alternatives under the preemption doctrine to preserve its security and safety, even at the expense of traditional notions of "sovereignty." This would no doubt precipitate serious debates within Indonesia over how to handle relations with the United States, which could be cast as a rogue superpower. A severe deterioration in relations and even a strategic realignment could not, in those circumstances, be ruled out.

Ultimately, the real battleground in the war on terrorism will be in the hearts and minds of that large moderate Islamic majority in Indonesia that seeks entry into the global community of nations and resents the violence that undermines the development of their society. Indonesia's status as the largest Muslim nation and a young democracy thus presents a critical challenge and opportunity for the United States. Although the Indonesian people are becoming more Islamic in self-identification, they are not necessarily becoming more radical or anti-American as a result. It will be a test of U.S. policy toward Indonesia, and of its fight against jihadist extremism more broadly, to prevent worst-case developments in the relationship—and instead promote a sense of partnership, based on a common set of values and interests, that induces Indonesians to view alignment with the United States as the most effective method to preserve Indonesian dignity and development.

Notes

[1] Dewi Fortuna Anwar of the Indonesian Academy of Sciences in Jakarta, in "How China Is Building An Empire?" *Far Eastern Economic Review* 166, no. 46 (November 20, 2003): 33.

[2] Raymond Bonner. "Indonesian Criticizes U.S. over the War in Iraq," *New York Times*, December 9, 2003.

[3] Remarks of Hadi Soesastro, executive director of CSIS-Jakarta, at a conference, "China-Indonesia Relations and Implications for the United States," sponsored by the United States-Indonesia Society (USINDO) and the Sigur Center for Asian Studies of the Elliott School of International Affairs at George Washington University, November 7, 2003.

[4] Indeed, Megawati was the first national leader to visit the United States after September 11.

[5] Acceptance of punishment as a method of "cleansing oneself of sins" is a standard tenet of Islamic faith.

[6] Indeed, in the spring of 2003, a U.S. F-18 jet entered Indonesian airspace inadvertently, leading some in Indonesia to worry that the United States was "up to something."

[7] President Bush reportedly apologized for his use of the term "crusade" during his October meeting in Bali with Indonesian religious leaders. It is unlikely that such an apology will have any impact on public memory or sentiment within Indonesia on President Bush's foreign policy intentions.

[8] Author's interview with Rohan Gunaratna in Singapore, November 11, 2003.

[9] Two different interlocutors questioned, for instance, why the United States paid so much attention to three U.S. citizens killed by Palestinians in Gaza in October 2003 and not on the U.S. activist crushed about the same time by an Israeli bulldozer as she sought to protect Palestinian homes.

[10] Indonesians will remind a Western interlocutor that when the 1997 financial crisis undermined Indonesia's economic stability, the United States at first seemed relatively disinterested in its well-being and then pushed hard for International Monetary Fund (IMF) intervention that imposed severe hardships on Indonesian society. A photograph of an IMF official standing authoritatively, with arms folded, behind President Suharto as he signed the IMF agreement was a symbol of deep national humiliation, and the strong, harsh hand of the IMF was associated fundamentally with the United States.

[11] Author's interview with Edy Prasetyono, head, Department of International Relations, Centre for Strategic and International Studies–Jakarta, November 14, 2003.

[12] Author's interview with Nusron Wahid and Wachid Ridwan, youth leaders from Muhamadiyah and Nadhlatul Ulama, respectively, in Jakarta, November 14, 2003.

[13] Interestingly, when one raised rumored U.S. involvement in the 1965 Suharto coup and the massacre of communists that followed as also potentially impacting the views of Indonesians toward the United States, Indonesian interlocutors tended to dismiss this period as irrelevant to the perceptions of their compatriots, calling these events purely an internal affair among Indonesians.

[14] Author's interview with senior Indonesian government official involved in counterterrorism cooperation with the United States, November 14, 2003.

[15] Ibid.

[16] One might note Australian prime minister John Howard's comment in 1999 about being America's "deputy sheriff" in Asia, and President Bush's echo of this sentiment ("we don't see it [Australia] as a deputy sheriff, we see it as a sheriff") during a press briefing in flight on the way to Southeast Asia in October 2003. Although both speakers regretted their comment and immediately sought to retract and apologize for it, such statements have encouraged development of a mind-set in the region, including in Indonesia, that closely associates the policies and actions of the two nations.

[17] Kalinga Seneviratne, "Megawati Irked over Close Australia-U.S. Ties," Global Information Network, October 10, 2003.

[18] Ibid. Quote from Andrew Jakubowicz, a sociologist at the University of Technology Sydney.

[19] The two sides signed agreements not only to boost military cooperation but also to help Indonesia develop its budding space program. The Russian news agency Rosbalt commented: "Faced with a U.S. arms embargo and wide differences over the war in Iraq, Indonesia is turning back to Russia, aiming to rebuild the close ties forged in Megawati's father Sukarno in the 1950s." The report asserted that the two nations had more in common than just opposition to U.S. actions in Iraq: "Both are still recovering from the fall of totalitarian regimes, dealing with rampant corruption and trying to lay to rest separatist conflicts." Rosbalt News Agency, "Indonesia, Russia: Reviving a Soviet-Era Relationship," Rosbaltnews.com, April 29, 2003.

[20] David Isenberg, "Indonesia, Russia Cozy up over Arms Sales," *Asia Times*, December 2, 2004.

[21] Ibid.

[22] Agence France Presse, "China, Indonesia Look for Ways to Boost Military Ties," November 5, 2004, as accessed on http://www.acheh-eye.org. Such comments follow similar rumblings two years earlier. In an interview shortly after the visit of the Chinese defense minister Chi Haotian to Jakarta in September 2002, Indonesian army chief of staff Sutarto commented that "Indonesia may buy arms from China to compensate for a U.S. embargo on weapons sales. We are considering China as one of the alternative arms suppliers. . . . Indonesia will not continue to be dependent on one source, which has imposed an embargo for the past few years." Virtual Information Center, "Special Press Summary: China-Indonesia Defense Cooperation," November 5, 2002, http://www.vic-info.org/RegionsTop.nsf/0/c7640cec3cbda9710a256c3e000430c9?OpenDocument.

[23] Anthony L. Smith, "From Latent Threat to Possible Partner: Indonesia's China Debate," in *Asia's China Debate,* ed. Satu P. Limaye (Honolulu, Hawaii: Asia-Pacific Center for Security Studies. December 2003), p. 7-4.

[24] Soesastro, remarks at conference, "China-Indonesia Relations," November 7, 2003.

[25] "In Brief," from *China Daily*, April 19, 2004, p. 10.

[26] Ibid.

[27] Smith, "From Latent Threat to Possible Partner," p. 7-5.

[28] Hadi Soesastro, "Indonesia China Relations—But Where Is the Beef? An Economic Analysis of Hadi Soesastro." Kompas CyberMedia, April 1, 2002, http://www.kopmas.com/kopmas-cetak/0204/01/ENGLISH/indo.htm.

[29] Author's interview with senior Indonesian government official.

[30] Ibid.

[31] Author's interview with Sidney Jones, Southeast Asian project director, International Crisis Group, in Jakarta, November 13, 2003; author's interviews with Wahid and Ridwan. Wahid and Ridwan made particular note that former President Clinton was viewed personally with very high esteem in Indonesia as a "humanitarian," despite aforementioned reservations about the U.S. approach to Bosnia under his watch.

[32] Author's interview with Prasetyono.

[33] Author's interview with senior Indonesian government official.

[34] Indonesia held legislative elections on April 5, 2004, and the first round of its first-ever direct presidential election on July 5. Since no candidate received 50 percent of the vote in the July polls, the top two vote-getters—Megawati and Yudhoyono—faced off in another election on September 20. Yudhoyono's inauguration occurred on October 20. The "election season" is thus viewed as spanning virtually all of 2004.

[35] Ibid.

[36] On this occasion, President Megawati said the following: "Although they [the terrorists] are a small splinter from the large Indonesian community of Muslim[s], the perpetrators of those terrorist acts represent a branch of international terrorism. The motives and justifying arguments of their movement apparently arise from the prolonged unjust attitude exhibited by big powers toward countries which inhabitants profess Islam, particularly in resolving the Middle East conflict. . . . It is difficult to refute the impression that the policy on conflict resolution in the Middle East is not only unjust but also one-sided. . . .Whatever the reason held by anyone of us, we all must admit that the absence of a just attitude, exacerbated by a feeling of being sidelined and ignored, in addition to the deficiency of formal means to channel aspiration, has cultivated a climate of violence to grow. In our view, this is actually the seed and root of the problem . . . and among others leads to even devastating and tragic acts of terror. . . . In order to deter or eradicate the problem of international terrorism, I should like to propose that the countries . . . should review their conventional anti-terrorism policies, particularly in dealing with the Arab-Israeli conflict. . . . Indeed, so many eminent Muslims in Indonesia believe that once the major powers behave in a more just manner and make clear their impartiality in the Middle East, then most of the root causes of terrorism, perpetrated in the name of Islam—which in any circumstances cannot be justified—would have been resolved." Address by the President of the Republic of Indonesia at the 58th Session of the United Nations General Assembly, New York, September 23, 2003.

[37] Greg Fealy, "USINDO Brief: Election Year Series," August 4, 2004.

[38] Exact evaluation of the success of "Islamic" parties in the 2004 elections is limited by the vague definition of what constitutes an Islamic party in Indonesia.

One commentator divided the term into two categories, "Islamist" political parties and "pluralist Islamic" parties, defining the former as ideologically based on Islam with overwhelmingly Muslim leadership and membership, and the latter as led by self-consciously Muslim community leaders but who are committed to the nation's secular constitution and are inclusive in their party membership. Ibid.

[39] The Prosperous Justice Party ran successfully on a "clean government" platform despite a radical Islamist core. The party played down the latter issue and promoted its moderate side to electoral victory.

[40] Ibid.

[41] Paul Dillon, "Profile: Susilo Bambang Yudhoyono," AlJazeera.net, July 4, 2004.

[42] In an interview shortly after his inauguration in October 2004, he commented that "the main issue is no longer whether there is or is not such a formal organization called Jemaah Islamiyah. . . . We will undertake all of our effort to prevent and fight against terrorism. We will take stern action. We will not give room for terrorists to develop and perform acts in Indonesia." Eric Ellis, "Shock Therapy to Defeat Terrorism," Times Online (London), November 8, 2004.

[43] The ascension of Vice President Kalla to the Golkar party chairmanship may change this dynamic somewhat, providing Yudhoyono the foundation of a governing majority in the legislature. Whether Yudhoyono ultimately shapes the coalition or the coalition shapes him is to be determined.

[44] Author's interview with Prasetyono.

[45] Ibid.

CHAPTER FIVE

PAKISTAN AND THE UNITED STATES: A PARTNERSHIP OF NECESSITY

Marvin Weinbaum

INTRODUCTION

Few countries outside of Afghanistan have been more widely affected as a consequence of September 11 than Pakistan. Policy adjustments have shaped its strategic alignments and chances for political stability. Domestically, decisions taken have influenced the possibilities of democratic governance, the shape of Islamic politics, including security concerns posed by extremist groups, and the viability of Pakistan's economy. Regionally and internationally, President Pervez Musharraf's choices after September 11 bear directly on the prospects for armed conflict and dialogue with India and participation in the global war on terrorism.

Pakistan has emerged as a pivotal state for the United States. Washington gained an ally for operations against Al Qaeda and the Taliban, and new leverage in curtailing Islamabad's export of cross-border insurgency to Indian Kashmir. Pakistan, with its U.S. partnership, reacquired much of the strategic importance lost at the end of the Cold War, redeemable in the form of military and economic assistance and greater American interest in facilitating resolution of the Kashmir dispute. With the blessing of the United States, the Musharraf regime could again hope to tap the resources of the international creditor community and see the lifting of the last of the U.S. sanctions imposed after the military coup of October 1999. Above all, the prospect of long-term cooperation with the United States in confronting terrorism and Washington's heightened concerns about nuclear proliferation seem to ensure a more sustained American engagement in the region than has occurred during the last half century.

Deepening and strengthening ties between Pakistan and the United States nevertheless carry limits in a post–September 11 world. At times, Pakistan's internal requirements and U.S. strategic objectives and priorities do not mesh, creating tensions and ambiguities in the relationship. Whether Pakistan's leadership can continue to defend its policy reorientation hinges in part on Washington's expectations and the demands placed on Islamabad. Pakistanis will continue to weigh the fruits of cooperation with the United States, and Musharraf will need ways to justify his far-reaching commitments, especially within the military. His freedom of action may also be determined by his degree of success in controlling and accommodating Islamic political forces and his willingness to reconstitute a moderate political center to support a progressive agenda.

As the United States assesses the relationship, the gap between Pakistan's words and deeds remains wide. With Pakistan's realignment likely more a matter of practicability than principle, commitments are subject to recalibration. Because those commitments are, moreover, identified so personally with Musharraf, they are necessarily contingent on his physical and political survivability as well as on his political acumen. In a larger sense, Pakistan may be a weak reed on which to rest a productive partnership without a stronger foundation in democratic institutions and civil society, or in the absence of progress on critical socioeconomic reforms.

To date Musharraf has essentially stayed the course he set after September 11. Pakistan provides logistical support for American forces operating in Afghanistan and continues to exchange intelligence and participate in the pursuit of Al Qaeda activists and Taliban leaders. Musharraf's domestic decisions have at times disappointed Washington and seemed to undermine the relationship. But even the revelations about Pakistan's having shared nuclear technology and equipment abroad have failed to shake the conviction that Musharraf and his military offer the best vehicle to serve U.S. interests in the region. In turn, Musharraf's heavy personal investment in a partnership with the United States precludes any actions designed to check or balance the exercise of U.S. global power. Although he leverages ties with Washington in hopes of winning support for his domestic and foreign policy objectives, Musharraf finds opportunities to demonstrate that Pakistan has signed on to the American bandwagon for the duration.

PROFILES OF PARTNERSHIP

At least six distinguishing features depict the history of alliance between Pakistan and the United States. First, it has been an *interrupted relationship*. After a decade of Cold War alignment to contain the Soviet Union, the United States withdrew military and economic support to Pakistan following its 1965 war with India over Kashmir. U.S. economic assistance soon resumed, but military aid remained restricted even as relations warmed in the early 1970s. Pakistan's facilitating role was indispensable to the U.S. opening to China in 1971, and in 1975 the arms embargoes on both Pakistan and India were lifted. But Prime Minister Zulfikar A. Bhutto's decision after 1974 to pursue a nuclear option to match India's program kept relations ruffled. His nationalization programs and attempts to join Pakistan to the nonaligned movement were also not welcomed.

The army's overthrow of the Bhutto regime in 1977, and General Zia ul-Haq's suspension of promised democratic elections occasioned strong rebuke from Washington. The general's refusal to halt a nuclear reprocessing project invoked a congressionally mandated provision to end all assistance aside from a food aid program in 1979. Only a year later, however, in the wake of the Soviet invasion of Afghanistan, the Carter administration offered military and economic assistance to bolster Pakistan's security. Zia held out for a more generous aid package, which he received from the new Reagan administration.

There followed the now well-documented years of collaboration in support of the Afghan mujahideen that allowed the Pakistani military to siphon off weapons. But in 1990, the year after the last Soviet soldier had left Afghanistan, aid was again cut off because of increased activity in Pakistan's nuclear program. Further sanctions were imposed as a result of Pakistan's nuclear tests in May 1998 and the military coup against Prime Minister Nawaz Sharif that brought General Musharraf to the helm in October 1999. These various sanctions were all in place on September 11.

The episodic partnership between Pakistan and the United States, marked by sharp swings in feeling between the governments, has also been a highly *mercurial relationship*. It has been described as veering "between alliance intimacy and cordiality, and times of friction and tension."[1] At still other times the relationship is best characterized as close to indifference, emanating more from the American side. The prevailing tone often bears the personal touch of individual leaders in both countries and may be conditioned by public mood swings, especially in Pakistan. In any case, widely shifting feelings usually owe their origin to contrasting or converging perceptions in Washington and Islamabad over their separate national security concerns.

The bilateral relationship between the United States and Pakistan has been a *limited engagement*. For all the array of agreements on military equipment sales, training, and personnel exchanges, and the earmarked economic and development assistance, neither party has been restrained from pursuing an independent foreign policy, not necessarily to the liking of the other partner. American decisionmakers have always asserted that policies toward India and Pakistan stand on their own and that one is not the reciprocal of the other. Over the decades, Pakistan's relations with the United States coexisted with its ties to China and Iran, even when these countries were viewed unfavorably in Washington. Importantly, the commitments of the United States and Pakistan have been narrowly construed. The United States had no sense of obligation to directly assist Pakistan in its 1965 and 1971 wars with India any more than Pakistan's participation in the war on terrorism obligates it to assist American peacekeeping in Iraq.

It has been an *asymmetrical alignment*. Objectives of the two countries, as already observed, have been at times dissimilar. Even while offering mutual benefits, the relationship has usually not been similarly or equally advantageous. As a result of the jihad against the Afghan communists and the Soviet Union, Zia ul-Haq was able to secure his grip on power, but the cooperation between the United States and Afghanistan more directly reflected and profited U.S. national interests. Pakistan's earlier membership in the Central Treaty Organization (CENTO) and the South East Asia Treaty Organization (SEATO) also primarily served U.S. Cold War strategies. Although Pakistan's stability may be furthered in bringing its Islamic radicals to heel, the domestically risky policy more closely suits American priorities and concerns in the region. By contrast, the generous economic and military assistance provided to Pakistan over the years has returned disappointing dividends for the United States. Still, most of the time when the United States and Pakistan have used their relationship to pursue different aims with unequal payoffs, their objectives have at least been compatible. For instance, the $5 billion in economic and military assistance that the United States has provided Pakistan was in the national interest of both nations; although it facilitated Pakistan's growth to the twelfth largest armed force in the world, it also provided the United States with a security buffer against Soviet expansionism and a military ally close to the oil-rich Persian Gulf.[2]

Throughout, it has been a *contingent partnership*, subject to continuing recalculation and reformulation responding to a changing regional and international environment and trends in domestic public sentiment. The strategic equation on which U.S. cooperation with Pakistan rested was sharply altered with the Soviet invasion of Afghanistan in December 1979, and again after the United States had accomplished its major objective in getting the Soviet Union to pull its forces from Afghanistan a decade later. If September 11 provided another watershed event, to a lesser but significant degree Pakistan's withdrawal from the Kargil sector of Kashmir two years earlier also forced reassessment of the partnership. Pakistan's assumptions about U.S. and international leverage in helping resolve the Kashmir conflict had to be revised. In setting a course for Pakistan on both Kashmir and Afghanistan, Musharraf has continued to modulate policies to please Washington without running afoul of limits posed by his elite and popular constituencies.

There is much that suggests this as an *unrequited relationship*. Both countries have repeatedly expressed disappointment with the other. Neither has demonstrated the will or capacity to deliver fully on what either promised or what was perceived to be committed. Not infrequently those expectations were unrealistic. In any case, Pakistanis have been apt to stress the unreliability of the Americans and their absence when Pakistan needs them most, as well as their failure to deliver fully on what was promised in exchange for cooperation. For its part, the United States usually points to Pakistan's untrustworthiness and how it has shown less than full faith in meeting commitments.

EXPECTATIONS AND INCENTIVES

Pakistan's leadership has felt increasing pressure post–September 11 to respond to U.S. expectations by cooperating with U.S. forces and law enforcement personnel in the apprehension of Al Qaeda and Taliban fighters; ending assistance to cross-border militancy in Kashmir; making serious efforts to curb domestic Islamic radicalism; strengthening Pakistan's democratic institutions along with liberalizing reforms; and introducing the requisite financial discipline and adhering to other conditions set by the international creditor community. U.S. expectations have included assurances that Pakistan is not engaged in the proliferation of nuclear technology and that it can be trusted to protect its nuclear arsenal. After the revelation in February 2004 that for many years Pakistani scientists had been sharing nuclear know-how and the means to produce fissile materials with North Korea, Iran, and Libya, Washington sought reassurance that transfers had stopped and that information gathered in investigations to uncover proliferation networks would be shared. Once President Musharraf revealed Pakistan's involvement in the proliferation of nuclear know-how, Secretary of State Colin Powell was dispatched to Islamabad to further question Pakistan's leader and obtain proof that the dissemination of nuclear knowledge had ceased and that all parties involved were no longer a part of Pakistan's government.[3]

Overall, Musharraf's public endorsement of U.S. policy expectations has rarely been at issue. At times his sincerity is questioned but, more often, doubts are raised about whether he is prepared to expend the requisite political capital and take the personal risks necessary to satisfy expectations. The gap between promises and delivery offers the terrain over which diplomacy between the United States and Pakistan mainly takes place.

The United States has little to fear that under Pakistan's current leadership Islamabad will back away from its commitment to fight terrorism. Yet despite a deployment of Pakistani troops to Afghan border areas under orders to flush out Al Qaeda and Taliban fighters, Musharraf has resisted allowing American forces to cross freely into Pakistan in pursuit of terrorists, or invited the U.S. military to mount a full-scale military campaign from within Pakistan to hunt for Osama bin Laden and his associates. In fact, President Musharraf has publicly said there is "no possibility" that he would allow for American troops to enter Pakistan in their search for Osama bin Laden, adding that it was "a very sensitive subject."[4] Nor has Pakistan, despite its apparent cessation of support for militants' infiltration into Kashmir, relinquished its armed option by decommissioning jihadi fighters, heretofore financed, trained, and armed by Pakistan's security forces.

After two nearly successful assassination attempts in December 2003, Musharraf is widely believed to be ready to act more decisively in dealing with the country's Islamic extremists. He has banned several prominent jihadi groups, and again vowed to move Pakistan in the direction of a moderate Islamic state. Nevertheless, it remains uncertain how far Musharraf is prepared to go to cripple these organizations, and authorities have yet to arrest their popular leaders. Periodic crackdowns ordered by Musharraf have in the recent past seemed curiously timed to the visits of leading American diplomats or in direct response to public complaints by high U.S. officials.

Pakistan is now also less likely to ignore concerns about securing its nuclear technology and assets. Musharraf is anxious to allay fears both in the United States and the international community, and internal investigations can be expected to produce some information that will be of value. Yet Musharraf also remains sensitive to domestic criticism that investigations are only undertaken to satisfy foreigners, particularly the United States, which many Pakistanis believe is determined to deny Pakistan its nuclear option.

Because Pakistan's leadership understands that American assistance is a reward for joining the war on terrorism, it has reason to believe that Washington will settle for less on other issues. Repeated expressions of appreciation from the highest levels of U.S. officialdom for Pakistan's efforts in helping to combat terrorism have encouraged Musharraf to believe that his policies are modulated sufficiently to keep the United States appeased without alienating his critical domestic policy elites or the public. Musharraf finds that he can play off sectors of the U.S. government that differ over whether cooperation against terrorists should preempt possibly risky democratic liberalization and a diminished role for the army in politics. Musharraf may, in deference to Americans and Europeans, hesitate to dissolve the country's unruly parliament, but he feels assured that he will not be pressed to turn over meaningful powers to an elected government. If there were any doubt about American priorities, the willingness of the U.S. State Department to absolve Musharraf and the Pakistani military of responsibility for the proliferation activities admitted by A.Q. Khan demonstrated the lengths that the United States is willing to go to avoid weakening Musharraf and his generals.

With Pakistan's policy reversals, U.S. sanctions—namely, those imposed in 1990, 1998, and 1999—have been lifted, providing substantial economic and military support. The United States rescheduled $3 billion in debt and supported the International Monetary Fund's rescheduling of $9 billion of Pakistan's approximately $38.5 billion of external debt. For fiscal 2003, $305 million was allocated, $200 million of which went for direct budget support, with the remaining $105 million divided between program assistance and military aid. For 2004, the assistance rose to $400 million, $300 million in economic and $100 million in security assistance.[5]

Of the total U.S. economic assistance that went to Pakistan in 2003 and 2004, only $100 million was planned for development assistance such as education. Most of the rest was for debt relief, largely intended to offset the costs to Pakistan of the antiterrorism campaign. In 2004, $73 million was earmarked to assist in the border program that included helicopters, surveillance aircraft, communications equipment, and 1,000 ground vehicles. Beginning in 2005, the United States allocated $3 billion over five years in aid divided equally between economic assistance and security or defense assistance. The new package leaves just $20 million a year specifically earmarked for education—a sector supposedly singled out by Washington to receive high priority.[6] After years of balking, Washington announced in March 2005 the intention to renew the sale of F-16s in an unspecified number. Islamabad also hopes that the United States will furnish or facilitate purchase of an airborne early warning system to counter the one being offered by the Israelis to India. Above all, Pakistan sees its access to military hardware as well as programs of military personnel exchange, bilateral exercises, and regular strategic dialogue as offering the litmus test of the American commitment.

Realistically, Pakistan in general and Musharraf in particular may have few good alternatives to a U.S. partnership. Renewal of economic and military assistance is widely appreciated as critical to reviving the country's economy and furthering its national security. Agreements with Pakistan's international creditors are also believed to have been contingent on satisfying the Americans. Any hope of enlisting Washington's diplomatic leverage on behalf of Pakistan in its disputes with neighboring states similarly rests on close alignment with American policies. Justification for Musharraf's remaining in power has at its core his presumed ability to alone access these external resources for Pakistan.

THE MUSHARRAF FACTOR

For the present, post–September 11 events have resulted in increased executive authority in Islamabad. Musharraf's decision to call a March 2002 referendum to extend his presidency and, months later, to impose by fiat constitutional changes—incorporating most into a parliament-approved 17th amendment—designed to enhance his powers, no doubt grew out of his personal belief that his leadership had become indispensable to the Pakistani nation. He shows few signs of relaxing his determination to keep former prime ministers Benazir Bhutto and Nawaz Sharif out of politics or to desist from dividing their already disorganized, secular, mainstream parties. Nor was he deterred from presiding over the intimidation and bribery of nominees preceding the parliamentary elections in October 2002. Self-confident and facing only restrained criticism from abroad, Musharraf has wrested virtually all policymaking initiatives from the parliament and civilian government. In a supreme exercise of executive power, he succeeded in late 2004 in getting a majority of elected representatives to free him from his pledge to shed his role as army chief, a promise exacted by a coalition of religious parties as their price for supporting the 17th amendment.

Significantly, Musharraf has refrained from using the United States for domestic political advantage. Instead, reflecting his personal investment in the relationship, he has regularly sought to minimize his differences with Washington. At the same time, Musharraf is not averse to using public opinion in Pakistan to elicit greater understanding from the United States. It is often suspected that he deliberately allows radical Islamic groups to publicly vent their opposition to policies to demonstrate the difficulties he must overcome in trying to satisfy American expectations.

Overall, Musharraf seems particularly adept as a marginal satisfier. He exhibits a remarkable ability to calibrate competing demands, both domestic and foreign, and to keep everyone at least minimally satisfied. He has shown a keen sense of limits on how far he can go in cooperating with American law enforcement in searching for terrorists and in knowing what jihadist groups will tolerate while he tries to appease Washington on controlling militants. Musharraf has had notable successes in placating both the military establishment and large sectors of the political class. His decisions reflect widely acknowledged tactical skills even while he is often held as deficient in strategic vision.

Musharraf has been twice spared the negative fallout of politically difficult, if not dangerous, decisions. The first came when the United States and Britain failed to press for a second UN resolution on Iraq shortly before commencing military operations in March 2003. Withdrawal of the resolution by the United States and Great Britain—acknowledging a failure to muster the needed nine Security Council votes—spared Musharraf from having to assume personal responsibility if Pakistan threw support behind the United States. Even if Pakistan's vote was not required to reach the nine necessary, an abstention would have been deeply unpopular among Pakistanis.

Musharraf also managed a discreet way out of a potentially damaging choice when Washington called on Pakistan to send troops to Iraq for peacekeeping operations. Knowing that any deployment of forces would be bitterly and almost universally condemned domestically, Musharraf was only prepared to go as far as telling the United States that in principle Pakistan was ready to make its contribution. India's decision to link its participation to the UN's adoption of a clear mandate authorizing troops gave Musharraf some political cover. Even after passage of a UN resolution, Musharraf insisted that before he committed Pakistani troops, a set of conditions must be met, including that they be part of an Islamic force and be approved by an Iraqi government. He also expected to fend off American pressures with the argument that, as Pakistan was now a democracy, he would be obliged to submit any decision to the popular will, presumably in a parliamentary vote.

International demands that Pakistan own up to its involvement in nuclear transfers and deal with those responsible offer the most recent and perhaps challenging test of Musharraf's tactical skills. The United States, the International Atomic Energy Agency, and others have once again given him slack in what is, by most standards, the most serious of all possible violations among nuclear-capable nations. Under different circumstances, the most severe of international penalties would have been exacted. But Musharraf has managed the crisis in a fashion that, however transparently contrived, has avoided worse political fallout at home and provided sufficiently believable assurances to policymakers abroad. In the end he traded on the unattractive alternatives for the international community and the promise of unraveling a network of illicit suppliers to gain freedom from prosecution for a national hero while simultaneously immunizing the army from culpability. Indeed, the virtually clean bill Musharraf won from Washington is widely viewed in Pakistan as a vote of confidence in the military's preeminence.

Pakistan's army largely approves of Musharraf's foreign policies. The corps commanders accepted his reasoning on the Taliban and later on acceding to American pressure to restraining jihadist operations in Kashmir. Pakistan's army continues to pride itself on being a disciplined, professional organization. Not unimportantly, Musharraf, as army chief since 1998, has had opportunities to staff his senior ranks with individuals who are considered personally loyal. Indeed, a number of his corps commanders were once his students. His position was further strengthened with the October 2004 retirements of the two generals who, as his closest peers, were generally regarded as possible successors.

Many senior officers nevertheless believe that Musharraf has ceded too much to the Americans and that he is perhaps too anxious to please the American president. Throughout the ranks there is reportedly resentment of the U.S. military presence at Pakistani bases and misgivings about American operations on the Afghan frontier.[7] Ambivalence toward the United States deepened after the invasion of Iraq by the American-led coalition. In recent years, several dissident mid-level officers have been arrested for plotting against Musharraf, and it is suspected that the nearly successful assassination attempts required collaboration between extremist groups and individual members of his security detail. Still, Musharraf feels confident that threats to his power and person do not originate from within the army.

Musharraf's generals appreciate that his removal would be strongly opposed by Washington and could very possibly jeopardize whatever advantages have accrued to the military from the reversal of policies after September 11. Prospects for an attractive U.S. defense package remain a powerful incentive to support Musharraf. His ouster would take a near consensus among the corps commanders that he had become a liability to the institutional well-being of the army. His stewardship would certainly be questioned if he failed to protect the army's resources and privileges or in the event of a humiliating military defeat to India. Otherwise, only a serious political misstep—most probably a popularly perceived sellout of Kashmir or Pakistan's territorial sovereignty—could threaten his tenure.

PAKISTAN'S DOMESTIC REALITIES

Although Musharraf has not allowed his domestic critics to deter him from casting his lot with the United States, they do nevertheless broadly circumscribe his actions. His sudden turnaround in abandoning the Taliban was not by itself a popular decision. Describing it as a "Pakistan First" policy, Musharraf succeeded in winning over most Pakistanis, but only because he publicly made a convincing case that Pakistan had no practical alternative. Any other choice, he contended, would leave Pakistan on the wrong side in the looming attack on Afghanistan's Taliban. Unstated was the possibility that to refuse Washington could conceivably drive the United States to tilt decisively toward India. Pakistan's interests, Musharraf argued, were served by cooperating with the United States because of the promise of winning new U.S. and international economic and military assistance and possibly enlisting the

United States and others to pressure India to open a dialogue on the Kashmir dispute.

Although the events of September 11 have profoundly altered Pakistan's relationship with the United States, they have not changed the widely held conviction that the U.S. approach to Pakistan is tactical—that is, once American interests are exhausted, most of all with the elimination of Al Qaeda's presence in the region, Washington will again turn away from Pakistan. Pakistanis regularly cite the unwillingness of the United States in the past to interpret its military-to-military relationship as obligating the United States to come to Pakistan's material assistance in armed conflicts with India. The imposition of economic and military sanctions on Pakistan over the "rediscovery" in 1990 of a nuclear program is seen as particularly hurtful in light of Islamabad's close cooperation in the anti-Soviet jihad through the 1980s. Pressure from Washington in July 1999 that led to Prime Minister Sharif's withdrawal of Pakistani troops fighting in the Kargil sector of Indian-controlled Kashmir is viewed by the military and a wider public as just another occasion when the Americans let Pakistan down or, according to some, stabbed it in the back.

Anti-American sentiment, already pervasive in most sectors of Pakistani society, has intensified since September 11 with the growing popular perception that U.S. policies, as manifested toward Israel and Iraq, are at root hostile to Islam—repressive and intent on humiliating Muslims. These actions have engendered both anger and insecurity and have helped fuel religious extremism. There is also a widespread sense that Pakistan had been oversold on the rewards to be reaped for its cooperation with the United States on Afghanistan and that it has paid too high a price for its policy reversal. Given unrealistic expectations, Pakistani policymakers were bound to be disappointed with the levels of debt relief and development assistance thus far provided. Disappointment also stems from the continued denial of relief from protectionist U.S. textile import quotas. Highly restrictive U.S. visa procedures and deportations of Pakistani nationals have also caused bitter criticism, as many believe that Pakistan, as an ally in the war on terrorism, should be treated preferentially. Finally, the military leadership in Islamabad is especially frustrated by Washington's reluctance to supply Pakistan with more sophisticated weapons at a time when India seems to be acquiring an increased conventional military advantage.

For more than a year after Pakistan's 2002 parliamentary elections, the opposition parties effectively disrupted the legislative process. Early in

2004, in a deal struck with the coalition of religious parties, Musharraf agreed to relinquish his army command before the end of the year in exchange for the legislators' legitimizing the constitutional powers he abrogated earlier through executive proclamation. Although the president effectively retained his political dominance over elected representatives, his negotiated agreement accorded new credibility to the very parties who most oppose close cooperation with the United States. In the past, elected governments in Islamabad and compliant legislators mostly deferred to the military on core foreign policy issues. Although it is doubtful that the military is willing to relinquish its grip on foreign policy decisionmaking, it is under greater pressure than ever to accommodate criticism.[8]

The religious parties (in a six-party alliance known as the Muttahida Majlis-i-Amal or MMA) have greatly capitalized on public dissatisfaction over American policies. In part, this explains the success of the Islamists in the national and provincial elections of October 2002. Their parties have never reconciled to abandoning the Taliban and aligning with the United States to destroy Al Qaeda and the Taliban. They also portray Musharraf as overly deferential to American preferences on Kashmir, Israel, and Iraq. The religious parties have a platform in the parliament from which they hope to exercise oversight, scrutiny, and guidance on foreign policy. Strong debate on foreign affairs can, in the near future, be expected to focus on whether cooperation with the U.S. military comes at the expense of Pakistan's territorial sovereignty or involves ceding control over the country's nuclear program.

The religious parties have brought foreign policy issues to the forefront of domestic politics. In hopes of tempering objections to his pro-American sympathies, Musharraf has slowed some promised reforms, including the enforcement of the registration of religious schools and curriculum revisions. Although Musharraf publicly blames the lack of progress on resistance from the lower rungs of the Pakistani bureaucracy, few doubt that forcing changes on the country's hard-line religious schools would hamper continuing efforts to induce the religious party alliance to soften their opposition to the government. Were this strategy to blunt criticism to succeed, the chances of reforming the schools or changing the controversial laws on blasphemy and women's rights would become even more remote.

Musharraf singled out several radical Islamic groups following September 11. The authorities hoped to demonstrate compliance with U.S. demands that Pakistan break the links between extremist groups, Al

Qaeda, and the Taliban, as well as act to defuse mounting tensions with India. Several groups were outlawed as terrorist organizations, their leaders and hundreds of workers were arrested, and their recruiting and fund-raising activities blocked. But having demonstrated its resolve, the government soon relaxed curbs on the ability of the groups to organize and promote propaganda. Although less transparent, the military's assistance to militants' infiltration resumed, and the level of violence inside Kashmir rose. A December 2001 terrorist attack on the Indian parliament in New Delhi prompted the full mobilization of Indian forces along the Line of Control (LOC) in Kashmir and the international border with Pakistan. After a further high-profile incident in Kashmir in May 2002, an impending full-scale war was averted by U.S. diplomatic intervention in early June. India accepted President Musharraf's pledge to the Americans that Pakistan's assistance to jihadist cross-border activities would end.

Militants continue to be told that cross-border operations are only on hold while diplomatic means with India are pursued and that the cause of Kashmiri freedom will not be sacrificed. By keeping these groups co-opted, the Pakistan government hopes to contain their militancy. To seriously disband their training camps would, it is reasoned, disperse an angry, violent force into the country's urban areas. Musharraf and the army believe that if they can wean meaningful Indian concessions on Kashmir through negotiations, there will be popular backing later to marginalize or repress the hardliners. Meanwhile, the Pakistani leadership is anxious that India appreciate that renewed assistance to armed insurgency remains an option should talks break down.

THE REGIONAL IMPACT

Pakistan is a participant in the campaign against Al Qaeda along its border with Afghanistan. In the two years following the defeat of the Taliban government, Islamabad boasted of having turned over to the United States more than 500 members of the organization. Pressed hard by Washington, Pakistani military operations broadened and intensified during 2004. Scores of foreign militants were rounded up or killed by the Pakistani army in an extended campaign launched in the tribal area of South Waziristan. Pakistan was expected to give special urgency to finding Osama bin Laden through coordinated intelligence and joint U.S.-Pakistani military operations in the border region with Afghanistan.

Until American insistence that cooperation in this theater be raised
to a new level, Pakistan's efforts against the Taliban and other anti-Kab-
ul elements had been inconsistent and unconvincing. Notwithstanding
the difficulties encountered in the rugged, porous border areas, Pakistan's security forces had done little to monitor and control the movement of those who continued to launch raids into Afghanistan from
sanctuaries in Pakistan. Even now, efforts to apprehend higher-level Taliban inside Pakistan are hardly detectable. Leaders of the Taliban have
been allowed to move freely, giving press conferences and making other
public appearances. The Taliban and their allies have reportedly established training camps and terrorist cells in and around Quetta and Pe-
shawar. Extremist groups in Pakistan have been encouraged to help
finance and facilitate these operations.

The coordination of U.S. and Pakistani forces along the unfriendly
Afghan frontier has forced changes of historic proportions in both the
activities of Pakistan's military and in the tribal belt. The penetration
has given Islamabad the long-sought opportunity to extend its writ into
tribal areas previously outside its authority. Pakistan's Pashtuns share
with the Taliban and their Afghan allies not only ethnic but cultural and
ideological identifications and, for some, financial interests. All feel deep
antipathy toward the United States for its Afghan policies since September 11. Madrassas in the border provinces of Pakistan, many affiliated
with the MMA party component Jamiat Ulema-i-Islam, help supply
new Taliban recruits to attack American forces and their supporters in
Afghanistan and undermine the Karzai government. National political
imperatives constrain Musharraf from removing an MMA-led provincial government in the North-West Frontier Province that has challenged
Islamabad with its radical Islamic legislative agenda and bitter opposition to American operations in Afghanistan.

U.S. expectations for Pakistan on Afghanistan are political as well as
military. Washington is concerned that the Islamabad government will
pursue policies that will inadvertently destabilize the Kabul government.
A politically stable Afghanistan, able to secure the flow of commerce, is
preferable to any immediate alternatives. Pakistan has publicly champi-
oned the Karzai regime and offered it modest financial and development
assistance. However, this has not stopped Pakistani officials, through
agents in Afghanistan, from befriending certain Pashtun regional commanders and other local influentials and backing their demands for greater representation in Kabul's governing structures, especially the Ministry

of Defense. A pro-Pashtun policy serves as insurance against the possibility of a failed government that could result in regional powers acting to claim their perceived spheres of influence inside Afghanistan.

The implications of September 11 also have significance for Indo-Pakistani relations. After September 11, Pakistan was placed on the defensive with India as New Delhi could now more easily link militant activities in Kashmir with wider threats from Islamic radicalism and terrorism. Islamabad has found it more difficult to convince an international audience of the distinction between "freedom fighters" and terrorists. Without disavowing the legitimacy of the freedom fighters, Pakistani officials have for some time been willing to acknowledge that some attacks in Kashmir and India proper constitute terrorism. Ties to the militant groups have no doubt become less transparent in deference to American sensitivity to Islamic extremists. Pakistani policymakers are also aware of U.S. concerns that a major crisis with India could force the redeployment of thousands of Pakistan troops from the Afghan frontier.

The Indian government's decision to desist from mounting a military campaign against Pakistan over the period from December 2001 through October 2002 can be partly credited to the presence of U.S. military and intelligence personnel within Pakistan after September 11. Although massive Indian forces had mobilized along the international border and LOC after a high-profile attack by terrorists alleged to be linked to Pakistan, Prime Minister Vajpayee's decision to accept U.S. mediation reflected his concern over the risk of escalation resulting from an Indian-initiated military assault. But Indian planners had also likely taken into consideration the disrupting effects of an armed incursion on the Pakistani-dependent U.S. antiterrorism campaign. Moreover, in the event of hostilities, Pakistan was expected to find shelter for its combat aircraft at those several bases in the country with an American military presence.

The dramatic improvement in Pakistani-Indian relations that began with Vajpayee's April 2003 speech, a Pakistani-initiated cease-fire along the LOC, and plans for a high-level composite dialogue have all occurred without visible American footprints. India, which has also sought negotiations with moderate Kashmiri separatist parties, continues to resist international mediation. But U.S. emissaries have repeatedly pressed both India and Pakistan to enter discussions and be willing to show greater flexibility. India's acknowledgment of U.S. success in getting Pakistan to curtail militant infiltration removed a key obstacle to India's acceptance of talks. Should the discussions progress to serious bargaining on hard issues, few doubt that finding mutually acceptable solutions will require increased U.S. and international facilitation.

Post–September 11 changes have raised the possibility of improvement in Pakistan's soured relations with Iran over Afghanistan. Pakistan's backing of the Taliban served as the principal factor precipitating differences between the two countries. Since the Taliban's demise, despite efforts to mend relations, suspicions run high. Not the least of the reasons are Sunni-Shi'a sectarian violence within Pakistan and Musharraf's alignment with the United States. Pakistan's Shi'a groups are believed to have Iranian financing and direction. The probable long-term presence of the American military in Afghanistan leaves Iran uneasy, especially with U.S. troops closeby in Iraq. Still, for all the differences between Tehran and Islamabad, a more aggressive U.S. policy against Iran would not be welcomed in Pakistan.

Although China is viewed in Islamabad as Pakistan's most dependable ally, the emergence of terrorism as a global threat has tempered Beijing's political support for Pakistan. China expects Pakistan to do more to contain its radical Islamic influences, lest they spill over into China's western provinces. As witnessed during the Kargil crisis, though Beijing still views Pakistan as a strategic partner, it discourages Islamabad from pursuing an adventurous foreign policy. Pakistan has also watched with some apprehension as Sino-Indian trade has blossomed in recent years and as China's publicly articulated views on issues of concern to Islamabad, including Kashmir, appear to be evolving.

Pakistan had long resisted establishing links with Israel, even as several Arab states either launched diplomatic relations or softened their position on recognition of the Israeli state. Although the Zia regime had been willing to purchase arms from Israel through third parties during the Afghan anti-Soviet jihad, nothing came of the link. It took the strengthening military and economic ties between Israel and India, much of which occurred after September 11, for Pakistan to seek a way to counter or neutralize the growing nexus. No doubt intending to placate the U.S. Congress following his June 2003 visit to the United States, Musharraf announced that he would entertain a domestic debate on the pros and cons of adopting a new approach toward Israel. Curiously, though he heard criticism from the expected Islamic quarters, opposition to Musharraf's initiative was not nearly as vehement as some had predicted. But as long as the peace process between Israel and the Palestinian

Authority remains stymied, there exists little chance of any policy redirection toward Israel in the foreseeable future.

CONCLUSION: SOLICITING THE WILLING PARTNER

Whereas some countries that initially sided with the United States after September 11 have since reevaluated their political and security interests, Pakistan has remained largely consistent in assessing the worth of its partnership with the United States. Others long-aligned with Washington may see benefits in building coalitions to balance or mitigate perceived U.S. unilateralism and global hegemony, but Pakistan's leadership goes out of its way to show its willingness to side with the United States—in word if not entirely in deed. Plainly, policies deemed necessary for domestic political survival will always trump foreign commitments. Pakistan's leaders have nevertheless accepted reasonable risks in trying to keep the United States content. Historically, Pakistan refrained from joining any alignment of countries against the United States, even during periods when relations had cooled. Similarly, Islamabad today avoids giving the impression that it is working alone or with others against American interests.

Since September 11, Washington has taken the view that virtually any change from the present leadership in Pakistan is likely to set back the prime objectives of the United States in the war on terror. In turn, Musharraf has staked much of his political future on his close ties with the United States and the benefits it can bring to Pakistan. With American interests hanging so critically on Musharraf's remaining in power, Washington, however, may have shortsightedly tied the future too closely to a single individual. A bilateral relationship so personality-dependent is unavoidably fragile, its survival subject to outcomes over which the United States may exercise little or no control.

Washington and Islamabad at times hold unrealistic expectations about each other. The American side often underestimates the political pitfall for Musharraf in trying to deal more vigorously with Pakistan's Islamists or the political costs at home for Musharraf's apparent deference to the United States. For its part, Pakistan believes that Washington has greater influence than it actually has on New Delhi in pressing for talks over Kashmir or that the United States can be induced to be more generous with its economic and military aid in exchange for Pakistan's cooperation. No doubt a better appreciation of the potential mutual returns for the United States and Pakistan would contribute to a more stable and durable relationship by leaving less room for future disappointment, claims of hurt, and even betrayal.

If Musharraf unexpectedly were to depart the political scene, constitutional provisions provide for civilian succession. In reality, power would shift toward the military as one or more generals from among the top commanders could be expected to step forward to ensure an orderly transition, possibly at the head of a martial law regime. To allay fears in Washington and the international community, Musharraf's successor(s) would declare in favor of continuity in policies combating terrorism. Still, a whole new set of understandings with the country's political groups would have to be brokered. Were Musharraf forced out under popular pressure, the generals in charge might have no choice but to placate an opposition likely to be spearheaded by Islamists. Failure over time to develop productive contacts with the religious parties and other opposition groups would leave Americans with little leverage over the new regime.

For the present, Pakistan's strategy is to retain the deep involvement of the United States in the region. Pakistan concluded long ago that only when American stakes are palpably strong is the attention and support it seeks likely to be retained. To the more cynical, Pakistan's spotty record of cooperation with the United States in military operations against Al Qaeda and the Taliban leaders is one way of ensuring a long American presence. For only while a threat from terrorist elements exists do Pakistani leaders feel assured that the United States will not turn away as it has in the past.

U.S. inconstancy may not be repeated. Although it would be going too far to say that September 11 has transformed the interrupted partnership between the United States and Pakistan over the past half century, their relationship may have entered a new and different phase. For with September 11, the partnership, though still contingent and often difficult, may have become more durable than at any time in the past. Afghanistan will continue for some time to remain potentially fertile ground for terrorist groups to operate, and no strategy to eliminate them can succeed without Pakistan's cooperation. Nor is the United States likely to divert its attention very far now that Pakistan has demonstrated how easy it is to become a source for nuclear technology and materials transfers. So long as the major differences between nuclear-armed Pakistan and India—namely, over Kashmir—remain unresolved, the United States cannot overlook the possible consequences of an escalating armed conflict. A possibly expanded role for Islamic parties in Pakistani politics should ensure that Washington does not lose interest in Pakistan's domestic scene. In the worst case, a regime dominated by Islamic extremists could align with elements dedicated to resisting U.S. strategic interests on terrorism. Should the United States desert the country, a jihadist scenario for Pakistan becomes more conceivable.

Warranting more concern in Washington is the possibility that the leadership in Islamabad, despite assistance programs, will fail because of misplaced priorities and misguided policies. Although the United States can do a great deal to ensure that a friendly government survives in Islamabad, it cannot save a leadership from its own errors or insulate it against overwhelming domestic dissatisfaction. A good case can be made that longer-term chances for a constructive relationship between Pakistan and the United States rest on Pakistan's measurable progress in dealing with its economic and social ills, and on its gains toward building responsible government in a moderate, progressive Islamic society. A relationship with Pakistan that fails to address economic development, educational, and health goals, and neglects to strengthen civil society, may leave the United States with a weak and ultimately unreliable strategic partner.

Although some insist that American interests are best served under an ascendant military, others believe that over the long run only sustained democracy and the legitimacy it can provide places the relationship on solid footing. In the absence of progress in reviving and strengthening Pakistan's democratic institutions, extremists are most likely to prosper. There is already evidence that a military-led government, in propagating a half-hearted democracy and marginalizing the mainstream opposition, has succeeded in strengthening radical forces inclined to sever cooperation with the United States. The Pakistani military's long history of coddling selective extremist groups allows governments to use the threat these Islamists pose to justify resistance to liberalization and unscripted elections.

Since September 11, interdependency between Washington and Islamabad has had a profound effect on setting expectations and fashioning attitudes in both countries. But the clearly preeminent U.S. goal of gaining Pakistan's cooperation for an antiterrorism agenda has dominated and effectively distorted the relationship. Whereas the interests of both countries would seem to rest on seeing progress in Pakistan over a range of issues—not the least of which are strengthening democratic institutions, improving social investment, and better managing domestic extremism—they have been subordinated to satisfying narrower security demands. In so doing, leadership in both countries has failed to appreciate opportunities to advance needed reforms or the interconnections among policies.

Because U.S. policy toward Pakistan in recent years is so fixed on Islamabad's cooperation in the war on terrorism, sustaining its resolve and ability to participate takes highest priority. The measure by which the United States gauges its demands on Pakistan is usually reduced to how likely they are to strengthen or undermine Musharraf. Thus rather than admonish Musharraf for actions (or inactions) that might otherwise have occasioned vigorous criticism and perhaps triggered renewed sanctions, the United States finds it necessary to heap public praise on Musharraf to spare him domestic political damage. Paradoxically, Washington's publicly unqualified backing is believed responsible for creating a sense of overconfidence that has contributed to Musharraf's most telling domestic political errors and setbacks.

The United States has meanwhile forfeited the considerable leverage it holds over Pakistan's leaders to encourage them to pursue structural changes both pleasing to Washington and in Pakistan's own long-term national interest. Policies aimed at improving the quality of life and realizing a just society through democratic means may be the firmest guarantee against radicalization or state failure. The United States arguably has the tools to further these developments through generous, carefully tailored aid programs that are also strongly conditional. More certain is that a U.S. engagement with Pakistan popularly perceived as merely a payoff for help in combating terrorists invites distrust and suspicion, and ultimately fails wider U.S. objectives in the region.

Notes

[1] Dennis Kux, *Disenchanted Allies: The United States and Pakistan 1947–2000* (Baltimore and London: Johns Hopkins University Press, 2001), p. 359.

[2] Ted Galen Carpenter, *A Fortress Built on Quicksand: U.S. Policy toward Pakistan,* Cato Policy Analysis no. 80 (January 5, 1987), (www.cato.org/pubs/pas/pa080.html).

[3] CNN World News, "Powell Wants Pakistan N-assurances," March 16, 2004 (www.cnn.com/2004/WORLD/asiapcf/03/16/powell.nuclear.ap/?headline=Powell~wants~Pakistan~nukes~pledge).

[4] CBS News, "Pakistan Slams Door on U.S. Troops," January 29, 2004 (www.cbsnews.com/stories/2004/01/24/terror/main595582.shtml).

⁵ BBC News, "Analysis: How Lifting Sanctions Helps Pakistan," September 23, 2001 (news.bbc.co.uk/1/hi/world/south_asia/1559277.stm), and T. Christian Miller, "U.S. Improves Ties with Pakistan: Change Means Greater Access to Weapons, Loan Guarantees," *Los Angeles Times,* March 19, 2004.

⁶ Dennis Kux, "Looking at U.S. Aid to Pakistan," Middle East Institute Policy Brief, September 24, 2003 (www.mideasti.org/articles/doc146.html).

⁷ Malcolm Garcia, "Many Pakistanis Criticize Musharraf for Going after Al-Qaida," Knight Ridder, March 26, 2004.

⁸ "Bushra Asif and Teresita C. Schaffer, "Pakistan: Parliamentary Elections and After," *CSIS South Asia Monitor,* no. 66 (January 1, 2004) (www.csis.org/saprog/monitor.cfm).

CHAPTER SIX

RUSSIA: THE ACCIDENTAL ALLIANCE

Andrew S. Weiss

INTRODUCTION

In the immediate aftermath of September 11, a qualitatively new U.S.-Russian relationship emerged, marked by unprecedented dynamism and cooperation in the diplomatic, military, and intelligence spheres. In a matter of months, U.S.-Russian relations achieved levels of strategic cooperation not seen since World War II. The fledgling U.S.-Russian neo-entente quickly became a signal accomplishment of the initial phase of the Bush administration's war on terrorism and stood in stark contrast to the fractious, often competitive relationship that dominated the Clinton administration's second term.

President George W. Bush was personally responsible for much of what transpired in the aftermath of September 11, having set a cooperative tone for U.S.-Russian relations some five months earlier at his first meeting with Vladimir Putin in Ljubljana in June 2001. Bush had made headlines at the time for an off-the-cuff, much-derided comment about having glimpsed the Russian president's soul. But the unexpectedly friendly tone at the meeting, which surprised some of the president's own advisers, helped counteract the corrosive effects of Bush's stridently anti-Russian campaign rhetoric and a generally unfriendly, distrustful view of Russia within his core national security team.[1]

The Ljubljana meeting was a great triumph for Putin, the public culmination of a months-long attempt to ingratiate himself with the new American president. In the waning days of President Clinton's administration, Putin had deliberately withheld cooperation on pressing issues such as amending the Anti-Ballistic Missile (ABM) Treaty, preferring instead to try to create a new relationship with the incoming administration.[2] Putin's core priorities from the earliest stages in his presidency had been almost entirely domestic policy–related, and he showed considerable realism about the kind of U.S.-Russian relationship he needed to help accomplish them. In particular, Putin aimed to revitalize the Russian economy, rebuild and reassert the authority of government institutions battered during the era of Boris Yeltsin, and, above all, promote order and stability throughout the country. Yet he also wanted to accomplish these objectives without having to change the centralized, bureaucratic, semiauthoritarian nature of the Russian state system along Western lines.[3]

As viewed from the Kremlin, fostering a close relationship with Bush was important, if not essential, for achieving these broad goals. The Americans, in Putin's eyes, could help ensure a benign international environment. With American help, Putin could minimize the number of challenges Russia faced in foreign affairs, giving him greater ability to concentrate on problems closer to home and to promote a period of relative calm as reforms took hold. By building a friendship with the leader of the Western camp (who also was gatekeeper for the key institutions of the global economy), Putin could help spur Russia's economic recovery and integration.

Bush had his own motivations for closer ties with Putin in the run-up to Ljubljana. His team's overwhelming focus in its dealings with Russia had been tied to the missile defense issue, and Bush was keen to probe Russia's willingness to work with the United States on discarding the restrictions imposed by the ABM treaty. In the first half of 2001, Putin had signaled that he wanted to defuse the issue, though he also called for negotiations on reductions in both sides' nuclear arsenals via a new strategic arms control treaty. Still, it was far from obvious that the Russians would be willing to give Bush everything he wanted on ABM and clear the way for a more expansive missile defense system. Russian cooperation, or at least acquiescence, on this issue was a key White House goal, and Bush's public embrace of Putin at Ljubljana effectively settled a disagreement inside the administration about whether it was worth going the extra mile diplomatically with the Russians to find a cooperative solution.

The public friendship between Bush and Putin established at Ljubljana, though eerily reminiscent of the "Bill-Boris" relationship that preceded it, was to remain a key stabilizing force in U.S.-Russian ties. But beneath the public portrayal of Russian-American friendship and bonhomie at the highest levels, there was surprisingly little success at converting that goodwill into tangible activity. Why did this happen? How did a relationship that looked so promising after September 11 atrophy so quickly?

Retracing the evolution of the U.S.-Russian relationship in the post–September 11 period helps explain why it proved so difficult to sustain the levels of cooperation that were forged from that crucible. Above all else, the intense disagreement between Washington and Moscow over the Iraq War prompted Russia to side with the Bush administration's fiercest European critics and effectively forfeit its status as a founding member of the antiterror coalition. The Bush administration's blunt style of diplomacy and lack of interest in building a durable coalition for what it portrayed as a multi-front war on terror also contributed to this outcome. At the same time, a fundamental divergence of interests closed off potential avenues for U.S.-Russian cooperation in the post–September 11 international environment.

A TRANSFORMATIVE MOMENT

It is now commonplace to view the impact of September 11 on U.S. foreign policy as comparable only to the attack on Pearl Harbor. In the emotionally charged weeks and months following the attacks, the Bush administration was quick to formulate new objectives and priorities for U.S. foreign policy. The first priority was to deliver a fierce blow against Al Qaeda and the Taliban regime that harbored it, an objective the Russians were quick to embrace and to which they contributed modestly. Throughout fall 2001 and 2002, U.S. and Russian intelligence officials stepped up the pace of information sharing on counterterrorism, coordinated covert military and financial support for the Northern Alliance, and worked cooperatively on ensuring the success of Operation Enduring Freedom.

But differences between Russian and American priorities emerged almost immediately as the Bush administration expressed an equally vehement determination to counter the spread of weapons of mass destruction to rogue regimes, a danger that the administration directly connected with the threat posed by jihadist terrorism.[4] Part of the problem was that at least two of the regimes of greatest concern to the Bush administration, Iran and Iraq, had long-standing cooperative ties with Russia, and there was little enthusiasm in the Kremlin for a snap reappraisal of these relationships.

Still, the U.S. view of the threat of weapons of mass destruction and Saddam Hussein was never too far in the background, even in the earliest phases of Bush's war on terror. In an address to the nation on September 11, Bush announced, "We will make no distinction between the terrorists who committed these acts and those who harbor them."[5] According to Bob Woodward's book *Bush at War*, Bush told his advisers at Camp David on September 15, 2001, that although he believed Iraq had been involved in the September 11 attacks, the lack of evidence meant that Iraq would not be targeted during the first phase of the war on terrorism. Vice President Cheney recounted that in the first moments after the attacks he had immediately worried about what the impact would have been if the terrorists had had access to weapons of mass destruction. Deputy Secretary of Defense Paul Wolfowitz triggered an early controversy over the administration's nascent policy framework with his suggestion about "ending states who sponsor terrorism" just two days after the attacks.[6] The administration's new strategy found fuller expression in the president's State of the Union address in January 2002, where he lumped Iraq, Iran, and North Korea together as part of an "axis of evil."[7] After months of semiofficial press leaks and briefings for foreign governments, the preemption doctrine was formally enshrined in the National Security Strategy, issued on September 17, 2002.[8]

SEPTEMBER 11 THROUGH PUTIN'S EYES—AND BLINDERS

Given the numerous indications of the direction that Bush intended to impose on U.S. foreign policy, how and when did the Russians take heed? How accurately did Russian policymakers anticipate the new course of U.S. foreign policy, the crystallization of the Bush doctrine of preemptive war, and, perhaps most important, the impact on U.S.-Russian relations? The public relations machinery of the Bush administration and the Kremlin both made much of the fact that Putin was the first world leader to call the White House in the immediate aftermath of the attacks.[9] Putin's call fit well with his pattern of behavior before Ljubljana and his desire to create a close bond with the new U.S. administration. In his more grandiose moments after the Ljubljana meeting, Putin was reportedly prone to thinking that "Russia and the U.S. could rule the world together . . . . He saw the possibility of a Moscow-Washington axis."[10]

But Putin's motivations for reaching out to the White House also had domestic political motives. "At that juncture, Putin was still beholden to Boris Yeltsin and [members of his influential retinue known as] 'the

Family.' He wanted to strengthen his position at home both within his own circle in the Kremlin and 'the Family' by becoming a first-class international statesman."[11] Since Putin could not do that by attacking "the Family" directly, he saw the relationship with Bush as an important source of leverage in this internal political tug of war.

A more controversial explanation for Putin's reaction to the attacks on the United States may lie in the Russian leader's own personality and temperament. Putin has a tendency to become deeply emotional and volatile during private discussions of terrorism or the war in Chechnya, a characteristic that was on display repeatedly during this author's tenure on the National Security Council staff. Equal parts coarse and ill-tempered, this side of Putin's personality often led him to make bold assertions or to lock himself into policy choices. The first public manifestation of Putin's inclinations in this regard were in September 1999, early in his tenure as prime minister, when Putin famously remarked, "We will pursue the terrorists everywhere. Forgive me, but if we find them in the toilet, we will rub them out in the shithouse." Since then, his public outbursts, often in the form of take-no-prisoners comments about terrorism, have revealed an impetuous side that is at odds with Putin's carefully cultivated persona as a calculating, former counterintelligence operative.[12]

Regardless of his motivations, the lopsided separation of powers in the Russian political system gave Putin, like Yeltsin before him, considerable room for maneuver on foreign policy issues. In a few short weeks after September 11, Putin completely rewrote the parameters and norms that had guided Russia's international behavior for the preceding decade. With little public or elite debate, Putin cast Russia as a willing and enthusiastic partner in the U.S.-led war on terrorism and helped the United States launch military and intelligence operations against the Taliban regime. He also quietly acquiesced, without clear public acknowledgment, in the establishment of an open-ended U.S. military presence on the territory of the former Soviet Union, a move that contradicted one of the core tenets of post–Cold War Russian foreign policy.

It is particularly important to examine how the latter decision was made. The U.S. desire for access to airfields and staging areas in Central Asia was conveyed almost immediately after the attacks by Bush and then in more detail by Deputy Secretary of State Richard Armitage, who visited Moscow for a previously scheduled meeting of a joint working group on Afghanistan. The request was unsettling for many of Armitage's interlocutors from the foreign ministry, intelligence services, and defense ministry who found it hard to contemplate the prospect of U.S. military deployments on Russia's doorstep. As U.S. diplomatic pressure mounted on Russia and Central Asian governments, a split in the Russian ranks appeared. A hard-line group, led by Defense Minister Sergey Ivanov, one of Putin's closest advisers, and Chief of the General Staff Anatoly Kvashnin, argued that Russia had enough residual influence to persuade the Central Asian governments to reject the U.S. request. Less than 10 days after the attacks, Kvashnin conducted a tour of front-line Central Asian capitals to make the case directly to regional leaders. These diplomatic activities and a series of well-publicized public comments created growing unease and annoyance inside the Bush administration. At one point, Ivanov publicly asserted that there was "no basis for even a hypothetical possibility" of a U.S. military deployment in Central Asia,[13] and Kvashnin suggested that Russia would not take part in "acts of revenge" in Afghanistan.[14]

Putin himself shed light subsequently on the intensely polarized reaction inside the Russian government at a 2003 press conference at Camp David with Bush where he said:

> When counterterrorist operation began in Afghanistan, we were approached by people, through several channels, we were approached by people who intended to fight against the Americans in Afghanistan. And if by that time President Bush and I had not formed an appropriate relationship, as we have, no one knows what turn the developments in Afghanistan would have taken.[15]

The internal Russian battle culminated at an angry, high-level conclave at Putin's Black Sea residence in Sochi on September 22. During the marathon meeting, it fell to Putin personally to cajole attendees into agreeing to—or at least into not actively opposing—the U.S. deployments.[16] At the meeting Putin was able to take advantage of a split within the so-called power ministries. Putin and members of the security and foreign policy establishment had for years portrayed the vast area lying along Russia's southern frontiers as an "arc of instability," where the forces of radical Islam were laying siege to Western civilization. In numerous public statements, Putin had singled out the Taliban regime as posing a major threat to weak Central Asian governments and to Russia itself.[17] But in the Sochi meeting, Putin argued that it was abundantly clear that Moscow could not deal with the Taliban threat on its own.

Russian security and military personnel, after all, had had only limited success in the preceding three years in helping Central Asian counterparts oppose the low-grade insurgency led by the Islamic Movement of Uzbekistan (IMU), an Al Qaeda–affiliated group that enjoyed sanctuary and support in Taliban-controlled Afghanistan. At Sochi, Putin made the case that although he found the proposed American military presence deeply disturbing, the least unpalatable option was to let the Americans fight Russia's battles for it.[18] He also argued that there was no reason to be confident that Russian pressure on the Central Asian states would ever dissuade them from accepting American troops.

Yet Putin's unveiling of Russia's participation in the antiterrorism coalition—and its costs—to the Russian people did not address any of the painful dilemmas that the discussions in Sochi had revealed about Russia's weakness and its challenging geographic location, let alone the difficult decisions that Putin had pushed through the government. Rather, Putin's speech to the nation was an awkward mish-mash of muted, almost begrudging, support for the coalition.[19] As a starting proposition, Putin asserted that the international community's reaction to the attacks showed the need to strengthen the role of institutions such as the UN Security Council, rehashing the standard Russian line about the Security Council's preeminence in decisions about the use of force. Putin dealt with the key topic of the U.S. deployments in Central Asia only cryptically, saying that Central Asian leaders "do not rule out for themselves the possibility of offering the use of their airfields."[20] Putin explained that Russia's role in the coalition would consist of intelligence cooperation, military assistance to the Northern Alliance, and use of Russian airspace for humanitarian missions. Yet to avoid associating himself with the extremely controversial decision on U.S. military deployments, Putin left it up to his foreign minister and defense minister to make the formal announcement a few days later.

The attempt to skirt unpleasant domestic political repercussions was classic Putin. Clearly, he was willing to take a great risk on the foreign policy front and displayed a degree of tactical flexibility that surprised foreign interlocutors and domestic political allies alike. But he mysteriously resisted making a persuasive case to the Russian elite and general public that would have justified his actions at this crucial moment in history. Putin's overall approach, especially the decision to acquiesce to the U.S. military presence, was guaranteed to be controversial with most of the Russian elite. The most effective means available to Putin to rebut such sentiments would have been to tackle publicly the myths about Russia's great power status and superpower nostalgia cherished by large segments of the Russian elite, to announce that he and Bush had fundamentally reinvented the nature of U.S.-Russian relations, or to demonstrate that he had wrung major concessions from the Americans in exchange for Russian support. Putin had chosen the second course, yet failed to announce it to his fellow citizens.

Putin appears to have demanded relatively little from the Bush administration in exchange for Russia's cooperation. First and foremost, he sought to arrange a public assertion by the Bush administration of equivalence between the war in Chechnya and the menace of Al Qaeda and jihadist terrorism. It was a gamble that reflected Putin's long-standing desire to establish himself as a close ally of the Bush administration as well as his deeply held feelings about terrorism. Unlike Pakistan, Russia was in the midst of an unprecedented economic revival and was not desperately looking for handouts from the United States or international financial institutions. To Putin, it was far more important to confront a common enemy than to negotiate concessions on the more mundane topics that dominated the U.S.-Russian bilateral agenda.

Although Putin's approach was a major departure from the tried-and-true habits of Russian diplomats who seldom missed an opportunity to create linkages between unrelated topics, it also reflected a sophisticated calculation that a generous Russian response in America's hour of need was more likely to establish Putin as a leading force in the new U.S.-led coalition. And it is fair to suspect Putin and his team anticipated that the exigencies of a U.S. foreign policy oriented solely around the fight against terrorism would lead to greater tolerance of repressive regimes that were part of the antiterror coalition. For all of Putin's shrewd insights about the gains he could achieve by joining the antiterror cause, he failed badly to communicate these important considerations to Russian opinion makers or the general public. At no point in the months and years that followed September 11 did he give a speech that clearly outlined the dramatic changes he was overseeing in Russian foreign policy and relations with Washington. This hope would come back to haunt him later. In the meantime, however, he restricted himself to frequently highlighting Russia's most important reward for joining the antiterrorism coalition—the dramatic change in the Bush administration's tone on his handling of the bloody war in Chechnya.

The American shift was not a small one, and, for Putin, it was deeply gratifying. He had fruitlessly lobbied international leaders and public opinion for years, trying to win support for the Kremlin's self-serving view of the conflict. Russian propaganda, typically in the form of lurid press accounts and briefings by the security services, had long attempted to focus Western attention on the role of foreign Islamic militants and terrorist organizations, especially adherents of the Wahhabi sect of Islam, while downplaying the historical grievances and nationalist aspirations of many Chechens.[21] Since the September 11 attacks, Putin has insisted on drawing a direct comparison between them and events in Chechnya. In an interview with American journalists in September 2003, when speaking of the outbreak in 1999 of the second Chechen war, Putin said, "Who were these fighters who attacked Dagestan?[22] They were essentially people who were closely connected with Al Qaeda, with other such organizations, who trained at their bases and armed themselves on their money. Essentially the same people who two years later attacked American cities."

But as has been well documented elsewhere,[23] there is more to the roots of the conflict than simply an expansion of jihadist activity in the Caucasus. The antipathies stretch back a century and a half and were, in origin, a matter of ethno-nationalist resentment at Chechnya's incorporation into the Russian Empire. In the last decade, the conflict has become increasingly colored by ethnic and religious hatred. In particular, this trend intensified after Russia granted Chechnya de facto independence in 1996, following Russia's defeat in the first Chechen war. Among the groups that gravitated to the region to stoke the conflict were supporters of bin Laden and other radical jihadists, including Ayman al-Zawahiri, the leader of Egyptian Islamic Jihad who is now bin Laden's deputy. By embedding themselves in the fabric of local communities, they built religious and educational institutions in the predominantly Muslim parts of the north Caucasus, funded economic development and antipoverty programs, and promoted the Wahhabi interpretation of Islam.[24]

The role of foreign fighters and clerics was given great prominence by Russian officials who sought to persuade Western governments that Russia was on the front lines of a radical Islamic terrorist assault on the "civilized world." Putin's public comments as well as private discussions with Western officials about the conflict and the wave of terrorist bombings emphasized these ideas as well. Putin published an article in the *New York Times* in November 1999 that reiterated the themes from his meetings with President Clinton and National Security Adviser Samuel Berger in Auckland, New Zealand, six weeks earlier. He wrote:

> We know that a great deal of the violence emanating from Chechnya is financed from abroad. The same terrorists who were associated with the

bombing of America's embassies [in Kenya and Tanzania] have a foothold in the Caucasus. We know that Shamil Basayev, the so-called Chechen war-lord, gets assistance on the ground from an itinerant guerrilla leader [the Jordanian militant Khattab] with a dossier similar to that of Osama bin Laden. And one of your television networks recently reported that—according to United States intelligence sources—bin Laden himself is help-ing to finance the guerrillas.[25]

Although the Clinton administration did not take all of Putin's claims at face value, there was recognition at senior levels that the Chechen war was cross-pollinating in an unhealthy fashion with the forces of interna-tional terrorism, including the Al Qaeda network. The arrival of foreign fighters in the area was aggravating the conflict and outside financial support from radical Islamists had been exacerbating matters in the north Caucasus since the perestroika period.[26] Attention centered on the role of Khattab, a leading Chechen field commander of Jordanian or Saudi origin who had fought alongside bin Laden and operated terror-ist training camps inside Chechnya in the 1996–1999 period; Khattab was widely presumed to be a member of the Al Qaeda network.

As a presidential candidate, Bush's line on Chechnya had been hard-edged, calling for the United States to punish Russia financially by cut-ting off support from the International Monetary Fund and the U.S. Export-Import Bank for "bombing women and children."[27] His top for-eign policy adviser Condoleezza Rice had been even more scathing about Russian conduct in Chechnya, arguing that Putin had used the issue to stir up dangerous nationalist sentiment and lay the groundwork for his political ascendancy.[28]

But that line of argument died swiftly after Putin's September 24, 2001 announcement of Russia's contribution to the antiterrorism coali-tion. The initial change may have been somewhat subtle: during a daily press briefing, Bush spokesman Ari Fleischer had highlighted and en-dorsed a specific passage in Putin's statement calling on the Chechen leadership to cut all ties to Osama bin Laden and the Al Qaeda net-work,[29] effectively introducing a parallel between Russia's military cam-paign in Chechnya and the Bush administration's moves against Al Qaeda and the Taliban. As the war on terror progressed, the adminis-tration's depiction of what Russia was up to in Chechnya became far less nuanced and careful. As Bush himself put it at a meeting with Putin at the G-8 summit in Canada in June 2002:

President Putin has been a stalwart in the fight against terror. He understands the threat of terror, because he has lived through terror. He's seen terror firsthand and he knows the threat of terrorism. . . . He understands what I understand, that there won't be peace if terrorists are allowed to kill and take innocent life. And, therefore, I view President Putin as an ally, strong ally in the war against terror. And his actions are more than—speak louder than his words. He has been a man of action when it comes to fighting terror, and I appreciate that very much.[30]

For Putin, the White House's initial shift, even if couched in terms of support for the Kremlin's avowed (yet obviously disingenuous) support for a political solution to the Chechen crisis, was a source of great personal vindication. Within the State Department concerns persisted about Russian human rights violations, the use of excessive force, and other conduct that was repugnant and undermined chances for a peaceful resolution of the conflict. Yet expression of such concern was repeatedly muzzled and its advocates publicly contradicted by the White House. For example, Alexander Vershbow, the U.S. ambassador to Russia, was mildly critical of Russian handling of the deadly Moscow theater siege in October 2002, saying that Russian secrecy about the gas used to subdue the Chechen gunmen had probably led to unnecessary deaths among the hostages, including an American citizen. Administration officials in Washington, however, declined to echo Vershbow's concerns, and in a subsequent interview with Russian television network NTV, Bush praised Putin's handling of the crisis:

I recognize that any time terrorists come to take life, a leader must step forward. And the fact that 800 citizens could have been killed by terrorists put my friend Vladimir Putin in a very difficult situation. And he handled it as best he could. He did what he had to do to save life. And people—I heard somebody the other day blame Russia. No, the people to blame are the terrorists. They need to be held to account.[31]

In short, since the shift in the Bush administration's public stance on Chechnya, the president has unfailingly stood by Putin on the issue.

In practical terms, the months following September 11 saw the Bush administration build upon preexisting efforts to cut foreign financial flows to Chechen militants and to shut down sources of terrorist financing.[32] There also was increased concern within Western governments that the north Caucasus, both Chechnya and Georgia's remote Pankisi Gorge, was becoming a magnet for terrorists, including some who had been put to flight by the international antiterrorism campaign. Prominent terrorism experts such as French magistrate Jean-Louis Bruguiere identified the region as an important source of terrorist training, including in the area of chemical weapons.[33]

Still, it was in Pankisi that the limits of the Bush administration's accommodating line on Chechnya were exposed. Russia's stated willingness to use force unilaterally to expel Chechen fighters and Arab sympathizers from Pankisi provoked a brief crisis in U.S.-Russian relations in autumn 2002. Putin's threats to launch air strikes inside Georgia raised grave doubts inside the Bush administration about the Russian leader's intentions toward his neighbors, concerns that have only grown more pervasive in the intervening period. By deploying hundreds of U.S. Special Forces troops as part of a deal to resolve the crisis, the Bush administration removed any of the ambiguity about the precedent established by the U.S. military presence in Central Asia or Washington's determination to prevent the use of force by Russia to resolve disputes in the post-Soviet space.

For Putin, the U.S. move to deploy troops to the Pankisi region was both a sharp rebuke and painful testimony to the asymmetrical nature of Russia's relationship with the United States. In Russian eyes, Washington and leading European powers had by themselves decided upon the standards of behavior by which Russia would be forced to abide, even in combating Al Qaeda–related security threats. To the Russians, these standards were significantly different from what the Western powers had arrogated for themselves and certain trusted allies. The crisis revealed once again the dismal condition of the Russian military. Although the Kremlin had made a big show of preparing military options to deal with the Pankisi crisis, serious observers of the Russian military were highly dubious that such attacks would have been successful. As prominent Russian military analyst Aleksandr Golts put it, "Russia does not have the capacity to conduct a large-scale anti-terrorist operation and contain terrorists within a large territory. Putin will never admit this publicly."[34]

A GLOBAL MISMATCH

Although the views of the Kremlin and the White House appeared to converge, at least superficially, on the question of Chechnya and global terrorism, the gap separating them on the broader nature of international relations—and, even more important, America's role in the world—became a source of considerable strain after September 11. For his part, Putin had distinguished himself, beginning with the Ljubljana meeting, by implicitly recognizing America's global preeminence and abandoning an approach to foreign policy that had been both overtly hostile to the United States and out of sync with the realities of Russia's post-Soviet decline. After the September 11 attacks, he had gone even further and made common cause with Bush.

But in Moscow there was growing discontent within the Russian government and elite circles with Putin's approach because of the lack of tangible benefits. Critics pointed out that Russian cooperation with the Bush administration had not led to any obvious economic benefits such as early Russian entry into the World Trade Organization or changes in American behavior during debilitating trade disputes over such issues as steel and poultry. (A highly public fight over the latter issue effectively torpedoed Russian hopes of congressional action to revoke the Jackson-Vanik amendment, a step promised by Bush shortly after September 11. Although Jackson-Vanik has had no practical impact on U.S.-Russian trading relations, many Russians are convinced that it is proof of enduring Cold War thinking in Washington.)

The list of blows to Russia's prestige caused by what was seen in Moscow as the heavy-handedness of the Bush administration was extensive—and growing. The Bush team had plowed ahead after September 11, with little apparent regard for Russia's sensitivities or concerns, on the unilateral abrogation of the ABM treaty and construction of a national missile defense system. At the Prague summit in November 2002, NATO membership was extended to the three Baltic States. As noted earlier, in autumn 2002 the Bush administration expanded its deployment of U.S. Special Forces troops to Georgia for a train-and-equip mission (GTEP) in the Pankisi Gorge. To most Russians, the image of the United States's encroaching on Russia's home turf was hard to overlook. At best, many in the Russian elite believed Putin looked like he was valued solely for his willingness to follow Bush's lead (or, in the memorable phrase of Russian commentator Aleksey Pushkov, to be "a jackal at the side of the American lion").[35]

The simmering discontent inside the Russian establishment was in many ways the natural by-product of Putin's long-standing reluctance to engage public opinion about the merits of his post–September 11 policy agenda. Thus, when the Bush administration began gearing up to make the case for war in Iraq, Putin had no significant base of support at home in favor of U.S.-Russian rapprochement, and he was soon confronted by a political class eager to teach the United States a lesson about the need to acknowledge the reality of a multipolar world and a more equitable relationship with Moscow. This alternative view was deeply entrenched in the Russian political debate and had been codified in numerous official documents, including the June 2000 Foreign Policy Concept of the Russian Federation.[36]

On no issue was this tendency to act as a spoiler in opposition to U.S. foreign policy objectives and initiatives more apparent than on the use of force and America's uneasy relationship with the UN Security Council. In a previous showdown at the United Nations over Milosevic's aggression in Kosovo, the Russians had threatened to veto any resolution authorizing the use of force. However, as the debate on the Iraq War intensified, Putin's position remained surprisingly fluid, and he sent conflicting signals about whether Russia would oppose a Bush administration decision to go to war. Russia had worked cooperatively with the United States in November 2003 on Resolution 1441, which held Saddam Hussein in material breach of his disarmament obligations and gave him a last chance to comply. The Russian vote for 1441 led an angry Hussein to cancel Lukoil's valuable contract to develop the West Qurna-2 oilfield in mid-December. During a visit to Kiev in early 2003, Putin put the onus of compliance with Resolution 1441 squarely on Hussein, saying, "If Iraq resists these inspections, if it creates problems for the inspectors, I do not rule out that Russia may change its position. And we intend to work with other Security Council members, including the United States, to work out other decisions—I won't say what kind, but tougher than the existing decisions."[37]

The Bush administration, banking on these signals as well as the close personal relationship between the two leaders, had good reason to believe that it could coax the Russians into taking a position similar to China's—that is, an abstention on an expected key vote in the Security Council to authorize force followed by limited public criticism of the U.S. invasion. In late February 2003, Putin's influential chief of staff, Aleksandr Voloshin, visited the White House for previously scheduled meetings with National Security Adviser Rice. Their talks included a brief appearance by Bush, and the most important topic was the diplomatic end-game on Iraq. Voloshin confided that he believed that Russia would abstain from a crucial pending vote in the Security Council. The core of Voloshin's message to the White House was that the Kremlin wanted to avoid a major dust-up in U.S.-Russian relations over Iraq and to protect its long-standing economic interests in post-conflict Iraq.

Inexplicably, the Bush administration did not deepen its dialogue with the Russians during these fateful weeks. Neither Powell nor Rice visited Moscow to explore what Russia expected in terms of guarantees of its economic interests, deciding instead to let the Russians come to them with specific requests. France and Germany filled the void left by the Bush administration and intensely lobbied the Russians to join what came to be known as the "Coalition of the Unwilling."[38] The first meeting of the three countries' foreign ministers in Paris in early March 2003 was hastily arranged after the Turkish parliament's surprise rejection of a proposed U.S. troop deployment. The three ministers believed that the diplomatic momentum had swung dramatically in favor of the antiwar camp, and they publicly committed themselves to blocking adoption of a second UN Security Council resolution, a move that effectively doomed U.S.-UK diplomatic efforts in New York. The Paris meeting between Igor Ivanov, Dominique de Villepin, and Joschka Fischer launched the so-called Coalition of the Unwilling and was an important milestone in France's and Russia's desire to create a lasting counterweight to U.S. global preeminence.

The contrast between Voloshin's message in Washington and Igor Ivanov's anti-American theatrics in Paris one week later provides a vivid illustration of Russia's dysfunctional foreign policy–making apparatus. Competing arms of the Russian bureaucracy had staked out diametrically opposing views on the most important foreign policy issue of the day and then proceeded to act independently on matters that went to the core of Russia's most important bilateral relationship. Pressure on Putin from prominent business figures such as Yukos CEO Mikhail Khodorkovsky, who had weighed in repeatedly with a pro-American assessment of the crisis, added to the confusion in Moscow.[39] Yet the failure to agree on a coherent Iraq policy had great importance in the flurry of end-game diplomacy. It meant that when it came time for Russia to tell the White House its price for abstaining in the Security Council, there was only silence. And the Russian silence was all the more remarkable given the billions of dollars of contracts held by Lukoil and other Russian companies to develop Iraqi oil fields, contracts that clearly would be at risk as a result of Russia's noncooperative stance.

What calculation guided Putin's decision to tilt in the direction of his newfound European soul mates, Gerhard Schroeder and Jacques Chirac? Did he really believe that the ad hoc anti-U.S. coalition could stop the Bush administration from going to war by withholding UN authorization or buying more time for the UN weapons inspectors? Was he trying to win a high-stakes bet on establishing the preeminence of the Security Council? Or was he simply trying to inflict a cost for American high-handedness? Each of the leaders of the Coalition of the Unwilling, with varying degrees of *schadenfreude*, appeared to believe that a U.S.-led invasion of Iraq would radicalize the Middle East and that U.S. forces would soon become bogged down in Iraq. Still, the dramatic debate on Iraq in the Security Council was in many ways a debate between conflicting visions for the new international environment—and America's role in it. Russia's national security establishment welcomed Chirac's and Schroeder's efforts to inflict the maximum damage on the United States in front of international public opinion, believing that it was safer for Russia to let long-time U.S. allies lead the charge. Yet the key *policy* question facing the Kremlin was whether a rupture in relations with the United States over Iraq was a risk worth taking, given Washington's fundamental importance for Putin's foreign policy framework.

Egging Putin on were large anti-American constituencies in the security services and military-industrial complex. These groups, which had been on the defensive since September 11, shared the French desire to try to cut the United States down to size and impose a more equal U.S.-Russian partnership on Washington, regardless of the consequences. And the opportunity to split the United States from its European allies, a tactic that had been a mainstay for Russian and Soviet diplomats alike, was simply too tempting to pass up. Those who advocated making common cause with France and Germany eagerly fed Putin's anger at Bush and Blair with slanted intelligence reports and misleading diplomatic cables. Russian Foreign Ministry and intelligence specialists on the region had largely advanced their careers working with the Baathist regime and piled on. They insisted—without firm corroborating information—that the United States would not go to war until all diplomatic options had been completely exhausted, a view that gave additional impetus to the delaying tactics that Russia, France, and Germany embraced in the Security Council debates. Intelligence reports persuaded Putin that the Iraqis would fiercely resist the U.S. invasion and that Bush would eventually be forced to plead for help from Russia and France.[40]

Putin also factored domestic political considerations into his decisions. Like German chancellor Schroeder and South Korean president Roh Moo Hyun before him, Putin's advisers believed that anti-American posturing might prove popular with the Russian public on the eve of parliamentary and presidential elections. In late February, opinion polls showed upwards of 90 percent of Russians opposed to the war.[41] (Tellingly, only 30 percent believed that European/Russian diplomatic efforts would have any effect on the United States.) The Kremlin's feel for the mood of the electorate was vindicated when representatives of the nationalist fringe of Russian politics were the big winners in the December 2003 Duma elections.

Putin's advisers also marshaled half-baked economic arguments, pointing out that Russian trade turnover with Germany was double that with the United States and that European foreign direct investment outpaced that of the United States. These arguments conveniently glossed over the fact that Moscow's newfound European allies had routinely played hardball with Russia on sensitive problems like Kaliningrad and EU-Russia trade disputes. In joining with France and Germany, Putin seemed to jettison or ignore Russia's broader economic and trade interests. In addition to discarding the valuable oil exploration contracts in Iraq, Putin was making common cause with two states that had done little or nothing to support his top priority—the revitalization of Russia's economy. For example, at the time of the Iraq War, Russia was the largest economy still outside the ranks of the World Trade Organization, and Russian exports were a major target for EU protectionists. For the first time in half a century, Russia had become a net exporter of grain, but EU trade barriers blocked access to European markets. Likewise, protracted negotiations on World Trade Organization entry at the time were being held up by, among other things, the EU's insistence on liberalization of the Russian gas sector apparently because of fears that Russia's abundant reserves would give its energy-intensive industries an unfair advantage in the future. But Putin made no attempt to negotiate practical benefits on trade or economics in exchange for his embrace of the antiwar agenda.

The breakdown in the Security Council and the start of the war took a heavy toll on U.S.-Russian relations. In the first days of the war, Putin denounced the U.S. invasion as illegal and called for an immediate halt to hostilities. Putin also reportedly had harsh words for Bush when the two leaders discussed U.S. intelligence reports that Russian companies had sent radar-jamming equipment and other materiel to Saddam's military in the run-up to the war. Tensions reached a peak when a Russian diplomatic convoy was mistakenly attacked by coalition forces, leading the Ministry of Foreign Affairs to suggest that the attack had been deliberate. After the course of the war turned decisively in Washington's favor, Putin began an awkward climb-down from his vocal opposition and issued a public statement on April 3, 2003, reaffirming his commitment to U.S.-Russian cooperation. As the Iraqi regime collapsed, it became clear that Putin remained angry about what he perceived as the Bush administration's arrogance in its dealings with Russia during the crisis as well as the personal embarrassment he suffered at home at the hands of Russian commentators who mocked the swift collapse of the assumptions that had undergirded Russian policy on Iraq. Putin vented his frustrations in public when Tony Blair visited Moscow in late April to lobby him on the UN's post-conflict role. Putin, visibly angry, mocked him in front of the international press corps, saying: "Where is Saddam [Hussein]? Where are those arsenals [of weapons of mass destruction]? If they were really there, what is happening with them? Maybe Saddam is sitting somewhere in a secret bunker and plans to blow up all this stuff at the last second, threatening hundreds of human lives. We don't know anything. These questions must be answered."[42]

The initial post-conflict period witnessed a gradual improvement in U.S.-Russian relations, thanks largely to the personal bond between the two presidents. Still, the formula of "punishing France, ignoring Germany, and forgiving Russia" propagated by Rice in spring/summer 2003 had unanticipated consequences. Many Russian officials and analysts soon speculated that the main lesson of the Iraq War was that Russia was able to get away with misbehavior, no matter how egregious, and might even be able to skirt criticism from Washington in the future if equally sharp disagreements emerged. And the failure of the Bush administration to mend fences with the Europeans meant that Russia would be able to take advantage of transatlantic tensions in the future. U.S. officials unwisely stoked this perception, with some arguing publicly that "less was expected" from the Russians than from the French, implying that the administration was prepared to bend over backward to cushion the impact of serious disagreements with the Kremlin.[43]

That forgiving tone helps explain why the Russians have been able to hold fast to their positions on post-conflict Iraq. The Russians lined up once again with the French and Germans in arguments with the Bush administration on the proper UN role in reconstruction and the timeline for returning full sovereignty to Iraqis. Likewise, the Russians refused pleas from the United States for a total debt write-off, suggesting

that concessions on the debt issue would require restoration of contracts for Russian oil companies inside Iraq.[44] Russia's obstinance on
this issue helped drag out contentious Paris Club negotiations on Iraqi
debt relief for more than a year. In a political gesture shortly after Bush's
November 2004 reelection victory, Putin agreed to write off approximately 92 percent of Russia's share of Iraq's sovereign debt. This partial
victory aside, the Bush administration has experienced great difficulties
in converting chumminess at the highest levels into active Russian support. For his part, Putin has remained rather conflicted in his reaction
to the worsening situation inside Iraq and hewed fairly closely to his odd
formulation of April 2003 that he does not wish to see the United States
defeated in Iraq.[45]

CONCLUSIONS

The inconsistencies and lack of focus that have dominated the Bush administration's management of the U.S.-Russian relationship have caused
recurring—and in many cases entirely predictable—difficulties for U.S.
foreign policy. Bush administration officials often appeared surprised
by Putin's chronic reluctance to embrace democratic norms, the rule of
law, or cooperative relationships with neighboring states. Of course,
Putin's manifest shortcomings on these issues were not new—they were
simply ignored by U.S. policymakers in the chaotic months following
the Al Qaeda attacks. Eager to distinguish themselves from the Clinton
administration—where several cabinet-level officials and the president
himself had seemed to vie for the role of leading U.S. engagement with
Russia—the Bush team early on de-emphasized Russia's importance in
overall U.S. foreign policy and largely discarded the Clinton-era approach of engaging the Russians proactively on major issues.

Putin's authoritarian tendencies and aggressive foreign policy behavior repeatedly put the Bush administration at a disadvantage whenever
disputes arose. On the one hand, the president personally sought to
minimize the impact of major disagreements or disappointments on his
close friendship with Putin or the stated benefits of the U.S.-Russian relationship. That reluctance persisted despite backsliding on democratic
principles during parliamentary elections in December 2002 and Putin's
reelection campaign in early 2003, the end of competitive elections at
the gubernatorial level, the Kremlin's vendetta against Yukos CEO
Khodorkovsky, and Putin's meddling in the disputed Ukrainian presidential election in late 2004. At the same time, Bush's glossing over of

problems was counterbalanced by top officials such as Secretary of State Powell, who were willing to issue public criticism of Putin's policies or make veiled hints about policy reviews. Still, it is hard to point to significant changes to the overall direction of the Bush administration's Russia policy since September 11 or any costs that Putin incurred as a result of the problems that beset the relationship since early 2002. If anything, the various crises in the U.S.-Russian relationship during this period reinforced a tendency toward disengagement and passivity on the U.S. side while fostering a deeply entrenched Russian view that the benefits of the relationship were too meager to justify making significant sacrifices to safeguard it.

One telling example of the distortions caused by the Bush administration's approach to managing relations with Russia is the fact that the most frequent visitor to Moscow during the first term appears to have been its point-person on nonproliferation, Under Secretary of State John Bolton. The administration's willingness to relegate high-level engagement with Russia to a figure with Bolton's portfolio (always a source of controversy in Russian policymakers' eyes) and hard-line political views clearly conveyed the issue's limited importance in Bush's foreign policy agenda. Nor has Bolton's prominence helped generate significant progress on one of the most important issues in his portfolio—Iran's nuclear program.[46] It is abundantly clear that overreliance on officials at Bolton's level and below to keep the relationship on track inherently limited development of the relationship with Moscow and left it highly vulnerable to the ravages of fate and external shocks. This chronic lack of high-level involvement has made it nearly impossible to inject dynamism or achieve course corrections in U.S.-Russian relations at key moments, let alone advance the U.S. interests at stake in Russia's transformation.

Thus, it is not entirely surprising that the U.S.-Russian relationship counted for little at key moments in the Iraq crisis. Of course, Putin also bears considerable responsibility for the tensions that eventually overwhelmed a once-promising opening in U.S.-Russian relations after September 11. Had he made the case to the Russian people about why Russia needed a more innovative approach to relations with the United States, he might have built the type of cushion that the relationship needed when tensions over Iraq erupted. And had Putin's efforts been matched by a concerted attempt on the part of the United States to show that the relationship was indeed mutually beneficial, the rift over Iraq might have been circumvented. Instead, the U.S. administration seemed to feel it was simply entitled to Russian support, and when that support waned, key members of the national security team hardly worked at trying to preserve it.

To the Russians, the ambitions and goals of U.S. foreign policy in the post–September 11 period moved too far, too fast, and the Bush doctrine of preemptive war threatened to create precedents they were loath to accept. Even on the issue of terrorism where U.S. and Russian views were the most compatible, there was little persuasive evidence that the Bush administration regarded Russia as a true ally, let alone one worthy of intense interaction or joint policy formulation. For all the emphasis on the personal chemistry between Bush and Putin, the Bush administration was simply unable—or unwilling—to convert it into closer, more substantive cooperation. It should be no surprise that Bush's team ended its first term just where it began, with an arms-length U.S.-Russian relationship and few fond feelings for a country many officials see as a marginal player in the post–Cold War world.

Notes

[1] This view was most forcefully expressed by Condoleezza Rice who had suggested in 1999 that the United States should "quarantine" Russia in light of its record of misdeeds and disruptive international behavior (quoted in James Carney, "Our New Best Friend?" *Time*, May 27, 2002). For an authoritative description of Russia policy during the early days of the Bush administration, see James M. Goldgeier and Michael McFaul, *Power and Purpose: U.S. Policy toward Russia after the Cold War* (Washington, D.C.: Brookings Institution Press, 2003), pp. 309–313.

[2] Strobe Talbott's memoir, *The Russian Hand* (New York: Random House, 2003) provides a detailed account of the frustrations that Clinton and his team experienced in trying to engage Putin during 2000 and the clear impression that Putin was, in Clinton's phrase, "treading water."

[3] Author's conversation with Liliya Shevtsova, Moscow Carnegie Center, January 20, 2004.

[4] See George W. Bush, "Address to a Joint Session of Congress and the American People," Washington, D.C., September 20, 2001, at http://www.whitehouse.gov/news/releases/2001/09/20010920-8.html.

[5] George W. Bush, "Statement by the President in His Address to the Nation," Washington, D.C., September 11, 2001, at http://www.whitehouse.gov/news/releases/2001/09/20010911-11.html.

[6] "DoD News Briefing—Deputy Secretary Wolfowitz," Pentagon, September 13, 2001, at http://www.defenselink.mil/news/Sep2001/t09132001_t0913dsd.html. In a precursor of the bitter debates that would later destroy the cohesiveness of Bush's

foreign policy team, Wolfowitz's comment was immediately refuted by Secretary of State Colin Powell. Quoted in Robin Wright and Doyle McManus "Bush Camp Split on Anti-Terror Policy," *Los Angeles Times*, September 21, 2001, p. 6.

[7] See http://www.whitehouse.gov/news/releases/2002/01/20020129-11.html.

[8] See http://www.whitehouse.gov/nsc/nssintro.html.

[9] Putin had actually spoken to National Security Adviser Condoleezza Rice; Bush himself was unavailable amid the confusion that delayed his return to Washington from an appearance in Florida. Putin told Rice that he was canceling a Russia military exercise in the Russian Far East, presumably in the hope that it would free up U.S. intelligence assets to respond to the urgent terrorist threat. See Dan Balz and Bob Woodward, "America's Chaotic Road to War; Part I: Bush's Global Strategy Began to Take Shape in First Frantic Hours after Attack," *Washington Post*, January 27, 2001, p. A1.

[10] Author's conversation with Shevtsova.

[11] Author's conversation with Sergey Karaganov, Council on Foreign and Defense Policy, January 2004.

[12] At a EU-Russian summit meeting in November 2002, Putin lashed out at a *Le Monde* reporter for critical questioning about Russian human rights abuses in Chechnya. Putin menacingly suggested that the reporter might want to "go all the way" and join the ranks of Islamic militants in Chechnya, but added that he should first travel to Moscow to be circumcised. The violent undertone of Putin's remarks ("I would recommend that he who does the surgery does it so you'll have nothing growing back, afterward") provoked official criticism from the EU as well as Muslim governments. Russian officials later ascribed Putin's performance to fatigue and frustration with the reporter's questions. Quoted in Associated Press, "Putin: Non-Muslims Target of Rebels," November 12, 2002. See also Michael Wines, "Why Putin Boils Over: Chechnya is His Personal War," *New York Times*, November 13, 2002, p. A16.

[13] Quoted in Michael Wines, "To Free the Way for the U.S., or Not? Either Way a Fateful Choice for Russia, *New York Times*, September 21, 2001, p. B2. See also Daniel Williams, "Putin's Tilt to the West Riles Three Key Groups; Powerful Constituencies Still Distrustful of U.S.," *Washington Post*, November 25, 2001, p. A24.

[14] See Avet Demourian, "Russian Defense Minister Denies Possibility of Anti-Terrorist Offensive Launched from Central Asia," Associated Press, September 14, 2001.

[15] Remarks by President Bush and Russian President Putin in Press Availability at Camp David, September 27, 2003, at http://www.whitehouse.gov/news/releases/2003/09/20030927-2.html.

[16] Author's conversation with Shevtsova.

[17] Putin himself had stirred up controversy in summer 2000 by threatening to launch airstrikes against the Taliban because of its support for Chechen militants. When questioned privately in June 2000 by a visiting President Clinton about the airstrike threat, Putin had suggested that making threats, even patently unrealistic ones, was one of Russia's only means of leverage on the Taliban.

[18] Author's conversation with Karaganov.

[19] See BBC Worldwide Monitoring, "Putin Spells out Russia's Stand on U.S. Anti-Terrorist Operation," Russian Public TV (ORT), September 24, 2001.

[20] Ibid.

[21] Curiously enough, many of Putin's lines of argument in the 1999–2000 period sound oddly prescient about the threat of jihadist terrorism even though they completely distorted the nature of the Chechen conflict. For example, during a visit to London shortly after he was elected president in April 2000, Putin told a press conference: "We aren't interested in enslaving the Chechen people. We are trying to free Chechnya from international terrorists and extremists who pose a threat not only to Russia but to other countries on the continent as well. I have every reason to believe that this international radicalism, hiding behind Muslim slogans, threatens several countries in Central Asia, in the Caucasus, and we can see its manifestations in several European countries." Joint Press conference of President Putin and Prime Minister Blair, April 29, 2000, at http://www.number-10.gov.uk/output/Page3559.asp.

[22] In summer 1999, a group of Islamic militants and Chechen fighters sought to overthrow the government of Dagestan in Russia's north Caucasus region. Following a successful counterattack by Russian military and security forces, many of the militants retreated into neighboring Chechnya, which shortly thereafter became the focus of a full-scale Russian military invasion.

[23] See Anatol Lieven, *Chechnya: Tombstone of Russian Power* (New Haven: Yale University Press, 1998), and Anna Politkovskaya, *A Small Corner of Hell: Dispatches from Chechnya* (Chicago: University of Chicago Press, 2003).

[24] For a balanced account of radical Islamic penetration of the north Caucasus, see Sharon LeFraniere, "How Jihad Made Its Way to Chechnya: Secular Separatist Movement Transformed by Militant Vanguard," *Washington Post*, April 26, 2003, p. A1.

[25] Vladimir Putin, "Why We Must Act," *New York Times*, November 14, 1999.

[26] See Ambassador-at-Large Stephen Sestanovich, "The Conflict in Chechnya and Its Implications for U.S. Relations with Russia," testimony prepared for the Senate Foreign Relations Committee, November 4, 1999.

[27] Interview with George W. Bush, *The Newshour with Jim Lehrer,* February 16, 2000, at http://www.pbs.org/newshour/bb/election/jan-june00/bush_2-16.html). Ironically enough, Bush's views were actually more or less in alignment with that of

the Clinton administration, which had taken steps to freeze assistance to Russia from the International Monetary Fund and credits from the U.S. Export-Import Bank early in the second Chechen war. For an account of these moves, see Stephen Sestanovich, "Where Does Russia Belong?" *National Interest* 62 (Winter 2000/2001).

[28] See Condoleezza Rice, "Exercising Power without Arrogance," *Chicago Tribune*, December 30, 2000. In the article, she also cast doubt on Russian assertions at the time about outside support for the Chechen cause by countries such as Saudi Arabia.

[29] See White House Press Briefing by Ari Fleischer, September 26, 2001, at http://www.whitehouse.gov/news/releases/2001/09/20010926-5.html). For an account of the internal Bush administration debate on altering its policy on Chechnya, see Alan Sipress, "U.S., Russia Recast Their Relationship; Anti-Terror Agenda Appears to be Framework for Future," *Washington Post*, October 4, 2001, p. A01.

[30] Remarks by President Bush and Russian President Putin in Photo Opportunity, Kananaskis, Canada, June 27, 2002, at http://www.whitehouse.gov/news/releases/2002/06/20020627-3.html.

[31] A more humorous yet telling illustration of the effects of the administration's inconsistent public posture was caused by tough-minded testimony about Chechnya by Ambassador Steven Pifer, deputy assistant secretary of state for European and Eurasian affairs, in September 2003. Shortly after Pifer's appearance, Putin was asked to respond during an interview with American journalists: "I wouldn't like to comment on mid-level State Department officials. I'll let Colin [Powell] deal with him. He is a pro and a very decent man. . . . But we have a proverb in Russia—in every family there will be somebody who is ugly or retarded. So if somebody wants to cast a shadow on the Russian-U.S. relationship, that's not hard to do."

[32] For descriptions of U.S. efforts to curtail foreign financial flows to Chechen militants, see Vladimir Isachenkov, "U.S. Ambassador: Washington Helped Cut off Aid to Terrorists in Chechnya," Associated Press, December 28, 2001. See also Vershbow's briefing at the Carnegie Endowment for International Peace, January 3, 2003, Federal News Service transcript.

[33] See Paul Quinn-Judge, "Surprise in the Gorge," *Time* (Time.com), October 20, 2002, and Sebastian Rotella, "Extremists Find Fertile Soil in Europe: Threat of War in Iraq Is Adding to the Pool of Potential Recruits for Al Qaeda and Others," *Los Angeles Times*, March 2, 2003, p. 1.

[34] Aleksandr Golts, "Time to Start Thinking," *Yezhenedelny Zhurnal*, November 5, 2002, pp. 18–19, Agency WPS translation.

[35] Aleksey Pushkov, "Interests and Principals Are One and the Same," *Nezavisimaya Gazeta,* March 21, 2003, translation by WPS Monitoring Agency.

[36] The Foreign Policy Concept of the Russian Federation, June 20, 2000, at http://www.ln.mid.ru/Brp_4.nsf/0/497C78AFB1AC61C44325699C00260A58? OpenDocument. According to one key passage of the document:

> There is a growing trend towards the establishment of a unipolar structure of the world with the economic and power domination of the United States. In solving principal questions of international security, the stakes are being placed on western institutions and forums of limited composition, and on weakening the role of the UN Security Council.
> The strategy of unilateral actions can destabilize the international situation, provoke tensions and the arms race, aggravate interstate contradictions, national and religious strife. The use of force by bypassing existing international legal mechanisms cannot remove the deep socio-economic, inter-ethnic and other contradictions that underlie conflicts, and can only undermine the foundations of law and order.
> Russia shall seek to achieve a multi-polar system of international relations that really reflects the diversity of the modern world with its great variety of interests.

[37] Vladimir Isachenkov, "Putin Raises Specter of Russia's Taking Tougher Line on Iraq," Associated Press, January 28, 2003.

[38] For a detailed comparison of the passive U.S. diplomatic effort and the actions of France and Germany, see Paul J. Saunders, "The U.S. and Russia after Iraq," *Policy Review*, June/July 2003.

[39] See interview with Khodorkovsky, "A Russian's Plea to Back America," *BusinessWeek Online*, March 14, 2002.

[40] See, for example, Pavel Felgenhauer, "The Russia Connection," *Wall Street Journal*, April 15, 2003, and Sergey Karaganov, "Crisis Lessons," *Moscow News*, no. 15 (2003).

[41] See February 27, 2003, Interfax report, "Russians Support Europeans Opposing War in Iraq," on results of nationwide poll by Public Opinion Foundation, at http://www.cdi.org/russia/johnson/7081a.cfm.

[42] Quoted in Associated Press, "Putin: UN Sanctions Should Not Be Lifted without Confirming Elimination of Weapons of Mass Destruction," April 29, 2003.

[43] See account of background briefing by senior administration official in Jonathan Wright, "Bush, Putin to Meet in Russia June 1," Reuters, May 5, 2004.

[44] See Christopher Marquis, "Russia Sees Iraqi Debt Relief as Link to Oil," *New York Times*, January 17, 2004, section A, p. 8.

[45] For an excellent description of the problematic issues raised by Putin's formulation, see Dmitriy Trenin, "Which Way Forward?" *Moscow Times*, April 30, 2004.

[46] The Bush administration pressed Moscow throughout the post–September 11 period to end Russian entities' cooperation with Iran's nuclear and missile programs and to support EU-led diplomatic efforts to coax Tehran back into compliance with its IAEA obligations. Initial U.S. hopes for a breakthrough on the Iran problem were fed by Putin's April 2001 decision to replace Yevgeny Adamov, the cantankerous and commerically aggressive head of Minatom. Yet Putin stopped

far short of ordering Adamov's successor Aleksandr Rumyantsev to halt Minatom's dealings with Iran and repeatedly expressed confidence in Iran's official denials about its nuclear activities. Thus, Putin was deeply embarrassed by revelations iin 2002 about secret Iranian uranium enrichment and heavy-water production facilities. He reacted nimbly to the new reality by throwing Russia's support behind international demands for a full accounting of Iran's nuclear activities, calling for strengthened IAEA safeguards and requiring Iran to return all spent fuel from the Bushehr reactor complex to Russia. However, the combination of the murky aftermath of the Iraq War, Iran's success in resisting international pressure, and widespread concern about the possibility of a military confrontation between the United States and Iran has allowed Putin to fend off U.S. demands for a tougher Russian approach.

CHAPTER SEVEN

DON'T STAND SO CLOSE TO ME: THE WAR ON TERROR AND U.S.-SAUDI RELATIONS

Jon B. Alterman

INTRODUCTION

The attacks of September 11, 2001, rocked the U.S.-Saudi bilateral relationship to its core. Over more than a half century, the two quite dissimilar countries had built a rich and complex relationship that had become central to each one's conception of its national security. The attacks and their aftermath provoked charges not only that the relationship had become a liability, but also that each country was a leading threat to the other's well-being.

The Saudi response to September 11 illustrated what many Americans viewed as Saudi ambivalence toward the bilateral relationship. Although Saudi government officials and clerics alike publicly condemned the attacks, polling and anecdotal evidence suggest that a large majority of Saudis took some satisfaction in the fact that the mighty United States had suffered, much as the United States had made others suffer around the globe. Others suggested that the United States had brought the attacks on itself by adopting a biased position in the Arab-Israeli conflict.[1] Most overwhelming, however, was a deep and persistent denial of Saudi responsibility for those attacks, ranging from widely repeated claims of a Mossad-CIA conspiracy to justify an attack on the Arab world, to a more sophisticated refusal to allow 15 individuals to define a nation of 20 million. Sorrow, mourning, and regret for the losses of a long-standing ally seemed hard to find.

In the American public sphere, many reacted to the attacks sharply, harshly, and with little ambivalence. Analysts and commentators

The author wishes to thank Neslihan Kaptanoglu, Kari Frame, and Alia Fattouh for their research assistance in completing this chapter.

from across the U.S. political spectrum sought to pin responsibility for the September 11 attacks directly on the Saudi government. Critics variously ascribed the attacks to internal political repression in the kingdom, to official and unofficial support for extremist proselytizing efforts in the kingdom and around the world, and to Islam itself. A slew of books, articles, and speeches called for the U.S. government to recast its relationship with the Saudi government, and many argued that nothing short of regime change in the kingdom could preserve U.S. interests.[2]

For most of its history, the government of Saudi Arabia has appeared obsessed with its external security needs, while judging internal politics to be mostly under control.[3] It persistently sought a close security relationship with the United States and demanded that its internal affairs were its own business. In the 1990s, however, a violent opposition arose with deep ties inside the kingdom and abroad. Now assaulted from within and from without, the Saudi government finds itself on the defensive in a new way.

With the end of the Cold War, the growing evidence of a more pacific Iran, and the ouster of Saddam Hussein in 2003, external threats to the Saudi government have diminished. At the same time, the country's perceived internal threats have multiplied, and the government's close relationship with the United States—previously a bulwark of Saudi security—appears to make it more vulnerable domestically. In the aftermath of September 11, Saudi public opinion has become even more skeptical of U.S. intentions, and too close an identification with U.S. desires puts the Saudi government's nationalist and Islamic credentials at risk, thereby undermining Saudi security instead of enhancing it.[4]

On the most basic level, the Saudi government appears not to see an alternative to an intimate continuing relationship with the United States. Several factors argue for continuing close ties. Saudis have a longstanding pattern of bandwagoning behavior that is unlikely to change, regardless of who is in power in the kingdom. Saudis also continue to feel vulnerable to regional instability and will seek an outside guarantor of Gulf security. An increasing sense of internal threat will create growing demands for technical assistance on domestic security. In all of these areas, U.S. power, influence, and expertise will continue to drive the kingdom toward an ongoing U.S.-Saudi partnership.[5]

The U.S. government is likely to continue to seek close cooperation from the Saudi government as well. Saudi Arabia remains not only a vital source of oil for global markets, but also the main swing producer whose actions can smooth fluctuations in oil prices. Saudi Arabia remains a vital regional actor, with important roles not only in Gulf security but also in areas as diverse as economics, religious life, and the media. Finally, Saudi intelligence cooperation is vital to the success of counterterrorism efforts in the kingdom and around the world.

Yet, the relationship cannot continue as it has been. Events of the last two years create two imperatives in each country. The first is to improve the working relationship on the technical level. A common sense of threat from violent groups suggests that technocrats from each side must jointly address the problems of internal security in the kingdom—narrowly, in a law enforcement sense, more broadly in terms of disrupting the violent networks with ties inside the kingdom, and even more generally in terms of promoting the internal economic and political reforms that many Saudis see as vitally necessary to enhance social harmony.

The second imperative is that each side must create more visible distance in the relationship. In part, this is because a frank assessment must admit that the areas of disagreement between the two countries are large and probably unbridgeable. Pretending otherwise exacerbates tensions rather than alleviates them. Perhaps even more important, however, is to free each side from domestic complaints that, by working with the other government, it is sleeping with the devil.

Refocusing the relationship on narrower yet deeper areas of cooperation will require a combination of effort, discipline, and political leadership, and it is not without its perils. A narrower relationship will further undermine political support in both countries for cooperation, and the United States could find itself tied ever more closely to a weakening government. Pursuing such a course, however, is likely to be the "least bad" option, as the need for tactical cooperation remains urgent and the external political factors that drive the publics apart appear unlikely to change dramatically in the near future.

THE ROOTS OF THE RELATIONSHIP

The Al Saud's effort to unite much of the Arabian Peninsula under its banner took almost two decades of hard-fought combat and skilled diplomacy. Land had to be conquered; tribes' allegiances had to be won. The unification that produced the Kingdom of Saudi Arabia was itself a more creative act than it appeared, for the peninsula itself had not been politically unified since the time of Muhammad.

Despite the challenges of its birth, however, the Saudi royal family has long perceived its primary strategic threats to be external rather than internal. The United Kingdom had been the guarantor of Gulf security since the late nineteenth century but had been retreating east of Suez since the end of the World War II. By the mid-1940s, it was clear to many Saudis—and many Americans—that a close relationship with the United States was the only way Saudi Arabia could counter its external threats. For this reason, the Saudi royal family nurtured a close strategic relationship with the United States despite obvious differences in background and approach.

Saudi policy in the 1940s, 1950s, and 1960s was essentially defensive, as secular nationalist revolutions swept through the Middle East, deposing monarchs and leaving young army officers in their stead. Egypt sought to be the tip of an Arab socialist spear that threatened the existing Arab order, and Saudi Arabia became the defender of that order, checking Egyptian interests, supporting monarchs in Yemen and beyond, and acting as an anticommunist bulwark in a perceived sea of instability.

For many Saudis, the highlight of the U.S.-Saudi relationship came during the Reagan administration, when Saudi Arabia played a key role quietly advancing U.S. foreign policy.[6] In the words of one scholar writing at the dawn of that period, "Because of the United States' role as the leading status quo and anti-Communist global power, there is a natural coincidence of political and strategic interests between the two countries."[7] Not only did Saudi Arabia guarantee stable oil prices during crises in Iran and beyond, but from Afghanistan to Nicaragua, Saudi officials quietly supported U.S. allies and proxies in the Cold War. Saudi aid most often arrived in cash, and it was not subjected to the prying eyes of a sometimes-skeptical Congress. Partly because of such aid, Soviet allies—and ultimately, the Soviet Union—fell.

Throughout this period, the U.S. government maintained a studied disinterest in domestic affairs in Saudi Arabia. Americans in the kingdom lived in separate compounds and, until just a few decades ago, were confined to the southern port of Jeddah and the oil-rich Eastern Province. Indeed, there appeared to be remarkably little interaction between most Saudis and most Americans, and Saudi "peculiarities" were accepted as such. Saudi students came to the United States by the tens of thousands. Many studied business or technical subjects, and although some stayed, many returned home enriched by their experience.

The 1990s were harder on the relationship, as events inside Saudi Arabia began to affect the security of Americans inside the kingdom—and toward the end of the decade, outside of it as well. At the same time, an Islamist opposition in Saudi Arabia became an increasingly vocal critic of the regime's relationship with the U.S. government. Americans were angered and saddened by the bombing of a U.S. military housing facility in al-Khobar in 1996 and the deaths of 19 servicemen. But equally troubling to U.S. officials was the way their Saudi counterparts treated the subsequent investigation. Saudi investigators barred U.S. investigators from interviewing suspects without Saudi officials present. The arrogance each side saw in the other's actions, and the resultant jostling back and forth, left a bitter taste in the mouths of many involved.

During this time, it was clear to many observers that a new kind of political opposition was rising in the kingdom. Resistance had emerged before, from the puritanical *ikhwanis* who opposed an end to raiding and conquest in the 1930s to the radical group that led the capture of the Great Mosque in Mecca in 1979. Heretofore, however, support for such groups had generally been sectarian or tribal, and also short-lived. The opposition that emerged in the 1990s was, on the whole, broad-based and ideological and in many cases had its roots in Saudi government institutions.[8]

The message of the new Saudi militants was something of a hybrid, combining traditional Wahhabi asceticism with a political activism that Muslim Brotherhood exiles from Egypt had imported during the 1950s and 1960s.[9] The resultant call for the overthrow of an insufficiently pious government owes more to the writings of the executed Egyptian militant Sayyid Qutb than to Saudi traditions, in which political ideology tended to play a minor role in justifying conflict.[10]

The immediate irritant appeared to be the presence of 20,000 U.S. troops pre-positioned on Saudi soil since 1990 to deter an Iraqi attack. Opposition, however, had been rising for more than a decade. It drew on a number of factors, including a heightened sense of cultural onslaught (brought on by a combination of information technology and the return of U.S.-educated graduates to the kingdom), dissatisfaction with the royal family, heightened parochialism among domestically educated religious graduates, and the first *intifada*. Many in the Islamist opposition viewed their government's relationship with the United States as compromising, making Saudis complicit in a fundamentally unjust world order. Although Al Qaeda has emerged as the best known and most violent of Saudi opposition groups, it is by no means the only one. Others, such as the Committee for the Defense of Legitimate Rights and the Movement for Islamic Reform in Arabia, were early pioneers of using faxes, videocassettes, and the Internet to generate opposition to the Saudi government.

Saudi dissidents did not advocate Western-style democracy at home, but they did attack the royal family and its conduct, and their voices proved hard to muzzle. Periodic arrests and rehabilitations (presumably following co-optation) of vocal religious critics of the regime challenged the system but ultimately appear to have fallen short of changing it.

In recent years, Al Qaeda's rhetoric has increasingly sought to justify the group's violent attacks by linking them to the Arab-Israeli conflict. Yet an examination of Al Qaeda's rhetoric and recruiting videos strongly suggests that the U.S.-Saudi relationship remains of far higher priority. On September 11, the 19 hijackers—15 of whom were Saudi citizens—appear to have attacked the United States because of its perceived role propping up the Saudi government. In the absence of U.S. support, the thinking went, the Saudi government would crumble, and a government that was more "properly Islamist" in their minds would come to power and defend Muslim interests in the Arabian Peninsula and throughout the world.

NEW PERSPECTIVES

The September 11 attacks fueled a shift in the Saudi government assessment of its security situation in two ways. First, the presence of so many hijackers from Saudi Arabia (followed later by revelations of the depth of operational support violent groups command within the kingdom and bloody suicide bombings in Riyadh in 2003) forced acceptance of the idea that tensions inside the kingdom were more serious than had been previously acknowledged. Most vexing for the Saudi leadership, those advocating violent overthrow of the regime appeared well ensconced in some sectors of the Saudi religious community. The rulers had always tied their popular legitimacy to their piety and their support of the clerics in the country, and what had been a sacrosanct domain came under immediate scrutiny.

Second, Saudis increasingly came to view the U.S.-Saudi relationship as a political liability—a view that was shared by many across the Atlantic. The relationship did provide external security to the regime and energy security to the world, but it also opened the Saudi regime up to internal accusations of hypocrisy and moral corruption. At the same time, the relationship opened the U.S. government to criticism that it was nurturing and protecting a government that bore a large portion of responsibility for the events of September 11.

Saudi cooperation with U.S. officials in the months following September 11 was often cooperative but, according to contemporaneous accounts, rarely swift or complete. Meetings could take months to arrange, and Saudi officials often complained that they did not have the institutional capacity to fully comply with U.S. wishes. U.S. desires for swift action and complete information often clashed with Saudi preferences for more deliberative processes, tolerance of ambiguity, and discretion that often looked more like secrecy.

One of the most commonly expressed feelings by Saudis in the months following September 11 was that they, too, were the victims of September 11. In their minds, Saudi Arabia had been a stalwart ally of long standing, yet the kingdom had suffered through an international campaign of harassment and suspicion, a frontal attack on Saudi charitable organizations, and an energetic drive for financial transparency.

These feelings of victimhood came to tragic fruition for Saudi Arabia on May 12, 2003, when suicide bombers attacked three housing complexes in Riyadh, killing 34 people. Again, on November 9, attackers drove two bomb-laden trucks into a Riyadh compound housing Arab expatriates. The attacks led not only to widespread acknowledgment in the Saudi government that they had a serious internal problem, but also a growing sense that the government's survival depended on confronting that problem squarely, energetically, and with a maximum of international cooperation. Voices calling for activism grew louder, while those arguing for the adequacy of extant efforts fell silent.

COERCION AND CO-OPTATION

The Saudi government's diverse approaches to the problem of terrorism all had their roots in the period before May 12, but its actions have become far more vigorous in the months since. Since then, the Saudi government has embarked on a range of activities that split the response to terrorism problem into two parts—coercion and co-optation.

Coercion encompasses law enforcement and intelligence activities. The Saudi government has redoubled its efforts to surveil, arrest, and sometimes kill members of radical groups whom they view as threatening to the safety of people in the kingdom. Although much of their activity remains out of view, one anonymous senior Saudi government official boasted to the Washington Post, "We have killed more Al Qaeda people than any other country in the world."[11] From outside government, it is impossible to determine just how complete Saudi law enforcement and intelligence cooperation has been, or whether there are areas of activity in which such cooperation has been lacking. However, U.S. government officials uniformly praise Saudi cooperation as "unprecedented,"[12] even if they sometimes fall short of calling it "complete."[13]

Cooperation has also been extensive in the area of financial transparency—especially in the area of monitoring cash flows to Saudi charities, which had been lightly regulated in the period before September 11. U.S. Treasury officials work closely with their Saudi counterparts, helping draft improved regulations to govern day-to-day behavior as well as cooperating with investigations of past behavior. In regard to the former, the Saudi Arabian Monetary Agency (SAMA) issued new regulations on May 27, 2003, to promote transparency and accountability of charitable accounts and to crack down on money laundering. SAMA's efforts were directly tied to implementing the so-called FATF 40+8 Recommendations, a series of measures recommended by the Financial Action Task Force to restrict the flow of illicit funds around the globe.[14]

The U.S. Treasury and the Saudi government jointly asked the United Nations to add four branches of the al-Haramain Islamic Foundation, a Saudi-based charity, to its list of terrorist-related entities.[15] The Saudi government had ordered the charity to close all its overseas offices in 2003, but Saudi and U.S. officials agreed that some offices had continued to function, often under different names. In taking joint action against the organization's branches in Indonesia, Kenya, Tanzania, and Pakistan, the Saudi government demonstrated a depth of cooperation that would have been hard to imagine in the not-so-distant past. The Saudi and U.S. governments have also established joint task forces on terrorism and terror financing, facilitating the exchange of people and expertise. Even so, many specialists view Saudis as more willing to promise than to follow through and see signs that internal political considerations sometimes appear to trump promises made to others. In the words of one critic, "U.S. officials' priority, then, is to get the Saudis to do what they've already promised to do."[16]

Co-optation involves promoting internal reform—political, economic, and religious—to ameliorate those conditions that are thought to drive young Saudis toward support for terrorist actions. Reform, however, is not purely the province of what are thought of as government reformers, and disagreements exist about the areas that need reform, the nature of reform that needs to take place, and the appropriate timetable.

Among the most visible areas of reform is the Saudi political system, which continues to emphasize the traditional concept of *shura*, or consultation, instead of elections. Political reform long predated September 11, starting with King Fahd's November 1990 announcement of his intention to establish a consultative council, or *majlis al-shura*. In the years since September 11, Crown Prince Abdullah has grown increasingly active leading two kinds of reforms on the domestic political scene. First, he has helped promote a plan to hold elections for the consultative council. Although all members of that council are currently appointed, the Saudi government has signaled the beginning of a process whereby elections would be held for half the seats on municipal councils in the spring of 2005, with consultative council elections to follow in due course. The Saudi plan, though clearly falling short of Western notions of democratic governance in the short term, nonetheless introduces unprecedented and important features of electoral politics.

In addition, Crown Prince Abdullah has been at the center of an effort to promote a "national dialogue" between different ethnic, religious, and political groups in the kingdom. The process is headquartered at the King Abdel Aziz Library in Riyadh, with which he is associated. An initial meeting in Riyadh in June 2003 brought together some 50 Sunni and Shi'a leaders, as well as liberal intellectuals, for a wide-ranging discussion. That meeting was followed by another session in Mecca in December 2003 that brought together 60 clerics and intellectuals (including 10 women) to discuss the topic "Extremism and Moderation." A third forum discussed "Women's Rights and Duties under Shariah," and women—who participated remotely—constituted half of the participants.[17] Although the national dialogue meetings are sometimes criticized in the local press for being closed, participants and close observers note that the frankness and pragmatic approaches that typify the meetings are a novelty for the kingdom and at least hold out the prospect for greater public discourse than has prevailed in Saudi Arabia up to now.

Some Saudis show impatience with the process of dialogue and complain that "there is too much consensus, and there is no leadership."[18] Those Saudis, and even loyal supporters of the royal family, argue that the only way forward is for the U.S. government to present the leadership with a set of specific tasks and specific deadlines to be met. "You understand the entire system," one explained, "and you are the only ones who can make it work."[19] What some Saudis are looking for is to preserve the present system of top-down rule, but to have the U.S. government shore it up by making it more effective and efficient. In a way, they are pleading with the United States to be a better monarch—wise, firm, but fair. At the same time, U.S. officials express impatience with what they see as passivity on the Saudi side, both among government officials and the public. Their hope is that the Saudis will become better democrats—innovative, entrepreneurial, and responsible. The result is impatience and frustration on both sides, as each seeks to mold the other into something it is not.

Thus far, the U.S. government has not played a role in Saudi political reform for fear that its endorsement of a step in any direction would delegitimize it. Such a reluctance is likely to continue, despite continuous rhetoric from Washington identifying broader political openness in the Middle East with U.S. strategic interests.

Another area for reform is the economy. In earlier decades, a generous system of subsidies and guaranteed employment, combined with the skillful co-optation of key groups and the maintenance of a strong security apparatus, had kept the system working. A key aspect, no doubt, was the fact that living standards were rising steadily, and children could look forward to a better life than their parents. Dramatic urbanization meant that people who had grown up in mud huts came to spend their middle age living in comparative luxury.

Yet, even before 2001, per capita income was on the decline, from a high of more than $28,000 in 1981 to about $8,000 in 2003. Some estimate the Saudi workforce to be growing by 5 percent per year, but job creation is growing at less than 1 percent a year.[20] The entry of an increasing number of women into the workforce, both by choice and economic necessity, makes that gap grow more quickly than overall population growth. The last time public sector salaries increased was 1977.[21] The numbers masked a harsh reality: that young Saudis were entering a job market with few prospects and few marketable skills. An increasing number were leaving school and entering a void. Some seeking adventure headed overseas to support Islamic causes in Afghanistan, Central Asia, the Balkans, and beyond. Many returned changed, but they faced an uncertain future.

The attacks of September 11, and the subsequent bombings in Riyadh, delivered a shock to the already ailing Saudi economy. Efforts to attract direct foreign investment in order to boost private sector employment for young Saudis were hampered severely, as a high-risk premium spooked potential investors. Some existing investors have pulled out altogether, such as Citigroup, which withdrew from Saudi Arabia after 48 years in the kingdom. In October 2003, the company announced it was transferring its half share in the Saudi-American Bank (SAMBA) to local management. By most accounts, the decision was prompted by reasons of security, not profitability.

Higher oil prices have thrust the Saudi budget into surplus in recent years—$26.1 billion in 2004, representing a third again over expenses. The sudden availability of capital has blunted some of the urgency of economic change, but has not removed its necessity. Left unaddressed, Saudi economic problems, and especially those facing the labor force, will only grow over time.

Although by no means driving economic reforms in Saudi Arabia, the United States has been playing something of an enabling role, working with Saudi counterparts for more than a decade to gain Saudi accession to the World Trade Organization (WTO). Some in the U.S. government have argued that WTO accession could be the trigger for a wide range of internal reforms—not only in Saudi Arabia, but also in other countries in which the political and economic systems are deeply intertwined and nontariff barriers add costs and inefficiencies to economic activity while providing a fertile environment for corruption. In this regard, U.S. government officials have worked to stoke Saudi interest in accession, at the same time seeking to ensure that the Saudis have to meet the same high bar as other countries.

A third area of activity is in educational reform. Although the Saudi educational system has expanded to encompass the vast bulk of the population and made illiteracy almost unknown among young Saudis, critics charge that religious instruction squeezes out time devoted to other subjects and that, even more important, the entire curriculum emphasizes rote memorization over reasoning skills. Reference works, technology, and other tools make memorizing information relatively less important for many jobs than creativity and flexible thinking, yet Saudis remain uncertain about abandoning traditional educational methods. On the curricular front, Saudis themselves have undertaken efforts to revise the textbooks used in school curricula, and the Shura Council's recently passed educational bill explicitly calls for an emphasis on moderation in religion classes. Efforts have also been undertaken to improve female education and to open community colleges and vocational schools for students who do not continue on to university.

Foreign involvement in educational reform, where it exists, has generally been out of public view. Saudis have conducted discreet discussions with foreign governments about foreign language teaching, for example, but changing the core curriculum remains the sole province of Saudis and, to a large extent, the clerical base.

A final area of activity, and certainly the most sensitive for the government, is religious reform. The government of Saudi Arabia has always reserved a unique role for the clerical establishment and has traditionally accorded clerics a wide ambit of freedom. Indeed, Al Saud rulers have been allied with religious reformers since the initial agreements between Muhammad ibn Abdel Wahhab and Muhammad ibn Saud in the eighteenth century, following through the second and third Saudi kingdoms. In recent years, however, the Saudi government has become increasingly concerned that some elements of the clerical establishment were working against the interests of the public good, through their embrace of radical teachings, their opposition to the continued rule of the Al Saud, or some combination of the two. As one government official put it recently, "The religious argue that we told you how to live, you don't, and we're not responsible."[22]

The government has been moving firmly to discredit what it considers "deviant" understandings of Islam and to damage the credentials of those who stray outside those understandings. Although a senior official's estimate that "99 percent of people consider them fanatics" is almost certainly overblown,[23] it gives a good indication of where government would like to go. In recent months officials have put a renewed emphasis on encouraging radicals to recant their beliefs and to appeal to others to renew their loyalty to official doctrine. According to one account, 2,000 imams have been suspended from their positions for "straying outside the bounds of religion and/or engaging in political activity," and another 1,500 have been referred to educational programs to ensure that their message is not one of extremism. Further, the government has encouraged Saudis to view those seeking the overthrow of the regime as "misguided youth," more in need of proper education than punishment.[24]

In addition to the fruit borne of this public relations effort, the Saudi regime may also be the recipient of some unintentional help from militants within the kingdom. Beginning with the May 2003 attack, the radicals carried out more than 15 violent actions, but the large number of the victims were Muslims, many of them Saudis. The extremists' decision to carry out an attack against the American consulate in Jeddah in December 2004—in which they killed only non-Americans—can be interpreted as a sign of chagrin, if not some desperation, that their violence has been failing to attract a broader constituency. That said, such violence has undoubtedly had a corrosive effect on confidence in domestic security among expatriates, particularly in the wake of several assassinations and the June 2004 kidnapping and beheading of Lockheed Martin employee Paul Johnson. This could yet lead to a damaging exodus of foreign workers, which may be a greater near-term threat than the jihadists themselves to Saudi Arabia, whose economy depends heavily on foreign-born talent.

ACTIVITIES ABROAD

Although the rising importance of an internal opposition is driving changes to Saudi security policy, Saudi Arabia's external environment, and particularly issues related to its bilateral relationship with the United States, looms large in its calculations. In this regard, two issues are primary. The first is the Arab-Israeli conflict. Historically, Saudi Arabia has been a steadfast defender of Arab rights in Palestine, and Saudi rulers from King Abdel Aziz ibn Saud to the present have consistently raised the plight of the Palestinians with American presidents. In the middle of the last century, Saudi Arabia barred Jews from visiting the kingdom, and for decades Saudi Arabia led an Arab League boycott of companies that did business with Israel.

Although figures are unavailable, official and unofficial Saudis, in private and public capacities, have contributed vast sums for Palestinian relief. The Saudi government has contributed between $80 million and $100 million to the Palestinian Authority every year, despite deeply strained ties with the late Palestinian leader Yasser Arafat. In September 2003, a *New York Times* article estimated that approximately half of the $10 million annual Hamas budget comes from Saudi donors, although Saudi government officials were swift to reassure that none of those donors are governmental.[25] Although not all the Saudi money that flows to Palestinian causes is intended to support acts of violence, some certainly does. In addition, some funds go to support the social wings of organizations that also carry out violent activities.

At least in conversations with Western interlocutors, Saudis are indignant at any suggestion that their support for Palestine constitutes support for terrorism. Such indignation arises in part because Saudi donors profess that their support for the Palestinians is primarily humanitarian rather than political; at the same time, the widespread belief in the legitimacy of armed resistance to the Israeli occupation suggests few Saudis view attacks on Israel as terrorism. For these reasons, private support for Hamas is unlikely to diminish, at least in the near term.

For the past two decades, however, Saudi Arabia has also been a significant supporter of Arab-Israeli peace efforts. Saudi officials have met prominent American leaders to discuss efforts at reconciliation, and they have quietly relaxed some of their support for boycotts and other efforts to isolate Israel. Most significantly, Crown Prince Abdullah introduced and secured passage of an Arab League initiative in March 2002 that promised Israel "full normalization for full withdrawal." Although the plan itself was overwhelmed by subsequent events—a suicide bombing at a Passover Seder that killed more than 20 Israelis and an Israeli incursion into the West Bank that produced scores of casualties—it represented a level of unprecedented Saudi creativity and activism for settlement.

In its efforts to support a peaceful settlement of the Arab-Israeli conflict, the Saudi government is almost certainly ahead of, rather than following, mainstream Saudi public opinion. Support for the Palestinian cause, the importance of Arab control over Muslim holy sites, and resentment at foreign control of traditionally Arab territories are ideas that are inculcated early and deeply in Saudi society. Indeed, 94 percent of Saudis polled in July 2003 held unfavorable impressions of U.S. policy toward the Arab-Israeli conflict.[26] Further, Saudis perceive their natural role—by reason of wealth and control of the holy sites of Mecca and Medina—as protectors of Arab and Muslim interests, of which the Palestinian cause is among the most central. If the Saudis were able to effectively lead the Arab world toward conciliation and could find an effective Israeli partner in that task, the nature of the Arab-Israeli conflict could change significantly.

At the same time, Saudi perceptions of American indifference to Arab-Israeli peacemaking are an irritant to bilateral relations. In the eyes of many, President Bush's use of the word "Palestine" in a November 2001 speech—the first ever by an American president—was part of an effort to allay concerns the Saudis raised the previous summer. Given the urgency and necessity of counterterrorism cooperation for Saudi decisionmakers, such cooperation is unlikely to end on account of perceived U.S. inaction on resolving the Arab-Israeli conflict. Still, the U.S. position on that conflict is likely to remain the central point of reference for U.S.-Saudi relations well into the future and could make cooperation on a wide range of issues of common concern far more difficult.

The other key diplomatic issue Saudi Arabia has been facing for the past decade involves Iraq. At first the donor of an estimated $25 billion to Iraq in its battle against Iran in the 1980s, the Saudis found themselves deeply threatened by the Iraqi invasion of Kuwait in 1990. The subsequent U.S. troop presence in the kingdom carried with it its own problems, however, and aroused considerable public opposition. As U.S. officials began to muse more openly in 1998 about the desire for regime change in Iraq, the Saudi leadership found itself caught. As defenders of the Arab cause, they could not very well come out openly for an attack on a fellow Arab country, but as members of a regime that felt itself in Saddam Hussein's sights, they strongly desired his early departure.

Saudis were deeply conflicted. Publicly, they opposed military action against Iraq and called on Iraqis to overthrow their government. Privately, they urged the United States either to mount an effective covert effort to depose him or to launch a lightning-fast military strike that would decapitate the regime but not provoke long-term resentment. The government's desires and its public imperatives made for some uncomfortable moments for all concerned, such as when Crown Prince Abdullah embraced then Iraqi vice president Ezzat Ibrahim al-Douri at the March 2002 Arab League Summit.

When the U.S. attack on Iraq came in March 2003, Saudi Arabia publicly remained above the fray, although the government quietly allowed U.S. Special Forces to mount ground operations out of bases in northern Saudi Arabia and allowed command and control, surveillance, refueling, and other logistical support to be carried out at the Prince Sultan Airbase at Al Kharj. It barred, however, attack aircraft from taking off from Saudi territory. In August 2003, U.S. troops turned over the facility at Al Kharj to Saudi Arabia and ended a military presence in the kingdom that dated to 1990. U.S. and Saudi officials hoped that the end of a U.S. military presence in the kingdom would help ease tempers in Saudi Arabia and in the United States.

Yet the U.S. presence in Iraq creates two problems for Saudi Arabia. First, most Saudis continue to view the occupation of an Arab land as an affront to Muslim dignity. Second, jihadist fighters—including veterans of the last decade's fighting in Afghanistan as well as a new generation of recruits—may be slipping across the border into Iraq, where they carry out attacks against U.S. troops. Over the longer term, they may also pose an internal security problem if they survive the fighting and return to the kingdom.

A third issue, which is more commercial than diplomatic but still has important diplomatic effects, involves Saudi Arabia's role as a swing producer of oil in world markets. Saudi officials have set a target band for oil at approximately $25 per barrel, and they have often acted to boost production when it rises to more than $28 per barrel. Higher prices could have severe repercussions and could slow world economic growth. Saudi interest in a stable price band is not completely altruistic, however. Slower economic growth could cut demand for oil, as it did in the Asian Financial Crisis of 1997–1999, which drove oil prices down into the mid-teens. The U.S. war against Iraq could have been part of a "perfect storm" of shocks to the oil market, as it disrupted shipments from Iraq and was accompanied by an oil workers' strike in Venezuela and civil unrest in Nigeria. Saudis boosted production by 1 million barrels a day, reassuring markets and significantly smoothing economic shocks to the global economy.

At the same time, the Saudi government appears to be taking some steps to diversify its relationships. Crown Prince Abdullah made an unprecedented trip to Russia in September 2003, presumably discussing, at least in part, production strategies with the world's second-largest exporter of oil and leading holder of natural gas reserves. In March 2004, Saudi Arabia signed gas exploration contracts with Russian, Italian, Spanish, and Chinese companies, but none with their U.S. counterparts. To veteran observers of Saudi actions, the inability of any U.S. company to win a contract was more than a coincidence.

THE LOBBYISTS ARE COMING

Besides their internal efforts to co-opt and coerce potential opposition and their labors to employ skillful diplomacy, Saudis have also embarked on a vigorous public campaign to mute criticism in the West. The Saudi government has hired a number of prominent Washington lobbying firms, including Patton Boggs and Akin Gump, and has engaged a public relations firm, Qorvis Communications. According to press reports, the Qorvis contract is worth $200,000 per month and covers both a short- and long-term media strategy for the kingdom.[27] Total spending for public relations, lobbying, and advertising in the two years since September 11, 2001, was reportedly $17.6 million.[28]

Saudis have certainly become savvier in their public relations. They stage an increasing number of joint appearances with their American counterparts that highlight their cooperation with counterterrorism efforts. In July 2003, when leaks about a classified chapter of a congressional report criticizing the kingdom hit the news, the Saudis appealed for the chapter's release. In so doing, they sent a message of openness and willingness to accept criticism, which helped their image. The report remained classified, and they did not have to publicly respond to the charges contained in it.

PROBLEMS FROM WASHINGTON

All of the tensions in the bilateral relationship cannot be traced to Saudi behavior, and some are far beyond Saudi control. The U.S. government's standing in Saudi Arabia is perhaps at an all-time low, and a rapid reversal in its fortunes appears unlikely. As suggested above, many Saudis feel aggrieved and even persecuted by U.S. actions. In addition, they see a campaign against Saudi Arabia under way within the U.S. government, ranging from leaks of Pentagon briefings calling for regime change to moves in Congress to push through a "Saudi Accountability Act" analogous to the "Syria Accountability Act" that passed late in 2003. Saudi officials complain bitterly that their direct interlocutors praise their cooperation, while shadowy critics call for their downfall.

One issue very much on the minds of the Saudi public is the fate of U.S.-held prisoners at Camp X-Ray in Guantanamo Bay. Saudis complain bitterly that such prisoners have been denied any semblance of due process and that the United States has little idea when or under what conditions it might free them.[29]

At the same time, law-abiding Saudis with long-standing ties to the United States argue that the rapid and dramatic tightening of visa procedures in the wake of September 11 makes it impossible for young Saudi males to visit the United States and develop the same kinds of ties to the country that their parents did. Their complaints partly concern the difficulty of getting a visa itself, but even more overwhelmingly concern the opaque and uncertain nature of the process, in which applications take months to process with little indication of when an answer can be expected.[30]

Most fundamentally, Saudis complain that these measures, combined with U.S. homeland security procedures, the investigations of Muslim charities in the United States and abroad, the invasion of Iraq, and U.S. government support for Israel, add up to a coherent plan to wage war on Islam and on Muslims. In this regard, some see any Saudi government move to accommodate U.S. concerns to be capitulating to U.S. designs of conquest. According to several interlocutors in Saudi Arabia, perhaps 60 percent of Saudis argue for the country to go its own way and to disregard its relationship with the United States, while some 40 percent favor moving forward within the rubric of that relationship.[31] Complicating matters still further, some view criticism of the United States as a proxy for criticizing the royal family in Saudi Arabia, a traditional taboo. At the core, some say, is the complete inability of the Al Saud "either to build support or build a vision for where they want to take the country."[32] Although that is likely true in part, if all criticism of the United States in the kingdom were indeed directed at the royal family, then the latter is far more unpopular than it is willing to admit.

WHITHER THE RELATIONSHIP?

Although the U.S.-Saudi bilateral relationship has clearly been damaged by the events of September 11, the challenge of dealing with internal politics in Saudi Arabia would have complicated the relationship even without a catastrophic terrorist event. Terrorist actions have exacerbated emerging political and economic challenges, but they have not created them, nor will eliminating the terrorist threat make them go away. Saudi Arabia is undergoing a process of change, and charting the future of the country will require a constant reevaluation of the Saudi government's internal and external relationship.

At the same time, the events of September 11 forced a reevaluation of U.S. security strategy that recast the relationship with Saudi Arabia. Although U.S. government officials had been aware of ties from the kingdom to individuals and organizations around the world, such ties were not thought to pose a direct threat to American citizens and to U.S. interests. After September 11, that determination changed.

Security strategies in both the United States and Saudi Arabia are in a state of flux and are likely to remain so for some time. In part, bureaucracies are in the process of adjusting to new challenges, determining both priorities and the methods to achieve them. Equally important, political leadership continues to grapple with the challenges of building a new strategy. They are particularly struggling to understand their adversaries' responses to their actions as well as the political costs of various courses of action. The learning curves in this regard are likely to remain steep for at least the next five years as new organizations are staffed, capabilities are built up, priorities are refined, and lessons are learned.

Despite the difficulties, the government of Saudi Arabia has little choice but to continue a close relationship with the U.S. government, and the U.S. government has little alternative but to do the same with the Saudis. It is not only a matter of shared interests and shared enemies but also the lack of a true alternative. As violent opposition to the relationship remains vigorous, only action on each side—and concerted action between both sides—can address that challenge.

Opening up Saudi Arabia to processes of internal dialogue and political openness is not a panacea, and it is a course that could go badly wrong. A more democratic Saudi Arabia would almost certainly be more wary of a close relationship with the United States, at least in the near term, and the U.S. ability to lead Saudi reform is highly constrained. Any U.S. efforts that would appear to represent an imprimatur on Saudi reform would almost certainly backfire.

What is needed in the relationship is visible distance, yet heightened cooperation behind the scenes. Striking such a balance is difficult, as news is increasingly hard to compartmentalize, opponents of the relationship speak loudly in each country, and proponents of the relationship seek support for their cause.

The dangers in such a course are clear. Most obviously, the lack of visible coordination can undermine political support in each country for the bilateral relationship, making further cooperation harder. Both sides need to work to define and develop areas of close cooperation that serve their domestic agendas, while not providing fodder to the enemies of such cooperation on the other side. One of the most difficult tasks in this regard will be striking a balance between U.S. leadership on the one hand and respect for Saudi counterparts on the other. Without both, longer-term cooperation will be difficult.

The other danger is what critics see as hitching one's wagon to a losing horse. Even friends of Saudi Arabia foresee the country continuing on a downward spiral for some time, and longtime observers of U.S. diplomacy in the Middle East predict a long dry spell before the United States regains credibility in the region. Voices on both sides argue that what is necessary is not engagement to produce slow evolutionary change, but a separation between the two parties so sudden and severe that it provokes a reassessment on the other side, including perhaps a change in government. Nongovernmental organizations have a role in addressing both dangers, building interests and enriching perspectives on both sides without the burden of official government sponsorship.

The U.S.-Saudi bilateral relationship has been difficult in the period since September 11 and will likely prove even more so in the years ahead. Despite the difficulties, however, the relationship is a vital one that will increase in importance in the next five years. Devising diplomatic strategies that integrate deepening intelligence, security, military, political, and economic relationships while responding to domestic pressures that will militate against such ties will be a tall order. Such strategies are necessary, however, and without them, neither government will be able to succeed in the coming years.

Notes

[1] In a widely publicized written statement upon the presentation of a $10 million check to New York City mayor Rudolph Giuliani, Prince Alwaleed bin Talal wrote, "At times like this one, we must address some of the issues that led to such a criminal attack. I believe the government of the United States of America should re-examine its policies in the Middle East and adopt a more balanced stance toward the Palestinian cause." Giuliani returned the check (www.cbsnews.com/stories/2001/09/18/national/main311676.shtml).

[2] James Woolsey, former director of the Central Intelligence Agency, told an audience in Los Angeles in April 2003, "We want you nervous. We want you to realize now, for the fourth time in a hundred years, this country and its allies are on the march and that we are on the side of those whom you—the Mubaraks, the Saudi Royal family—most fear: We're on the side of your own people" (www.avot.org/stories/storyReader$138).

[3] See Dale R. Tahtinen, *National Security Challenges to Saudi Arabia* (Washington, D.C.: American Enterprise Institute, 1978), which only deals with external threats.

[4] Author's interview with Saudi government official, Washington, D.C., September 10, 2003. The French author Eric Rouleau argues that Saudis "object to the entire thrust and tenor of Washington's foreign policy, which they see as arbitrary, unjust, and dismissive or contemptuous of Arab interests." Eric Rouleau, "Trouble in the Kingdom," *Foreign Affairs* (July–August 2002): 77. Crown Prince Abdullah was even more blunt: "In the current environment, we find it very difficult to defend America, and so we keep our silence. Because, to be very frank with you, how can we defend America?" "Saudi Affirms U.S. Ties but Says Bush Ignores Palestinians' Cause," *New York Times*, January 29, 2002.

[5] In the words of one Saudi official, "On the surface, there are alternative alliances, such as with Russia. But some peddle the idea that these relationships can be an

alternative to the U.S.-Saudi relationship in the long term. In fact, it would be a disaster for both countries" (author's interview with Saudi government official, Washington, D.C., September 10, 2003).

[6] Author's interview with Saudi businessman, Jeddah, Saudi Arabia, September 16, 2003, and interview with Saudi lawyer, Riyadh, Saudi Arabia, September 13, 2003.

[7] Adeed Dawisha, *Saudi Arabia's Search for Security*, Adelphi Papers no. 158 (London: International Institute for Strategic Studies, 1979–1980), p. 27.

[8] An interesting and relatively early argument that Saudi Arabia was ripe for political upheaval because of social and economic pressures can be found in Mark Heller and Nadav Safran, *The New Middle Class and Regime Stability in Saudi Arabia,* Harvard Middle East Papers, Modern Series, no. 3 (Cambridge, Mass.: Center for Middle Eastern Studies, Harvard University, 1985).

[9] The Brotherhood's members were seeking refuge from Gamal Abdel Nasser, who saw them as a threat. The Kingdom was a natural refuge, because it saw Abdel Nasser as a threat. Although the often urban and educated Muslim Brothers were sometimes a peculiar addition to the still mostly rural Saudi populace, they shared a compatible, yet not identical, attachment to Islamic orthodoxy. As the Kingdom sought labor to staff schools and hospitals and build governmental institutions during this period, it was Egyptians who supplied much the labor. Although they unquestionably helped build many of Saudi Arabia's modern institutions, they also brought with them ideas—such as the necessity of resisting unjust political power—that have had a lingering effect on Saudi society.

[10] The Al Saud have long sought to build out from a religious base, making an eighteenth century alliance with the theologian Muhammad Abdel Wahhab and maintaining it with his descendents, the Al Sheikh, to the present day.

[11] Peter Slevin, "Saudi Bombing Blamed on Al Qaeda," *Washington Post*, November 10, 2003.

[12] Meetings with U.S. government officials in Washington, Jeddah, and Riyadh, September and December, 2003.

[13] It is worth noting in this regard that State Department counterterrorism coordinator Cofer Black was quoted as saying, "I've personally seen great improvement in the cooperation," and Secretary of State Colin Powell referred to the fact that there is "good cooperation with the Saudis" and an "improving level of cooperation." Neither man was willing to characterize that cooperation either as complete or enthusiastic. John Mintz, "U.S., Saudi Arabia Fettering Charity Tied to Terrorism," *Washington Post*, January 23, 2004, p. A17, and Radio Sawa interview with Secretary Colin Powell, August 4, 2003 (www.state.gov/secretary/rm/2003/23005.htm).

[14] See Saudi Arabia Monetary Agency, Banking Inspection Department, "Rules Governing Anti Money Laundering and Combating Terrorist Financing," May 2003, reprinted in *Initiatives and Actions Taken by the Kingdom of Saudi Arabia in*

the War on Terrorism (Washington, D.C.: Royal Embassy of Saudi Arabia, 2003, pp. 30–86.

[15] See www.treas.gov/press/releases/js1108.htm.

[16] Matthew A. Levitt, "Charity Begins in Riyadh: Unfortunately It Often Ends in the Hands of Terrorists," *Weekly Standard* 9, no. 20 (February 2, 2004).

[17] Maha Akeel, "Next National Dialogue to Focus on Women's Rights, Says Al-Rajih," *Arab News*, January 11, 2004, p. 1.

[18] Author's interview with Saudi businessman, Jeddah, Saudi Arabia, September 16, 2003.

[19] Author's interview with prominent Saudi journalist, Jeddah, Saudi Arabia, September 15, 2003.

[20] See SAMBA and *Dallas Morning News*, July 16, 2003.

[21] *Financial Times*, December 1, 1999.

[22] Author's interview with Saudi government official, Washington, D.C., September 10, 2003.

[23] Author's interview with senior Saudi official, Riyadh, Saudi Arabia, December 13, 2003.

[24] Author's interview with secretary general of Saudi NGO, Riyadh, Saudi Arabia, September 14, 2003.

[25] Don Van Natta Jr. with Timothy L. O'Brien "Hamas Document Hints at Saudi Aid," *New York Times*, September 17, 2003 (www.iht.com/articles/110195.html).

[26] Mary E. Morris, "At a Crossroads: American Policy and the Middle East" (www.arabialink.com/Archive/GWPersp/GWP2004/GWP_2004_01_29.htm).

[27] Christopher Marquis, "Worried Saudis Try to Improve Image in the U.S.," *New York Times*, August 29, 2002.

[28] Joe Carey, "Saudis Spending to Improve Image in the U.S.," Associated Press, October 28, 2003.

[29] Author's interview with local Saudi official, Jeddah, Saudi Arabia, September 16, 2003.

[30] Author's interview with Saudi businessman, Jeddah, Saudi Arabia, September 15, 2003.

[31] Ibid.

[32] Author's interview with Saudi lawyer, Riyadh, Saudi Arabia, September 13, 2003.

CHAPTER EIGHT

TECTONIC SHIFTS:
A NEW GLOBAL LANDSCAPE

Julianne Smith

INITIAL INTERNATIONAL CALCULATIONS, EXPECTATIONS, AND INCENTIVES

In the days following September 11, the United States issued a global call to join, in the words of former Secretary of State Colin Powell, "a great coalition to conduct a campaign against terrorists who are conducting war against civilized people."[1] The response was overwhelmingly positive. Dozens of countries around the world swiftly promised unconditional support in the form of political, diplomatic, economic, legal, and in some cases, military assistance in a global fight against terrorism. New partnership initiatives both between states and within international organizations were launched almost daily in the weeks following the September 11 attacks. Many world leaders spoke of a new era of international cooperation.

But as the United States began to outline a concrete agenda for the war on terrorism, countries around the world, especially those that had a somewhat thorny relationship with the United States (China, Pakistan, and to a certain extent, Russia) were forced to determine just how deep their cooperation would run. Potential partners had to calculate both the costs and benefits of offering an array of military, political, and economic assistance in an environment where historical and operational norms seemed to disappear. Decades of classic state responses to U.S. behavior were superseded to a large extent by the impulses and emotions of national leaders who looked at this pivotal moment in history through a wide variety of lenses. Some leaders looked at the post–September 11 era as an extraordinary window of opportunity—a chance to improve bilateral ties with the United States and thereby enhance their global standing. Others were far more apprehensive or suspicious of U.S. motives.

Although no two countries shared the same formula in calculating their participation to the global campaign against terrorism, many of them relied on the same fundamental ingredients. Between September 11 and the war in Iraq, the strategic calculations that leaders made tended to be based on the following factors: the perceived existence of a mutual threat, domestic constraints, the real or perceived benefits of cooperation, the personal relationship between President Bush and other foreign leaders, and historical relationships.

Global threat perceptions concerning terrorism varied widely after September 11. Some countries, such as Indonesia, perceived the threat of jihadist-based terrorism to be a real and present danger, but did not necessarily believe it was targeted at them. In their eyes, U.S. policy was primarily what motivated the September 11 terrorists, and as a result, catastrophic terrorism was unlikely to occur on their soil (even if terrorist cells had been discovered inside their own borders). Others shared U.S. threat perceptions, a sense of victimhood, and the assumption that terrorism threatened their own internal security situation. These were mainly countries like Russia that had been tackling their own "terrorist problems" well before September 11. Still others were under pressure from their publics to discredit the threat altogether as a range of conspiracy theories surrounding the attacks on New York and Washington—often involving the CIA or Mossad—made their way into public debates. For example, despite the fact that a number of the September 11 hijackers were identified as Saudi nationals, many Saudis still felt the attacks were a Mossad conspiracy.

Both then and now, countries jump from one category to another, sometimes denying the threat and giving credence to conspiracy theories, sometimes expressing a fervent determination to combat a threat they perceive to be real, and other times conveying utter indifference. What is interesting to note, however, is that the correlation between the degree to which a country gives credence to the threat and a country's level of support for the war on terrorism has not been as strong as one would imagine. Some countries, such as China, pledged and provided strong counterterrorism cooperation despite skepticism about the threat. As a result, in the first few weeks and months following September 11, a shared sense of the threat was rarely *the* key driver in a country's decision to support the coalition's efforts. However, the U.S.

decision to invade Iraq in 2003, discussed later in this chapter, triggered fierce and heated international debates over threat assessments, causing many countries to question their commitment to the U.S.-led war on terrorism.

More influential than threat perceptions were the various domestic constraints that international leaders faced in joining the fight against terrorism. In Indonesia, for example, a combination of cultural and political constraints prevented President Megawati, a relatively weak leader, from establishing her country early on as a strong and steadfast partner in the war on terrorism. Indonesia's long-standing sensitivity to "hegemonism," rooted in decades of colonial rule and deep feelings of anti-Americanism, made it reluctant either to express support for the global campaign or to acknowledge the increasingly apparent presence of jihadist elements at home.

Domestic constraints also played a central role in Saudi Arabia's initial response to the call to join the war on terrorism. The relationship between the United States and Saudi Arabia, which had been strong for decades, became a poisoned chalice after September 11, opening the Saudi regime up to internal criticism that it was compromised, hypocritical, and morally corrupt. As a result, the Saudi authorities' relationship with the United States turned into a political liability, hampering (but not fully obstructing) that country's willingness to cooperate. The Saudi regime also had to address the widely held assumption at home that the United States is waging a war against Islam. Saudi officials therefore have taken great pains to avoid being seen as capitulating to U.S. designs of conquest when offering pledges of support, especially any promises to curb Islamic radicalization at home.

Almost without fail, the United States challenged its partners in the war on terrorism to take dramatic steps, often presenting national leaders with a precarious political dilemma, one that placed the interests and views of their constituencies directly in contradiction with U.S. requests for support. The degree to which heads of state were willing to find ways to balance those two sets of interests varied considerably. Unsurprisingly, some leaders, such as Indonesian president Megawati, found the risks of cooperating with the United States to be too high and chose to forgo broad promises of support in the name of salvaging their political careers. Others, like Pakistan's president Musharraf, have made a strategic decision to work with the United States, but have taken great pains to simultaneously placate their supporters (sometimes resulting

in promises of assistance that are heavy on rhetoric and light on substance). Still others have put the future of their political careers at risk
by supporting the war on terrorism with measures that dramatically
challenged the deeply held convictions of their constituents, their own
government, and, occasionally, their own party. For example, German
chancellor Gerhard Schroeder combined the decision to send German
troops to Afghanistan with a confidence vote in the German parliament, a move widely seen as a significant political gamble. Whatever
the outcome, the impulses and emotions of leaders clearly played a very
significant role.

If domestic factors constrained some countries' response after September 11, the real or perceived benefits of cooperation certainly enticed
others. Through public speeches and private meetings, the American
message has been clear: Partners in the war on terrorism can expect to
be rewarded. The forms this took included increased development and
economic assistance for many poorer members of the coalition, military training and bilateral exercises for the Georgians, military hardware such as helicopters and surveillance aircraft for the Pakistanis, or
technical assistance on internal security for the Saudis. These rewards
have helped a number of foreign leaders quell public opposition to
supporting the U.S.-led coalition and build sufficient acquiescence to
move forward.

Most foreign leaders have also created their own wish lists of rewards, which were not always openly discussed with U.S. policymakers.
In exchange for Russian support, President Putin wanted political cover for his handling of the terrorist problem in Chechnya and a change
in the Bush administration's tone on his management of domestic matters (that is, Putin's efforts to chip away at Russia's fledgling democratic
institutions). President Musharraf sought greater U.S. assistance in facilitating a resolution of the Kashmir dispute with India, the lifting of
U.S. sanctions against his country, and a large economic assistance
package. Georgian president Shevardnadze hoped for NATO membership; China believed that strengthening relations with the United States
would improve prospects for economic modernization and political
stability; and Germany, by cooperating with the United States, expected greater consultation on the formulation of U.S. policy and strategies
(which the Germans had perceived to be seriously lacking since President Bush entered office). In addition, the war on terrorism was widely
perceived to be a window of opportunity that would significantly increase the strategic importance of its coalition members.

In addition to anything that the United States might provide, some foreign leaders anticipated significant domestic benefits through cooperation with the United States. President Putin, for example, thought that his early support of the U.S.-led coalition would bolster his status as an international statesman and strengthen his position at home. President Shevardnaze of Georgia also hoped that close cooperation with the United States would bring him political gains back home. By ousting terrorists in the Pankisi Gorge, he had hoped to demonstrate real resolve in resisting Russian coercion and show the Georgian public that he was prepared to crackdown on criminal elements in that region. (Tacit public support for his counterterrorism strategy and close ties with the United States, though, failed to bring Shevardnaze the necessary political gains, and he was forced to resign in late 2003.)

Whether real or perceived, the expectation of rewards for cooperating with the United States frequently trumped domestic constraints, political risk, and skepticism about the threat in the decision to support the coalition.

President Bush's personal relationships with foreign leaders have also played a role in some countries' decisions to support or undermine the war on terrorism. Putin's successful visit with Bush in Ljubljana just three months before September 11, which left him optimistic about a new Moscow-Washington rapport, likely contributed to Putin's almost immediate decision to call the White House on September 11 with generous offers of support. In other cases, the president's relationships with foreign leaders have hampered cooperation. For example, in late 2002 it was said that German-American relations had become "poisoned," in the words of then U.S. national security adviser Condoleeza Rice. The Bush-Schroeder relationship got off to a rocky start with several transatlantic spats over missile defense, genetically modified organisms (GMOs), the Kyoto Treaty, and the International Criminal Court. Those issues were temporarily swept under the rug during the initial weeks following September 11 when Chancellor Schroeder pledged Germany's unconditional support for the war on terrorism, but tensions did not take long to resurface. The strained relationship between Bush and Schroeder, though it never halted cooperation entirely, certainly obscured any quest for common ground during the extraordinary transatlantic tensions of late 2002 and early 2003 over the Iraq War.

Finally, a country's behavior toward the United States before September 11—as one might expect—often provided clues in calculating its behavior after the terrorist attacks. Saudi Arabia had been a long-time "bandwagoner" before the attacks, frequently aligning itself with the United States on a multitude of issues over many decades. Its resolve to maintain a positive relationship with the United States came as little surprise despite unprecedented domestic constraints such as the widely held conviction among Saudis that the United States was waging a war against Islam. Similarly, over the past few decades, Pakistan has regularly refrained from joining any alignment of countries against the United States, even when its relationship with the United States has been cool. Since September 11, Pakistan has maintained this policy, taking great pains to show that it is not working alone or with others against U.S. interests.

Despite differences in threat perceptions, domestic constraints, and in some cases a poor relationship with President Bush, most of the world's major leaders opted to join the U.S.-led war on terrorism in one form or another. As mentioned earlier, the motivations and reservations for supporting the United States were wide-ranging, generating promises of support that varied in size and sincerity. In a matter of a few months, the United States had created a truly global campaign against terrorism, which spawned significant progress in law enforcement, intelligence sharing, terrorist financing, information sharing, and transnational crime, among others. As a consequence, a number of bilateral relationships between the United States and partner countries were enhanced, breeding stronger cooperation in other areas.

INTERNATIONAL RECALIBRATIONS

As the war on terrorism progressed and the U.S. administration began to focus on regime change in Iraq in the fall of 2002, several countries began to reassess their commitment and support. Perceived U.S. unilateralism, the Iraq War, developing trends in domestic public opinion, new terrorist attacks, and disappointment regarding Washington's rewards for support caused some countries to reduce their level of cooperation. Germany and Russia, two early backers of the war on terrorism, began to question publicly U.S. strategy and talked openly about banding together to balance against the United States.

The sea change in international support was first triggered by the global perception that U.S. unilateralism was on the rise. Germany and other major powers were hopeful in the months following September

11 that the Bush administration's newfound interest in coalition building would apply in other international areas such as global warming,
the International Criminal Court, arms control, and HIV/AIDS, re-
versing what many countries perceived to be a unilateralist direction in
foreign policy. There were also hopes that the Bush administration
would rethink its aversion to international treaties. However, a number of U.S. policies, including the U.S. withdrawal from the ABM treaty
with Russia in December 2001 and the release of the *U.S. National Security Strategy* in September 2002—with its highlighting of preemption—
made it clear that United States was not preparing to embrace a
stronger policy of multilateralism. Germany and other European allies
felt disillusioned and started to question the original deal they thought
they had struck with the United States in the weeks following the September 11 attacks.

Most damaging to the coalition, however, was the U.S. drive to go to
war in Iraq in late 2002. Few countries agreed there was a link between
the war on terrorism and the war on Iraq, and many warned that removing Saddam Hussein from power would only radicalize the Middle
East, bog down U.S. forces in Iraq, and fuel international perceptions
that U.S. policies are at root hostile to Islam. Eager to stop the Bush
administration from going to war and to buy more time for the UN
weapons inspectors, Russia, Germany, and France jointly agreed to
block the adoption of a second UN Security Council resolution, which
would have declared that Iraq had failed to disarm if it had not demonstrated full cooperation with UN inspectors by March 17, 2003, thereby offering a green light for military action against Iraq. That move
spurred perhaps the greatest rift in postwar transatlantic relations,
triggering fierce debates on state sovereignty, international law, U.S.
global preeminence, and the war on terrorism.

It was not long before several countries outside the Euro-Atlantic
area joined those debates, especially when it became clear that the United States planned on invading Iraq without a UN Security Council
resolution. While the United States argued that it had ample justification
to invade Iraq without further blessing of the United Nations, the war
was widely perceived by many states as an act of aggression without international legitimacy. More than a few coalition partners worried that
Iraq was only the first on a list of countries the United States was prepared to invade unilaterally and preemptively in its search for weapons

of mass destruction and terrorist cells. Under pressure from their publics, some political leaders, who had not done so before, began to voice support for a "multipolar" system aimed at balancing against U.S. power and authority. This "us versus them" worldview fractured the global sense of purpose that took root in the fall of 2001, giving way to an atmosphere built more on competition than partnership.

It is important to note, though, that not all members of the coalition were affected by the political drama surrounding the Iraq War. China, for example, maintained relatively high levels of cooperation with the United States both before and during the war, having concluded that any dramatic reactions to the war would get it nowhere and that the rewards of cooperation would continue to outweigh the risks. In other words, fear of U.S. encirclement among Chinese political elites was overcome by the hope that the United States might moderate its cross-strait policy in return for Chinese counterterrorism support. Similarly, Georgia's contributions to the coalition against terrorism also remained unaffected by the Iraq War. In fact, Georgia voiced strong support for the invasion even before Colin Powell presented his case to the United Nations in February 2003. Georgian officials felt that their unconditional support was necessary, given all that the United States had done for Georgia, and believed that their country only stood to benefit from further cooperation with the United States.

Moreover, most countries continued to cooperate with the United States in areas such as intelligence sharing, law enforcement, and terrorist financing even as their political leaders were questioning or even opposing military action in Iraq. Ironically, Indonesia and Saudi Arabia actually increased their support for the coalition to combat terrorism just before and during the U.S. invasion of Iraq. But such changes in support stemmed from terrorist attacks inside those two countries' borders. The murder of more than 200 in Bali in October 2002 and the attacks in Riyadh in May 2003 convinced the Indonesians and the Saudis of the danger that violent Islamist groups posed to the safety and security of their citizens. As a result, those two countries exhibited a greater willingness to partner with the United States and deal more decisively with Islamic extremists at home despite persistent criticism of U.S. action in Iraq.[2] The question is whether countries can maintain their counterterrorism support in the face of enduring political tensions.

One consequence of the Iraq War, though, was the damage it inflicted on the U.S. image throughout the world. With few exceptions, anti-

Americanism soared to new heights during and after the U.S. invasion of Iraq. The sole superpower, once considered a global leader, had become in many peoples' eyes a global menace. This surge in negative feelings toward the Bush administration and the United States writ large made it more difficult for many national leaders around the world to argue for greater cooperation with the United States, even in the war on terrorism. In fact, anti-American posturing was shown to bring big gains to parliamentary and presidential elections (most notably in Germany, where Chancellor Schroeder used it in the fall of 2002 to secure a narrow victory over his conservative challenger, Edmund Stoiber).

U.S. policy (or lack thereof, some countries would argue) regarding the Israeli-Palestinian conflict inspired further complaints about U.S. strategy and approach in late 2002 and early 2003. As the United States prepared to go to war in Iraq, many national leaders around the world stressed the need to negotiate an end to that conflict in order to combat religious extremism and anger in the Middle East. But the widely held conviction that the war on terrorism needed to start, not in Baghdad, but in Israel and the Occupied Territories (with a focus on the Middle East Peace Process) was not one to which the Bush administration subscribed. Instead it has argued that "getting Iraq right" is the top priority and that a democratic Iraq will exert a moderating influence on the entire region. The fear in many countries, though, was that U.S. security interests in Iraq were eclipsing all other aspects in the war on terrorism (including efforts in Afghanistan) and hindering the effectiveness of broader efforts against terror.

Furthermore, U.S. rhetoric about democratization in the Middle East has left more than a few countries in that part of the world, especially in late 2003 and 2004, worried that they could quickly move from being partners in the war on terrorism to being targets of unwanted reforms. The less those countries were consulted about U.S. strategy, the greater their suspicion and skepticism about U.S. intentions became. As a result, countries like Saudi Arabia have been placed on the defensive, at times tempering their enthusiasm for partnering with the United States when other factors, such as the terrorist attacks in Riyadh, give them good cause to do so.

Finally, disappointment about the rewards for cooperation in the war on terrorism has dampened enthusiasm for committing additional resources. Domestic critics in many partner countries (both at the elite and public level) have complained they have been oversold on the rewards to be reaped for their cooperation. Pakistanis in particular, feel they have paid too high a price for their policy reversal on Afghanistan. For example, that country continues to be disappointed with the levels of debt relief and development assistance thus far provided. Others such as Saudi Arabia have complained about the lack of preferential treatment in coping with the new, highly restrictive U.S. visa procedures. Deportations of Pakistani or Saudi nationals from the United States have done little to reassure those two countries that the United States values their partnership and cooperation. Russia also experienced a wave of disappointment when the United States deployed of U.S. Special Forces to Georgia for a train-and-equip mission in the Pankisi Gorge, highlighting the limits of the Bush administration's accommodating line on Chechnya. These incidents and others have heightened accusations that the United States is taking advantage of its partners and regularly failing to deliver promised benefits, which breeds mistrust and suspicion of U.S. behavior.

The shortcomings were seen as not just material. Many states began to complain that the coalition lacked a real sense of partnership, describing it as unbalanced and lacking transparency. Over the past two years the United States has been characterized as arrogant, overly demanding, and selfish—a superpower that takes but never gives. Furthermore, the Bush administration's "with us or against us" stance, it was complained, left little room for allied reservations or input on any particular course of action in the war on terrorism.

Of course, some of the frustration and disappointment mentioned above stems from unrealistic expectations on the part of U.S. partners. Although the United States could do more in terms of debt relief or development assistance, there are limits to what it can offer. Russia's cooperation in the war on terrorism has not led to early entry into the World Trade Organization, nor did it trigger changes in U.S. behavior during debilitating trade disputes over issues like steel and poultry. Although the United States has reversed its longtime opposition to selling new F-16 fighter jets to Islamabad, it is not prepared to provide Pakistan with all of the military support and hardware it needs to match India's conventional military advantage.

COALITION MAINTENANCE

More than three years after the September 11 attacks, the global coalition to fight terrorism is in need of repair. Despite a long list of achievements, the coalition is plagued with mistrust and deep divisions over strategy, threatening its overall effectiveness and cohesion. Assuming that the war on terrorism will not end soon, the United States should take a number of steps to revitalize the coalition's mission and morale.

First, the United States should promote a lasting sense of partnership and commitment with its coalition partners. That requires persuading partners that the positive relationships that have developed since September 11 will not evaporate once U.S. concerns or goals are met. China and Pakistan, in particular, worry that as soon as the United States declares victory, they will return to their pre–September 11 status as either states of concern or strategic competitors. It is important, therefore, that the United States stress its interest in long-term collaboration. Identifying additional areas of cooperation on issues unrelated to terrorism (health, the environment, etc.) would help ease concerns that U.S. cooperation, partnership, and friendship are likely to be short-lived.

President Bush did kick off his second term with a notable change in tone, particularly toward European allies such as France and Germany. But European allies are not convinced that a change of style will result in any substantive changes in U.S. policy. Therefore, the president's recent outreach efforts are viewed largely as superficial and insufficient.

Parallel to outreach efforts, the Bush administration should focus on countering international perceptions that the U.S.-led war on terrorism is almost exclusively tied to Iraq and largely anti-Islam through greater reception to and acknowledgment of partner antiterrorism strategies. Most countries around the world do not consider the war in Iraq to be a component of the war on terrorism and therefore feel that U.S. stabilization efforts in Iraq detract from the broader mission. Furthermore, a number of partner countries have called for the United States to put more resources toward nonmilitary means to neutralize and reverse the spread of terrorism. For example, Germany would like to see the United States focus more on the nexus between transnational crime and terrorism, the global spread of the jihadist worldview, education, radicalization, and the Arab-Israeli conflict. Demonstrating genuine resolve in combating these issues will be key to maintaining long-term international support.

Countering international concerns and skepticism about the overall direction of the war on terrorism will also require the United States, to the extent possible, to keep decision making transparent. As mentioned earlier, a number of coalition partners have complained about the lack of consultation in the war on terrorism. Wherever possible, the United States should work to keep the channels of communication open at the operational, strategic, and tactical level. U.S. initiatives that foreign leaders first learn about in local newspapers do little to instill a sense of partnership and trust. Coalition partners, particularly those in the Middle East, want to feel that they have a voice in crafting new measures and strategies instead of simply being ordered to act when it is convenient or critical to U.S. interests. Many governments believe that the United States frequently fails to capitalize on their regional expertise, cultural understanding, and economic and historical links to countries that the United States is actively trying to engage or influence (Iran, Syria, etc.). Enhanced U.S. efforts to seek the opinions and expertise of other nations would do much to dispel perceptions of American arrogance and foster a greater sense of partnership. These consultations should take place in person as a number of coalition partners have stressed that they would welcome increased visits by U.S. policymakers.

In addition to enhanced outreach at the policymaking level, some coalition partners would like to see the United States redouble its efforts to win "hearts and minds." They argue that improving America's image abroad might ease the challenge they face in supporting the U.S.-led war on terrorism and potentially increase pledges of support from around the world. Most countries do not want the United States to fail in its efforts to combat terrorism, and yet, at the same time, domestic resistance makes it difficult or impossible for them to help—a challenging paradox, to be sure. Although there is no magic bullet, much more could be done to improve America's image abroad. For example, the United States should significantly increase the resources available for public diplomacy, launch a major communications effort to reaffirm that the United States welcomes dialogue and is not conducting a war against Islam, develop a stable of American speakers both inside and outside of government who can travel to Middle East and other regions around the world to discuss U.S. policies and strategies, create and fund exchange programs between "next generation" young leaders, actively promote successful partnerships that are producing tangible results in the war on terrorism, and identify and cooperate with opinion leaders and media outlets in foreign capitals.

The United States may also want to exercise greater care in the signals it sends to foreign leaders. In some cases, the United States has instilled overconfidence in national leaders by signaling that positive and fruitful cooperation on the war on terrorism grants coalition partners the right to misbehave or bend the rules. For example, U.S. acquiescence in Russia's military operations in Chechnya, combined with the U.S. decision to "punish France, ignore Germany, and forgive Russia" after their opposition to the Iraq War, has left Putin feeling somewhat immune from U.S. pressure and influence. Similarly, constant U.S. praise for President Musharraf—intended to spare him from further domestic political damage—may have made him overconfident. (Of course, there are limits on how much the United States can influence the behavior of national leaders as they ultimately act the way they want to.) The fact that the United States appears to have given Musharraf a pass in the A.Q. Khan scandal regarding the transfer of nuclear technology has sent disturbing signals about accountability to global norms of behavior.

The United States should also remain realistic about the constraints under which other governments operate. Although it is in U.S. interests to promote domestic reform in countries like Saudi Arabia, Indonesia, and Pakistan, the United States should not underestimate the political pitfalls for some foreign leaders in trying to deal more vigorously with Islamist groups at home. Domestic political survival tends to trump international commitments to the war on terrorism when a partner's internal requirements and U.S. strategic objections do not match. Therefore, the United States should take proactive steps to ease the challenges some national leaders face at home in supporting the war on terrorism. These steps could include reducing or increasing the visibility of the country's relationship with the United States and providing greater rewards for a country's cooperation.

Finally, the United States should create foundations that support productive partnerships. As in the case of Pakistan, some countries' commitments to the war on terrorism are closely tied to a single individual, which is an inherently risky approach. Instead, the United States must create broader bases for long-term cooperation—these foundations must include strong democratic institutions and civil society. Obviously, motivating countries to take on the necessary socioeconomic reforms to create such foundations is often a difficult and delicate task, one that risks jeopardizing whatever cooperation currently exists. Pushing the Saudis, for example, to undertake dramatic and speedy democratic reforms would certainly curb the government's willingness to cooperate on the war on terrorism. But the United States should use its influence wherever possible to encourage gradual structural changes that are both in Washington's and the specific country's long-term interests—such as strengthening democratic institutions, improving social investment, and better managing domestic extremism.

It is difficult to predict how future events and trends will continue to test the coalition's cohesion in the months and years ahead, although the situation in Iraq and future terrorist attacks could all influence coalition members' behavior. It is therefore imperative that the United States reinforce its efforts today to foster strong and committed partnerships that can withstand the challenges of tomorrow. No single U.S. strategy will suffice to develop and maintain productive partnerships with all of the members in the coalition, but increased consultation and exchange, greater transparency, a stronger commitment to broaden the strategy beyond military efforts, and stronger public diplomacy efforts would go a long way toward ensuring the kind of cooperation the United States needs to prosecute the war on terrorism.

Notes

[1] See http://usinfo.state.gov/topical/pol/terror/01091488.htm.

[2] The results of the Spanish election after the 2004 terrorist attacks in Madrid, however, should caution U.S. policymakers against assuming that further attacks will automatically spur deeper commitment to the coalition to combat terrorism. Instead of moving Spain closer to the United States, the terrorist attacks actually provided the newly elected government with an excuse to disassociate itself from U.S. policy and strategy, specifically the stabilization efforts in Iraq that Spain believes have only diminished the security of its citizens. This shows just how problematic the issues became when Iraq and terror were intertwined.

INDEX

Page numbers followed by the letter n refer to notes.

187

ABOUT THE AUTHORS

Jon B. Alterman joined the Center for Strategic and International Studies in November 2002 as director of the Middle East Program. Previously, he served as a member of the Policy Planning Staff at the U.S. Department of State and as a special assistant to the assistant secretary of state for Near Eastern affairs.

Daniel Benjamin is a senior fellow in the International Security Program at the Center for Strategic and International Studies, where he focuses on issues of terrorism and the Middle East. He previously served on the National Security Council staff as both director for transnational threats (1997–1999) and foreign policy speechwriter and special assistant to President Clinton (1994–1997).

Bonnie Glaser is a senior associate at the Center for Strategic and International Studies in Washington, D.C., and an independent consultant on Asian affairs. Ms. Glaser has published extensively on Chinese foreign policy and East Asian security issues.

Carola McGiffert is currently a fellow in the CSIS International Security Program, where she helps manage Asia projects. She previously was deputy chairman of the International Trade Practice at Mayer, Brown & Platt. She served in the Clinton administration at the White House, the Commerce Department, and the Office of the U.S. Trade Representative (1993–1997).

Derek Mitchell serves as senior fellow for Asia in the CSIS International-al Security Program. He formerly served as special assistant for Asian and Pacific Affairs in the Department of Defense (1997–2001).

Julianne Smith is a fellow and deputy director of the CSIS International-al Security Program, where she focuses on questions of European secu-rity and defense and transatlantic relations. Before joining CSIS, she served as program officer for the foreign policy program at the German Marshall Fund of the United States.

Marvin Weinbaum is professor emeritus of political science at the Uni-versity of Illinois at Urbana-Champaign and served as analyst for Paki-stan and Afghanistan in the U.S. Department of State's Bureau of Intelligence and Research from 1999 to 2003. He is currently a scholar-in-residence at the Middle East Institute in Washington, D.C.

Andrew S. Weiss served as director for Russia, Ukrainian, and Eurasian Affairs on the National Security Council staff (June 1998 to January 2001), as a member of the State Department's Policy Planning Staff (September 1994 to May 1998), and as a policy assistant in the Office of the Secretary of Defense (March 1992 to September 1994).

Cory Welt is a fellow with the CSIS Russia and Eurasia Program. He served as a visiting fellow with the program's Caucasus Initiative during 2003–2004.